THEOLOGICAL CROSSFIRE

THEOLOGICAL CROSSFIRE

AN EVANGELICAL/LIBERAL DIALOGUE

CLARK H. PINNOCK
AND DELWIN BROWN

ZondervanPublishingHouse
Academic and Professional Books
Grand Rapids, Michigan

A Division of HarperCollinsPublishers

Requests for information should be addressed to:
Zondervan Publishing House
Academic and Professional Books
1415 Lake Drive S.E.
Grand Rapids, Michigan 49506

Library of Congress Cataloging-in-Publication Data

Brown, Delwin, 1935-
    Theological crossfire : an evangelical-liberal dialogue / Delwin
Brown and Clark H. Pinnock.
      p.   cm.
    Includes bibliographical references and index.
    ISBN 0-310-51441-X
      1. Theology, Doctrinal.   2. Theology—Methodology.
3. Evangelicalism.   4. Liberalism (Religion)—Protestant churches.
I. Pinnock, Clark H., 1937-   II. Title.
BT78.B865   1990
230'.046—dc20   90-43962
                                                        CIP

Edited by Robert D. Wood

Printed in the United States of America

90 91 92 93 94 95 / AK / 10 9 8 7 6 5 4 3 2 1

This edition is printed on acid-free paper and meets the American National
Standards Institute Z39.48 standard.

CONTENTS

INTRODUCTIONS

INTRODUCTION
BY CLARK H. PINNOCK

The major division in modern theology is not between Catholics and Protestants anymore but between liberals and evangelicals. Martin Marty has spoken of a two-party system with liberals on the left and evangelicals on the right. While one party enjoys the ascendancy, the other does not just disappear but hunkers down and holds on until circumstances change. At the moment, evangelicals seem to be prospering, but that does not mean you can ever write the liberals off.[1]

But the polarization is often so extreme that it is rare for evangelicals and liberals to talk to each other, much less try to understand one another in a sympathetic way. As Wuthnow reports, "Liberals look across the theological fence at their conservative cousins and see rigid, narrow-minded, moralistic fanatics; while conservatives holler back with taunts that liberals are immoral, loose, biblically illiterate, and unsaved."[2] The stereotypes are awful and the divisions very deep.

In addition, the polarization drives each side to extremes. For example, it makes evangelicals reluctant to admit that God's salvation is broad and comprehensive. And liberals sound as if they do not really care for continuity with the old Christian traditions in doctrine and ethics at all. The situation does not put either liberal or evangelical theology in a good or even true light.

---

[1]Martin Marty, *Righteous Empire* (1970). R. Stephen Warner describes the relationship in *New Wine in Old Wineskins: Evangelicals and Liberals in a Small-Town Church* (Berkeley: University of California Press, 1988).

[2]Robert Wuthnow, *The Restructuring of American Religion, Society and Faith Since World War II* (Princeton: Princeton University Press, 1988), 215.

9

An evangelical-liberal dialogue must begin to happen in our denominations and churches. We have to start talking to each other. Our two modes of interpreting Christian faith in the modern world need to confront one another for the good of the church—for purposes of reconciliation, self-correction, and mutual enrichment. This is obviously true in the Methodist and the Baptist contexts, which we two represent. How can we afford to live in complete isolation from one another when we have to rub shoulders day in and day out? Our denominations are something like political parties, playing fields where liberals and evangelicals engage issues and offer stimulation and correctives to one another. One faction has not won hegemony, is not likely to win it, maybe should not try to win it. Rather, we should figure out how to make the best of the situation of coexistence so that all are served.

Mark Ellingsen has recently written, "The relationship between evangelicals and the mainline churches may be *the* question for ministry and Christian unity in the next decades."[3] The evangelical movement is too strong to be ignored by the mainline, and the mainline is too important to be shunned by a separatist evangelicalism. This is not to say the dialogue will be easy, only that it is necessary. There will be difficulties and risks, but difficulties need to be faced and risks taken.

We agree with Donald Shriver when he said that there are things which liberals and evangelicals can teach each other and learn from one another.[4] For the sake of our Christian mission in the world, and on behalf of those who need to hear the Good News of God's grace and find wholeness in the love of Christ, the Savior of the world, should we not be trying to bear common witness as far as possible to Jesus our Messiah?

There is an example of what a dialogue between liberal and evangelical can be like in a book by David L. Edwards, in which he scrutinizes the thinking of John R. W. Stott, who has an opportunity to respond. Edwards is long-time editor of SCM Press, and a respected Anglican leader, and John Stott, of course, is a noted preacher and leader of the evangelical community. In the book, *Essentials: A Liberal-Evangelical Dialogue,* the dialogue between

---

[3]Mark Ellingsen, *The Evangelical Movement, Growth, Impact, Controversy, Dialog* (Minneapolis: Augsburg, 1988), 24.
[4]Donald Shriver, "What Can Liberals and Evangelicals Teach Each Other?" *Christian Century,* (August 12–19, 1987).

them is respectful, uncontrived, serious, mutually beneficial, and bridge-building. It stands as evidence that liberals and evangelicals can teach one another; and is a model for the style, tone, and temper of other such dialogues and of this present book. It is actually possible, it seems, for a liberal and an evangelical to discuss their differences in a charitable and Christian way.[5]

Such a dialogue works best between people who are moderates in their respective camps and share a common concern for the Christian tradition and the desire to face up to modern issues candidly. It would not work nearly so well if the protagonists represented more radical positions. A dialogue between a modernist like Donald Cupitt and a fundamentalist like Harold Lindsell would not accomplish much. The split would be too wide and the voices would be drowned out in the shouting. But the authors of this book are moderates in our respective camps, and share a mutual concern to respect Christian tradition and to engage pressing contemporary issues in an open way. There is a spirit of openness to change in both of us and a willingness to listen sympathetically to one another.[6]

One thing that facilitates our dialogue is a dialectic that is continually at work in Christian theology. All theologians find themselves constantly struggling with two poles or horizons that define their work. They strive to correlate the Christian message with human existence. Theology needs to wrestle with both to be worth much. Evangelicals are relatively more preoccupied with the message pole and liberals relatively more with the pole of human existence, but both are really interested in correlating and integrating both poles, wherever the emphasis is placed. Each of them cares deeply about fidelity to the original message and creativity in the face of fresh challenges.

Even though evangelicals tend to put a greater emphasis on conserving the achievements of the past (so that the Good News is not lost sight of) and even though liberals are particularly con-

---

[5]Richard J. Coleman sought to create a dialogue between liberals and evangelicals much earlier in *Issues of Theological Conflict, Evangelicals and Liberals*, rev. ed. (Grand Rapids: Eerdmans, 1980).

[6]Kenneth Cauthen distinguishes evangelical liberals from modernistic liberals in his book *The Impact of American Religious Liberalism* (New York: Harper & Row, 1962). In the same way, the dialogue here is between an evangelical liberal and an evangelical conservative, not between a modernist and a fundamentalist.

cerned that people hear the message in fresh forms of expression (so that they hear the Good News in vital ways), both concerns are surely valid ones. As responsible theologians we cannot ignore the past and cut ourselves off from the roots of our faith, any more than we can ignore the necessity to think through what these ancient doctrinal formulations meant and may mean for today. In some ways, the difference between evangelical and liberal theologians may be one of emphasis rather than substance, and a serious dialogue between us may benefit us and our communities. Ultimately, the sense of the faithful will have to judge the adequacy of the balance we strike with our two noncompeting concerns.

Another factor that enhances the dialogue is the diversity that exists within both liberal and evangelical camps. On the evangelical side, there is the rainbow of traditions we call denominations—the Lutheran, Anglican, Reformed, Wesleyan, Pentecostal, Baptist; and on the liberal side, in addition to all these, there are many other shades and types of liberal thinking. This means that there is a lot of room for us to move around in during any dialogue. Abundant treasures in both of our storehouses can be brought out by way of answers to the questions we will put to one another.

The terms "liberal" and "evangelical" when used in theology do not point to absolutely fixed positions that cannot and do not change. What it means to be liberal and evangelical is even now being worked out in modern history. Some liberals may raise their eyebrows at Brown's version of liberalism just as some evangelicals will frown at some of my suggestions about what it means to be evangelical. Even as we address each other, others will be looking over our shoulders, wanting to change this or that in what we say. This is simply to admit that history is still in the making and that perspectives change. Who knows what may be possible by way of more fruitful and considerate relationships in the future? Why close off positive possible outcomes, when it is not our place to do so?

But whatever happens in the future, the fact remains that "liberal" and "evangelical" do not point to the same thing theologically at present. There is a great gulf fixed between these theological approaches and differences, which cannot be papered over. Truth issues are at stake. Without denying this we can begin to try and create more understanding.

Who are evangelical theologians? In North America evangelical refers to those who belong to a diverse coalition or network of basically conservative Protestants that has risen since the Second World War. Evangelicals come in many shapes and sizes. We may be postfundamentalist, confessional Lutheran or Calvinist, traditional pietist or Wesleyan, etc., but we share some common concerns: not to see the church seduced from the truth of its formative message (2 Cor. 11:3). Evangelicals desire to stand in doctrinal continuity with the historic church and with the original community of Jesus and the apostles. We treasure a truth deposit that we believe we must guard and steward (2 Tim. 1:14; Jude 3). We object to liberal theology, which we feel, though it can be creative and original, stands in danger of losing the revealed truth deposit. We are much less open to theological revision and convinced that the main articles of the historic evangelical faith do not need changing.

What makes evangelicalism vital is its doctrinal continuity with the historic grammar of the church, which attracts people seeking deep meaning. The possibility of being able to confess one's faith confidently appeals to us more than the hesitancy of liberals who often seem to be unsure where they stand. The short-lived life span of radical proposals and the endless pursuit of relevance rather than truth have given evangelicals a certain advantage in recent years. Along with our cognitive orientation, there is a degree of vitality in evangelical religious experience that motivates people to share the faith with others and that leads to a steady stream of converts.

Who then are considered liberal theologians? They are creative people who are willing to run the risks of being discontinuous with Christian tradition. They may find such discontinuity necessary in order to make sense of Christian faith for fair-minded people today. They are much less worried about heresy (a term they do not like) than they are about idolatry. They seriously doubt that human beings are capable of possessing divine truth in such a way as to make them able correctly to label other people's convictions as false or damnable. They think that it is idolatrous to equate what we believe with absolute truth in this manner. And they believe that evangelical theology has consistently been guilty of doing just that. Liberals call for greater modesty in religion and theology. They work less deductively from the tradition and more inductively from our generally accessible human experience.

Liberal theology has its attraction. Many people can identify with their sense of the relativity of all things human, including things

13

theological and religious. We know from experience that to live is to change, and for that very reason many find they need to have their religion in a liberal form. Life is a pilgrimage; they do not expect to find theology free of uncertainty and risk.

We hope that the dialogue that follows will reveal the two methods and approaches at work on the major topics of Christian theology and will prove to be at least a study in contrast. If that is all that happens, it will have been worthwhile. But we will also be asking ourselves whether it is possible to dig a middle channel between liberals and evangelicals. We wonder whether one can be evangelical and liberal at the same time and actually avoid both heresy and idolatry. In any case the reader can judge these matters as we work through the issues.

On the one hand, we want to be authentic representatives of liberal and evangelical theologies and to defend those standpoints against unwarranted and ill-considered criticisms. On the other hand, we want to say fresh things, too, and not hide the weaknesses that exist in our own thinking. We intend to be candid and admit weaknesses in our positions where we see them as well as mention strengths we see in the other person's work. If we see the possibility of reforming either evangelical or liberal theology, we will try to do so. Neither of us is trying to win the argument here. It is a better mutual understanding that we seek and deeper truth.

We have already engaged in public dialogues on some of these matters and are familiar with each other's published work. So the essays that follow are not written in ignorance of each other's views. We were already somewhat familiar with how the other one thinks, and were able to frame the discussion in this book with the other one in mind. Thus the whole book rises out of dialogue and not just from the questions and answers at the end of each of the major presentations. At the same time, we wrote the major presentations independently of each other so as to preserve the saltiness of our individual perspectives.

INTRODUCTION
BY DELWIN BROWN

The wall that divides liberals and evangelicals in North America still stands, but cracks are appearing. A few Christians are beginning to remove a block or two from the wall, look across to the other side, and listen to what is being said there. Sometimes there is even an exchange. This communication, however, seldom occurs in society at large, where we simply glare if we notice each other at all. Nor does it occur frequently in our churches, where the other side is usually ignored. When it does take place, the communication between liberals and conservative Christians is most often a scholarly one.

The significant fact is that liberal and conservative scholars are no longer divided absolutely. The few very sharp distinctions that defined Christian theological disputes earlier in this century have largely disappeared. There is still a wide spectrum of theological views and along that spectrum there are many distinct differences. But our theological differences now do not make for the great divisions that once existed. Theological discussions today do not follow party lines.

Clark Pinnock's own recent work illustrates this fact, and it is this that first interested me in his views. A commitment to conservative or evangelical Christianity permeates his writings. But that commitment does not make him predictably "conservative" in current theological discussions. Always, on each issue that he addresses, he clearly is searching for the way to be committed and critical, faithful and open, Christian and sensitive to the modern world and its claims. If evangelicals now and again wonder aloud whether Pinnock's conservatism is "true," they are not nearly as numerous as one might think. This is the case because, as a whole, evangelical theology today is more open in attitude and varied in its expression than it has been for a long time. Certainly it is more open and varied than we liberals have claimed.

Current evangelical theology, it must be noted, is *not* represented by the monolithic and manipulative voice of the so-called conservative television evangelists. Much of what is called "conservative Christianity" in the media is scarcely either. More often than not it is an egoistic psychologism or a secularistic nationalism cloaked in quasi-Christian rhetoric. Authentic conservative Christianity is quite different. Its heritage has been a noble one. Its theologies have been intellectually careful and socially compassionate. These theologies have been self-critical and capable of change. They are becoming so again today.

Liberal theologies, too, are becoming more open. That statement sounds strange since "liberalism" and "openness" are often thought to be synonymous. While this is true in some areas, openness has not always characterized the liberal attitude toward conservatism. That, as I say, is changing. Liberal theologians are reading and thinking about conservative works. Publications by evangelicals are now showing up as assignments in courses at liberal seminaries, to be discussed, not simply dismissed. In part these changes may be due to the ascendancy of conservative Christianity in North America today. The power of the religious right forces the rest of us to take it more seriously, in all of its forms.

There is evidence, however, that much of the increasing liberal openness toward more conservative forms of Christianity stems from liberal self-criticism. In some cases what we liberals have taken to be "facts" have faded rather quickly. The meaning and implications of "secularization" for the role of religion in society is a conspicuous example. In other cases we have been blind to the full implications of our own presuppositions. The significance of our affirmation of human "historicity" is an example of this, a point I shall discuss later in this volume. Liberal self-criticism is a liberal tradition. Christian liberals have always resolved to seek the truth fearlessly, knowing that such a search must include the most stringent self-reflection.

Given this greater openness and the diversity on both sides, it is not surprising that dialogue between liberal and conservative theologians and other scholars is increasing. We are beginning to talk to one another because we are learning from one another. We are also talking because we continue to differ. But we usually find our differences to be stimulating and mutually enriching, or at least we are likely to find them so if we are clear about them and explore them together. Yes, we also find our differences to be irritating and painful, disappointing and threatening. These consequences, these risks, however, are a part of life. If theology is a part of life, we should expect to find them in theology, too.

The purpose of this book is to help bring the growing scholarly dialogue between liberals and conservatives into the churches. This goal probably has something to do with the authors' own histories. I, the liberal in this discussion, was raised in a small evangelical group. Clark Pinnock, the evangelical or conservative, was raised in mainline Protestantism. We share the fact that we intentionally, and largely for theological reasons, departed from our pasts. But we also share the fact that we left our traditions aware of their gifts, their strengths, as well as their shortcomings. We find it unfortunate that so many of our present allies, Pinnock's conservative colleagues and my liberal ones, are so thoroughly ignorant of the splendid histories and the inner realities of the other side. We are disturbed by the occasional smugness that perpetuates this ignorance. We believe that liberalism and evangelicalism are both inadequate as they are. We think that both would benefit from a dialogue with their counterparts in North American Christianity.

Among the inadequacies of liberal and evangelical Christianity today is a failure in our churches to love God with the mind. There is a dearth of serious theological reflection across the spectrum of North American Christianity. That is the fault of no one group; historical factors, too complex to sort out here, are the main culprit. Pinnock and I are not so foolish as to think that we can turn the historical tide, but we know of many others—clergy, laypeople, professors, etc.—who have a similar concern and who also are trying to encourage the renewal of responsible theology in our churches today.

For various reasons, some of which will become evident in the subsequent discussion, Clark Pinnock and I have concluded that significant theological thinking in the churches might best be encouraged if it takes the form of dialogue across the lines that have for so long divided us. The most prominent of these lines, in

Protestantism especially, separates liberal and conservative Christians. This book is our effort to contribute to the growth of a conservative/liberal dialogue.*

*For assisting my contribution to this book I am indebted to three Iliff colleagues in particular. Dennis R. MacDonald and Donald E. Messer read significant portions of my manuscript and offered several helpful suggestions. Sheila Greeve Davaney, a colleague in theology whose views differ markedly from my own, read everything I wrote and kept raising the questions that the best critic asks: "Is this what you want to say and ought to say, and is this the way to say it?" What I have said is my own, immeasurably improved, however, because of these friends.

PART ONE
THEOLOGICAL METHOD

SECTION 1

Delwin Brown's presentation on theological method, Brown's answers to three questions put by Pinnock, and a rejoinder by Pinnock to Brown's answers.

The issue we must address first has to do with what theologians call "theological method." This may be an abstract issue but it is a real one, implicit daily in the life of the thoughtful Christian. The issue can be stated as a set of questions: How should we go about the task of thinking as Christians? In other words, where should we go for our resources—the Bible, science, philosophy, experience, the church? How should we evaluate what we hear from these various quarters—on the basis of reason, prayer, conformity to Scripture, some modern consensus? In sum, what are the rules for, or at least the characteristics of, responsible Christian thinking?

In discussions between liberals and conservatives these questions usually move rather quickly to disputes about the authority and the nature of the Bible. There can be little doubt that we have differed markedly here. In some respects this is the basic division between liberals and conservatives. Even so, I do not think that what separates us here is quite so sharp as we sometimes think. In fact I will argue that our difference on this issue is best seen as one of emphasis, and I will go on to say that the liberal position, which I defend, must nevertheless incorporate something very important from the conservative point of view. I will also contend, however, that conservatism has something to learn from liberal Christianity, something it must affirm if it is indeed to be an authentically conservative Christianity in our time.

It is sometimes said that on questions of method the difference between more liberal Christians and more conservative ones has to do with faith and reason. "Liberals trust reason" and "conservatives rely on faith"—that is the alleged difference. There may be something useful about this distinction for differentiating liberals and conservatives, but historically it has not represented a definitive difference between us. Liberalism has sometimes been strongly oriented toward reason, rejecting anything that does not seem to be consistent with the rational quest. But conservative Christianity, too, has had its stalwart rationalists, as the nineteenth-century fundamentalist theologians of the Princeton School demonstrate. Furthermore, both liberalism and conservatism have had representatives who rejected reason. Romantic liberalism and pietistic conservatism illustrate this rejection, in the past and still today. The contrast between faith and reason, then, is not the key difference.

It is more helpful to see the difference between liberals and conservatives in terms of the relative balance each gives to the wisdom of the past versus judgments characteristic of the present age.

Every generation struggles between the "you have heard it said by those of old," on the one hand, and "but I (or we) now say to you," on the other. Every generation struggles between the judgments of the past and contemporary opinion, but this struggle became especially intense and fractious for Christians beginning three or four hundred years ago. A number of things began happening all at once (at least on the clock of historical time) to cast doubt on inherited Christian wisdom.

In the eighteenth century philosophers of the Enlightenment resolved to have done with superstition, to dismiss beliefs held on mere authority, and to scrutinize everything rationally. They declared that they would follow reason alone, confident that reasoning, objectively used, would bring about a better world and a clearer grasp of truth.

This rational quest moved in a number of directions. Biblical scholarship demonstrated, for example, that many traditional assumptions about the biblical text were simply not true, for example, the Mosaic authorship of the Pentateuch and the historical uniformity of the New Testament accounts of Jesus. Evolutionary theory made it exceedingly difficult to subscribe to the historic view of creation. The study of other religions produced astonishing results—adherents of Buddhism, Hinduism, etc., are remarkably intelligent and moral people with insightful views of the world though they differ radically from our own.

Today we might have made our peace with these particular controversies, but still they powerfully illustrate the problem before us. When the consensus of the best contemporary minds differs markedly from the most precious teachings of the past, which do we follow? To which do we give primary allegiance, the past or the present?

As I understand it, conservative Christianity at its best will say, "We ought to listen to the hypotheses of the present and take from them what we can, but ultimately the truth has been given to us in the past, particularly in Jesus, and the acceptance of that is our ultimate obligation. Everything the contemporary world might say must be judged by its conformity to biblical revelation."

Liberalism at its best is more likely to say, "We certainly ought to honor the richness of the Christian past and appreciate the vast contribution it makes to our lives, but finally we must live by our best modern conclusions. The modern consensus should not be absolutized; it, too, is always subject to criticism and further revision. But our commitment, however tentative and self-critically maintained, must be to the careful judgments of the present age, even if they differ radically from the dictates of the past."

It is this kind of liberalism that I want to discuss and defend against conservatism. But I will discuss it as much as defend it, explaining in the process why I think liberalism itself has had serious weaknesses that conservatism helps to reveal. In the final analysis, however, I advocate a liberal method in theology. While I do not particularly seek to convert those readers who may disagree with me, I do want to clarify why I am a liberal on the issue of theological method.

It should be noted, first, that in principle liberalism is open to many different forms of inquiry, as its own history demonstrates. Liberal theologians influenced by Kant or Hegel, for example, have sometimes relied on deductive reason as the path to truth. Other liberals have been empiricists, relying on sensory experience.

Usually theologians in this second group have combined experience with reason in a disciplined way, producing what could be loosely termed a "scientific method" in theology. Finally, since the eighteenth-century liberal theologians influenced by Schleiermacher have primarily trusted feeling or intuition in the human search for truth. For them, "religious experience" is central.

Liberalism must be willing to hear the case for any of these methods of seeking to know what is true, or, for that matter, any other methodologies that come forward. For liberalism the crucial thing is that every such candidate—reason, sensory experience, intuition, (more recently) praxis, or what have you—must be presented and defended in the arenas of our contemporary discourse. No method can claim privilege. Each method must be defended without special pleading. Whatever path the liberal chooses must be chosen because he or she concludes that this is the alternative that is most defensible according to the best criteria available in the present.

If asked to justify this attitude, a full reply would be complicated. One can reply generally, however, by pointing out that this is the attitude we all normally have anyway and that there are good pragmatic reasons for adopting it. When we want to wire a house, fathom the weather, or audit a business, we rely on the criteria most adequately defended in the contemporary setting. If we propose to depart from this generally accepted procedure, we recognize that we are obligated to justify ourselves; the burden of proof is on us. I have not yet heard any good reason to make an exception when we talk about God, the world, and human nature. What we have to say on these topics, as on any other, ought to make sense in terms of the best information available to us and our contemporaries. And if that means that we differ from the past, then we should do so and be honest about it.

But another point ought to be considered, too: What exactly is the alternative? "Appeal to the Bible" is not a clear option anymore (if it ever was!). Biblical scholarship has demonstrated to the satisfaction of most people (including many conservative Christian scholars) that the Bible does not present uniform theological positions on God, Christ, or human nature. If we accept the Bible as the Bible actually presents itself, we are faced with varying points of view. Therefore, even if we did turn to the Bible for "the" answer, what we would find instead are "answers." And how do we decide which of these biblical answers is central and normative? Do we not necessarily employ some extra-biblical principle in order to choose between biblical alternatives? But where does that principle come from? Is it not appropriate that we acknowledge our guiding principles and defend them, without special pleading, in the arenas of public discussion?

There is, in my judgment, no viable alternative to a tentative, self-critical search for truth guided by the criteria of knowledge defensible and defended in the arenas of our contemporary discourse. To this point, I think, liberalism is right.

Liberalism, however, has also been wrong in some respects and this becomes apparent in light of the kind of questions conservatives are likely to raise in response to the foregoing discussion. "If that is your view of the Bible," the conservative might say, "then why do you liberal Christians use the Bible at all? In fact, why do you even call yourselves Christians?"

We liberals have continued to call ourselves Christians, and we have continued to use the Bible. We have *felt* that we are correct in doing both, and I think we have been, but the way we have stated our view has made our actual practice puzzling. Why do we see ourselves obligated above all else to contemporary knowledge, and yet identify ourselves in terms of the Christian past? Why do we say what we say about the Bible, yet give it special place in our worship and practice?

The answer to these questions is to be found in our history. Liberal Christianity rose as a part of the Enlightenment spirit, to which I referred earlier. The fundamental assumption of the Enlightenment was that reason, based on available evidence, should be the ultimate arbiter in questions of truth. But individualism, too, was part of the spirit of the Enlightenment and thus a part of much of liberal Christianity as well. The reflective process in this tradition was conceived of individualistically. The reason appealed to was individual reason; the experience appealed to was personal experience. To be sure, other qualified persons were recognized as legitimate critics of the individual's reasoning, so some social dimension was acknowledged. But the qualifications of the *past* to function as a critic of contemporary reason and experience was not admitted. This meant for liberal theology that the Bible, because it is very much a part of the past, was dismissed as a serious critic of the present. The individualism of the Enlightenment was an individualism of the present age. "We (contemporaries) must be the arbiters in our search for truth"—that was the attitude.

In some respects I think that attitude is still admirable, and, in any case, it is hard to deny that it had profoundly beneficial results for Western culture. It challenged dogmatism, helped to topple entrenched authorities, and lifted up as an ideal at least a more free and democratic quest for knowledge. But this attitude also had its problems.

Ironically, one major problem of Enlightenment liberalism was already implicitly recognized in another claim of the liberal frame of mind, especially as it moved into the nineteenth century. Liberalism insisted on the historicity of human beings. We are historical creatures, products of our social pasts. That has been an insight common to liberalism, but it has not been adequately incorporated into liberal theology. When it has been incorporated, this insight has usually played a negative role rather than a positive one. The limitations that the past imposes on our thinking have been emphasized. The past as a positive resource has been neglected.

Conservatives, however, have recognized the positive importance of the past and they have manifested that importance in their practice. Thus, both their lives and their critique of liberalism have been reminders that we do not take seriously enough our own admission that human beings are indelibly historical, and that this can be positive as well as negative. Conservatism, in my judgment, is best viewed as the recognition that the past presents distinctive resources as well as limitations. Liberals can and should incorporate this recognition into their theology.

To be is to be cumulatively. The past is an inescapable and irreplaceable resource if we are to move ahead effectively. We do not move through time, as individuals or as religious communities, unless we appropriate our pasts. Our pasts form us, inform us, and are essential to our re-formation. We live in historical streams. They are not amorphous resources nor do they wait passively for us to take notice of them at our leisure. Our pasts come to us insistently, demanding our attention. More than that, they speak to us in structures that have identity and therefore that give identity to those whom they form. They come to us as "canons." This helps to explain why the Bible as canon is crucially important to all Christians, including liberals even when liberal theology has failed to account for that importance.

To be "a people" is in some way to live out of a canon. When Christians think of "canon," we think of the Bible. Historians of religions, however, point out that each religion has its canon. This is obvious with respect to religions that have scriptures, such as Judaism and Islam, but it is no less true of those religions whose roots are non-textual. The definitive resources, the canons, of these religious traditions might be a set of stories or a tradition of ritual.

A community is formed by a canon; the canon provides the basis for its identity. There is no other way for a people to live and move constructively into the future, except to live fundamentally (though not exclusively) out of the resources of the past. The well from which Christians drink is the Bible, as it lives through the traditions of interpretation, celebration, and meditation in the life of the community. Conservatives have been right, then, to emphasize the positive importance of the past. The Bible is that past for Christians.

Conservatives have been wrong, however, in their typical characterization of the Christian past. Apparently they have assumed that the unique importance of the Bible for Christians is somehow tied to the Bible's being consistent in theology, coherent in outlook, uniform in teaching. This is a false assumption, I think. In fact, the Bible, as conservatives have said, is uniquely important, but it is not consistent, coherent, and uniform in any very specific sense. The conviction that the Bible must be the latter has blinded conservatives to the Bible as it actually presents itself. About the Bible, in this respect, liberal biblical scholars have been correct; to this extent at least they have taken the Bible more seriously than have conservative Christians.

I began by explaining that in my view there is no viable alternative to a tentative, reasoned search for truth guided by contemporary criteria of knowledge. To seek truth in that way is, I said, fundamental to Christian liberalism. But this point has to do mostly with the adjudication of our differences, the proper method for deciding between competing truth claims. The search for truth, however, requires more than a method. It also requires resources. This brings us to the role of the past and, for Christians, the place of the Bible.

If to be a people is to live in relationship to some particular canon, then it should not surprise us that the resource for Christian identity (insofar as it is specifically Christian) is the Bible in celebration, meditation, and interpretation. That, I believe, is what it means to speak of the Bible's authority. The Bible "authors" our lives and identities as Christians. It teaches, inspires, unsettles, infuriates, comforts, and creates. In our varied relationships to it we continuously come to be who we are as Christians.

The power of the Bible to author Christian identity does not imply the kind of uniformity that more conservative Christians tend to attribute to it. Uniformity is not what we find in the Bible. An authentic conservatism should allow the Bible to be what it chooses to be. A people's formative past, its canon, is effective precisely in its manifoldness, diversity and playfulness, in its refusal to be controlled. Uniform pasts are dead pasts. Living pasts speak with many voices.

The Bible is alive, and enlivens us, because its traditions are multiple, conflictual, interactive, and challenging to each other and to us. Its conflicting ways of portraying the significance of Jesus, its many struggling voices on issues of justice, its apparent blindness on some occasions and its brilliance on others—all speak to us with a power and challenge that will not let us be content with who we are and will not let us change glibly. When we rest in a comforting legalism, for example, the Abrahams and the Pauls of the Bible speak of freedom and adventure. When we are seduced by antinomian illusions, a Moses or a Matthew reminds us of the value of order and discipline. When we are tempted to believe that we have triumphed, Mark says that salvation is faithful suffering. When we despair of the possibility of change, John says that we have already won, and Paul, like the writer of Revelation, proclaims the coming reality of a new heaven and a new earth. In short, when we think we have struggled through to the end with one of its voices, sinking comfortably into settled conviction, another voice begins its piercing preachments. The task of rethinking and reforming begins again within us. It is not so much that we feel obligated to go to the Bible; it comes to us, often when we wish it would go away. We can close its pages, but its voices then pursue us in art, music, story, sermon, commentary, ritual, even in supposedly secular sights and sounds.

To summarize my view, the Bible is not the criterion of truth. That criterion is fallibly developed in the always difficult, always tentative process of reflection as it is conducted in conversation with our comtemporaries. Judgments about truth in theology are made in the same kinds of discussions, employing the same open rules of evaluation, that are used in making judgments about the claims of history, science, philosophy, and common sense. To realize this is the contribution of liberalism to Christianity in our time. I believe it is an enduring contribution, one that conservatives ought to affirm. But if the Bible does not "norm" us, it does form us. It authors us. That realization is the contribution of conservatism to a viable Christianity today. It is a point consistent with the classic liberal insistence on our historicity as humans, but liberals have not fully appropriated it. Convervatives have. It is time for us to join them.

Even if we were to come much closer together on issues of method, however, many other differences would and should remain. Christians will be authored differently by their common past, and they will differ about what is and is not warranted according to the best judgments of the day. If there is diversity within the Bible, and it is good, then the variety of views within the ranks of Christians can also be good. We need not fear our differences. They can be helpful. The harm will come from a timidity that keeps our differences from encountering each other, and a disrespect that keeps them from being mutually enriching. If the Scripture in its diversity is a gift of God, can our own diversity not be the same?

> *Pinnock: I sense that the difference between us here goes deeper than just a matter of emphasis. What do you think the apostolicity of the church means? Wasn't the church's decision for the New Testament canon a decision to be ruled by this written witness to Jesus Christ in a somewhat stronger fashion than you suggest?*

Brown: Yes, the church of the first three centuries, in its theological declarations, did develop a "stronger" view of the "rule" of the Bible than liberal Christians have today. That liberal Christians now decline to accept the church's previous decisions as the rule to which our own views must conform should not be at all surprising. Still, I think I recognize the force of your point and I'll return to it in a moment.

First, however, I want to say something about what you are

doing, as it seems to me, in the way you pose your question. You are making the nature of the Bible's authority for Christians today dependent on the conclusions that some Christians reached in the second and third centuries. Since the church fathers thought of the Bible's authority in a certain way, you seem to be saying, then we should think of its authority in the same way. If that is your point, I want to ask why any contemporary Christian, an evangelical included, would want to give Christian theologians of those early centuries that kind of primacy? When evangelicals, for example, struggle to come to conclusions about God, Christ, sin, etc., they purport to go directly to the Bible; they don't stop in the third or second centuries and let the views they find there settle these matters for them. There is no reason, either, to let the ancient church determine contemporary Christian views on the nature of the Bible's authority.

But your basic point is about "apostolicity" and what it can or does mean for liberals. I can address the question best by acknowledging, again, that we liberals ought to make our statements of the Bible's role in our lives conform more closely to the actual practice in our Christian communities, assuming we think that practice to be appropriate. There the Bible does have a "specialness" that is not adequately acknowledged or explicated in our liberal theologies. I have characterized this special quality as the fact that the Bible does *author* Christian identity, and it does so both directly and indirectly in celebration and meditation as well as in interpretation. To say that the Bible is authority is to say that, in our continual wrestling with it, it continuously authors who we are and what we are for.

To speak of apostolicity is to speak of the fact that we as Christians never have direct access to our Scriptures. Obviously we can pick up the Bible and read it directly, but we read it with minds informed by the generations that preceded us. Inevitably the Bible for us is also in part what the Bible has been for them, as their views have shaped our own presuppositions. So to wrestle with the Bible is also to wrestle with the sensibilities of our forefathers and (to the extent that their witness has not been snuffed out by our predominately male history) our foremothers.

The Bible, in other words, is not simply a written document. For us, existentially or experientially, it is also the history of living with that document throughout the generations. To affirm the apostolicity of the church is to affirm that this history of Scripture is a part of Scripture itself for us, and to recognize, therefore, that in taking the Bible seriously we must also take seriously the long history of living with the Bible that has preceded us. The church's apostolicity is the fact that each generation of the church becomes constitutive of the generations to follow. To affirm that apostolicity is actively to affirm that history, both critically and appreciatively.

All of which leads me now to say that in this sense I do have the responsibility to acknowledge, too, the church decisions of the second and third centuries with respect to the nature of the Bible's authority. They do not "norm" my own view, but they are part of what forms my views today, both in what I can share with them and in what I think I see about their views that is deficient and sometimes even destructive.

> *Pinnock: I agree that in the last analysis a Christian must make up his or her own mind about things. But how do we avoid being swayed by current opinion and conformed to the world's agenda? I worry about the chauvinism of modernity and the tyranny of the present moment in this appeal to "reason."*

Brown: We know that nothing guarantees our freedom from chauvinism and tyranny. One of the more painful aspects of Christian history is the extent to which the very same people who have been exemplars of virtue in some respects have embodied the most despicable human qualities in other respects. Among these despicable qualities, embodied even by some of our "saints," is an arrogant self-confidence they have about their own views, an arrogance that is (when coupled with power) often tyrannical in its expression.

The arrogance to which liberalism is susceptible is obvious. It is a chauvinism of the contemporary, of what is "in" at the moment. It is evident in liberal theology and in liberal church life. Seen from one perspective at least, the course of liberal theology, during the past fifty years especially, looks like little more than a mimic of passing developments in the physical and social sciences. I think that is too cynical a view, but it is by no means without merit. And the fads of the mainstream and liberal church, too, parallel rather strikingly the ever-changing latest "advances" in popular culture.

31

This liberal propensity is rooted in the Enlightenment which, as I have explained, resolved above all to do away with the tyranny of traditional authorities. The various forms of authority rooted in the past, especially the authority of priests and kings, were categorically rejected in the name of freedom and autonomy. The persistent temptation of this liberal tradition, however, is the temptation to sacrifice its hard-won freedom and autonomy to the consensus of the present moment. In our time—due to the weakening of social stabilities, the pervasiveness of mass communication, etc.—this consensus is always rapidly changing. Being a liberal nowadays can be a dizzying experience!

But what puzzles me about your question is the implied supposition that the problem you speak of is rooted in modernity or reason, or both! What about the chauvinism of tradition and the tyranny of the past? What about being swayed by past opinion and being conformed to the ancient world's agenda? Christians, and conservatives in particular, wish to rest their hopes on a spotless revelation in the past. I think that ploy reflects a highly problematic understanding of the Bible and Christian revelation. But even if it did not, one would be hard-pressed to deny that the biblical revelation, however orthodoxly conceived, has been pervasively interpreted in ways that are tyrannical, chauvinistic, oppressive—indeed, even murderous.

The conservative can respond, as would many liberals, by saying, "But that does not result from an employment of the 'true' revelation nor is it inspired by the Bible as 'properly' considered." That response, I think, is too easy. After all, one could say the same, if one wished, in defense of the reliability of reason: "If the contemporary consensus is tyrannical, that is only because the modern mind has not been 'truly' rational or because modernity has not been 'properly' understood."

Liberalism rose in part because traditional Christianity, appealing to the absoluteness of its past, had become tyrannical. Conservative Christians today are right to shout their objections whenever Christian liberalism, pretending that the present is absolute, becomes tyrannical. But does this not provide us with an insight into the nature of tyranny? The problem is neither in attending to the past nor in attending to the present; the problem lies in attributing absoluteness to either of them. We have the impulse to become arrogant and try to impose our views on others whenever we think *we* possess, or just might possibly possess, or are just about to gain possession of, *the* final and flawless truth, whether we got it from the past or the present.

Tyranny is a danger in liberal Christianity and in conservative Christianity, and it is a danger for one—so far as I can tell—no less than another. A guarantee against this danger does not exist, but a guard against it might be the acknowledgement that our ways are not God's ways and that our views are not God's either. In other words, we are less likely to be tyrannical if we relinquish the pretense that we somehow have hold of absoluteness; if, instead, we accede to the insight that in the pursuit of truth, as in the pursuit of righteousness, we must depend finally on the grace of Another rather than on our own ability to get things right.

Pinnock: I sense that one explanatory cause of the declining fortunes of the Protestant mainline churches in North America is the loss of doctrinal clarity and conviction among them. Am I wrong in suspecting this?

Brown: No, I don't think you are wrong, assuming your important qualification that this is "one explanatory cause" among others.

The measurable fortunes (membership, wealth) of the mainline churches, however, are not the primary issue for me any more than they are likely to be for you. There is a story that Karl Barth was visited by one of his former students who began telling about the crowds flocking to hear his Sunday sermons, whereupon Barth is said to have interjected, "Then you must not be preaching the gospel!" The point, for me, is that the decline of liberal and mainline Protestantism (they are not the same, though they often coexist and often suffer the same weaknesses) rightly causes us to ask whether they are doing something wrong, but this decline does not answer that question "yes" or "no." Sometimes these churches, I believe, suffer decline because they preach the gospel! And I believe some other churches—many evangelical churches among them—flourish because they do not! Churches can be successful by secular standards precisely because they buttress the cultural status quo against prophetic challenge; because they cultivate self-satisfaction and the arrogance of race, class, and gender; because they condone laziness of mind by proclaiming "prevenient" certitudes; because they manipulate those who are vulnerable, etc. I am not a fan of most of the so-called successful churches. I know that a number of evangelical scholars have a similarly dubious view of these "operations." In short, the reader should be aware that—in my judgment, at least, and probably in yours, too—the most common criteria of success are unacceptable.

But I also think that liberal and mainline denominations fail according to more substantive and appropriate criteria, and I agree with your suggestion that these failings have to do with both a lack of doctrinal clarity and of conviction. In fact these failings in tandem are peculiarly endemic to liberalism. In some conservative churches there is doctrinal clarity without much conviction (they tend to be Calvinist) and in others (the Wesleyan ones) there can be the reverse. But whenever you find a church that lacks both clarity and conviction it will almost certainly be a liberal church!

The reason for this can be traced back to something I extolled as a virtue in answering your preceding question—the willingness to live without absolutism. It should be clear that we must forego absolutes, whether traditional absolutes of the past or modernist ones of the present. Christian liberalism to an extent has learned to live by "faith alone" in this sense, that is, without absolutes, often then to be plunged into a convictionless lethargy and an indifference to the life of the intellect. Conservatives frequently take this as evidence that Christianity must return to absolutism. Such a return would be untenable, unchristian, and immoral. It would be untenable because plausible absolutes simply are not there. This strategy would be unchristian because it amounts to a version of salvation by works alone. It would be immoral because, as I noted above, it creates tyrannies that oppress and destroy.

What conservative and liberal Christians together must do is seek theological understandings that show the interconnectedness of toleration and commitment, of tentativeness and zeal. The claim that they are interconnected, I maintain, has always been present among the voices of the Christian witness. Only in the modern age, however, have we been forced to give up the illusions of nonrelative, absolute claims to truth. Only now are we being forced to live with the realization that our thoughts are not God's thoughts but that we must choose, nevertheless, whom and what we will serve. The question before us today is whether we can live in true humility and also be committed, whether we can hold with conviction the things we claim only tentatively to be true.

I will say, frankly, that if we cannot, then the "liberal experiment" within Christianity is doomed. But if we cannot the doom will be broader. I am concerned about the viability of Western culture. A culture without conviction will die in a whimper of permissiveness. A culture without toleration will die in a blast of dogmatism. The problems you point to are real for us all and not merely for liberal Christianity.

• Pinnock's Rejoinder to Brown

First, I have to say right off the top, Bravo! I knew I had asked three good questions, but I had not been prepared for such excellent answers! Not only do you reply to my queries, you even explore assumptions hidden in the questions and turn them back effectively on evangelicals. This is the kind of dialogue we desperately need today.

Specifically, I accept your point about our not just accepting the authority of the New Testament because Christians in earlier ages did so. After all, large numbers of evangelicals do not accept Augustine's view of infant baptism or soteriological predestination. Nevertheless, I am still concerned about the apostolicity of the church in liberal theology. Jesus proclaimed that the kingdom of God had drawn near and that the power of God to save and heal had been poured out. The New Testament writers witness to this event and provide the crucial cognitive commentary on what is involved in terms of theism, anthropology, soteriology, and the like. In setting aside the New Testament documents as canon, the church decided that its identity would be and ought to be grounded in the message once and for all articulated by Jesus Christ and the apostles. My problem with liberal theology is its apparent willingness to break with the foundational proclamation, and your answer did not sufficiently allay my fear. It leaves the way open to reduce and distort the Word of God under the pressure of modern ideas. Nor is this merely theoretical when one sees liberals dropping the finality of Christ as the only Savior and when they reduce their assessment of his person from incarnation to inspiration, and in similar revisions.

I do not take your point though, that evangelicals are just as vulnerable to infidelity and accommodation as liberals are and have no reason to be puffed up. The works of the flesh operate in all of us indiscriminately. Nor do we have any right to level unfair accusations against liberals who often emphasize truths quite out of keeping with contemporary culture and pay the price for their courage. I can understand why liberals must resent evangelicals often for our crude attacks. At the same time, I have to register my conviction about the importance in principle of having the canon of Scripture as a solid truth deposit to stand against our potential idolatry. But I do hear you when you say that having such a Rule of Faith does not protect anyone from even gross disobedience. I appreciate the criticism, which is well founded and appropriate.

I do detect an element of rationalization, though, in your remarks about declining mainline Protestantism. Perhaps, as you say, the decline is partly due to faithfulness to Christ rather than bourgeois accommodation. Using Barth here was very effective. In reverse, perhaps the reason conservative churches are growing is precisely their enculturation not their vaunted confidence in the Scriptures. I have to agree that there are many factors that operate in all such developments of rising and falling. But I cannot quite accept a stalemate on this point, though I do appreciate your candidness as well about the problem of conviction and commitment in mainline churches. And my heart is moved when you speak about its being impossible for liberals simply to return to absolutes that they believe are not there to return to. I can only hope that my own theology in this book will help some of them to recover the evangelical essentials and renewed vitality in the Spirit of God.

SECTION 2

---

*Clark Pinnock's presentation on theological method,
Pinnock's answers to three questions put by Brown,
and a rejoinder by Brown to Pinnock's answers.*

Method in theology or any other discipline describes
the way the work is carried out. It is like the recipe for baking a fine
cake or the blueprint for constructing a sturdy house. The method
needs to be sound for the task at hand to be properly done. By
reflecting upon the procedures for doing theology, one can become
better at it. If we ignore the issue of method completely, we will run
the risk of being influenced by alien sources unwillingly and
unawares or of doing our work haphazardly.

Candidly, something in me as an evangelical theologian
objects to giving too much prominence to the subject of theological
method. I suppose it is the same inclination that made Barth
hesitate to include prolegomena in general. My instincts urge me to
put Jesus Christ first, ahead of any theory or discussion of method.
Is the Lord himself not the foundation of Christian theology?
(1 Cor. 3:11). Did Luther not urge us always to preach Christ?
Responding to this impulse, one could omit a discussion of method
or place it at the end of everything else (as Thomas Oden did in *The
Living God*).

However, method in a certain sense surely comes first, if not in
the order of doctrine, at least in the order of theorizing and it can

hardly be pushed aside inasmuch as it affects everything we do in theology subsequently. So it really ought to be discussed first, since it will certainly affect all that we say after, even though method obviously is not what we confess or proclaim.

Theological method has become a prominent subject for our discussion in recent years. There is a good reason for this. In earlier centuries, the method followed by most theologians was fairly uniform. The Scriptures were cited continually to establish sacred truth on the assumption that they, being inspired by God, comprised divinely revealed and inspired propositions. To appeal mainly to the Bible as the infallible authority seemed the only proper thing to do. But with the rise of biblical criticism, this assumption was called into question in many quarters and theologians were forced to ask new questions, such as how the Bible can be appealed to as an authority in the present circumstances. Even on the Roman Catholic side, the authority of the teaching office of the church has been widely challenged along with the Scriptures.

The result has been uncertainty and the rise of a plurality of methods in theology. Theologians generally have had to assume the burden of an assumption which has become prevalent, that all human understanding and sources of authority are historically conditioned and relative to time and place. But if so, how then can we pretend to be appealing to something infallible as we always assumed? The traditional authorities have been called into question by recent developments so that we have, not only a pluralism of methods in theology, but a pluralism of theologies as well.

This crisis goes very deep, too. The new pluralism has created a sense of nervousness in the churches. It feels to many Christians (not just to fundamentalists) as though theology has lost its bearings and come loose from its moorings. Even many moderate people have the feeling that something basic has changed and that Christianity cannot likely remain at all the same as it was. Theology seems now to be open-ended with no one being able to say where it may be headed. This affects evangelicals most especially because we care so much about the historic faith and have a sinking feeling about the changes we see happening. It seems to us as if the seamless robe of Christian truth is coming unraveled. We wonder where our identity is henceforth to be found.

As one who believes in God's lordship, I look for a silver lining in these dark clouds. I have to admit that the new emphasis upon the human dimension of the Bible and our theological traditions has brought a good deal of light to bear upon matters that had been hidden. It suggests many needed reforms. Evangelicals have had to ask ourselves whether we have not construed the authority of the Bible in too authoritarian a way in the past and unwisely mostly overlooked its human dimensions. I wonder whether our traditional focus has not been too limited to the Bible's authority as a source of doctrinal propositions and whether the new thinking does not actually place us in a better position to appreciate the actual nature of biblical revelation than when its historical character had not yet been opened up. It seems distinctly possible that the turn to the human, even in the area of the Bible and theology, is not going to spell only impoverishment but enrichment as well. Because of God's ability to use circumstances, even unpromising ideas to alert his people to uncompleted tasks, I do not think we need to despair but can seek ways to grow into theological maturity.

A POSITIVE ORIENTATION

Christian theology rests ultimately upon divine revelation in history. Along with the believing community, we confess the triune God who has revealed himself to humankind as the God of love and grace. In the scriptural narrative of salvation, we have caught a glimpse of the reality and character of the God of all nations. Therefore, in our theological method, we go incessantly back to this fundamental fact of revelation in which all of our sources are rooted and serve as various responses to it. Although the term "revelation" sounds like a peculiarly religious word, in fact it is not an odd idea at all. It refers to the sort of experience that people regularly have when they find that a particular truth or experience or event bestows meaning on the rest of their lives and illuminates everything for them. What revelation means for evangelicals is that we have seen God having been disclosed in history in the person of Jesus Christ for the purpose of reconciling and restoring the whole human race. This is the basic premise of historic Christianity, that God has revealed himself supremely in the face of Jesus Christ and this disclosure is necessarily the foundation of Christian theology.

For me revelation and the Bible are distinct and not just identical ideas. Revelation refers to the divine self-disclosure in history and in every human heart, particularly in the Christ event bringing salvation to sinners. Revelation is that to which the Bible bears testimony. It cannot simply be lifted off the surface of the Bible as from a flat plane. We have to seek God's revelation on the basis of the Scripture's witness, which sets forth the progressive unfolding of God's saving purposes still awaiting completion at the coming of Christ and the kingdom of God.

The sources for theology rise out of this fundamental fact of revelation and are essentially four: Scripture, tradition, experience, and reason. Because there are these four anchors, Wesleyans have spoken of this as a quadrilateral. What this means in essence is that God's revelation has generated and continually empowers a written witness (the Scriptures), a remembering community (the traditions), a process of existential appropriation (experience), and a way to test for internal consistency (reason). Let me discuss the four sources each in turn.

1. Evangelicals make a great deal out of the final authority of the Bible because they realize that Scripture alone gives Christians access to the original revelation. There is no other source like it. It would be necessary, even apart from other considerations, that the revelation of God would have to be fixed in writing, if it was going to be possible to pass it on to succeeding generations without major distortion and fading. (All world religions have scriptures for this reason.) They make it possible in the providence of God for those who come later to participate in the original revelation because it has been fixed for them in writing and made present to them in the form of documents.

Initially there was a period of oral tradition before the New Testament collection was gathered and circulated, but this was only temporary. So long as there were eyewitnesses of the Word and disciples of those who had known the apostles, the need for Scriptures would not be urgent. But, as soon as the distance between the original revelation and the present became too wide to be easily bridged by the original witnesses and their friends, written testimony necessarily came into play. The Bible itself anticipates this reality as when it tells of Moses writing things down and when it speaks of the charism inspiration in one way or another. It was practically inevitable that a body of documents would be collected in order to comprise a written record of the original revelation. Without such a scriptural canon, the danger would exist of people reinventing the revelation as they go and adapting it unwisely to the spirit of every age. Nowhere else than in Scripture does the word of the primary witnesses to God's revelation come to us with such authenticity and power. In the Bible we meet God and encounter his revelation afresh. This is both what the Bible claims and what one would expect. The message of saving grace is not left to chance or the whims of historical tradition but is inscripturated for our sakes.

Christians love the Scriptures because we hear God speaking in them. Christians have always found that the Scriptures empower and instruct us. The Bible is a source of renewal and we return to it again and again to be spoken to by God. It is the evangelicals' favorite sacrament and our most frequently used means of grace. We treasure the great and precious promises of God recorded in Scripture and take great delight in them. Evangelicals believe that acknowledging the full authority of the Bible is essential for the Christian faith to be healthy and strong. Therefore we accept Scripture as the norm that has no other norm above it.

However, it is also true that, out of reaction against liberal theology, which sees the Bible largely as a human source, evangelicals have often gone to the opposite extreme and exaggerated its divine character. We frequently distort the meaning of biblical inspiration in order to lift the Bible up to the heights of perfection and invoke it as if it were all on the level of a prophetic oracle. It becomes a book like the Koran to us, a text written in heaven and not a human witness to God's revelation on earth. We really need to listen more carefully to the Bible's own doctrine of inspiration, which is more modest in its claims, speaking more about its complete profitability rather than any scholastic perfection.

2. Evangelicals do not normally pay much attention to tradition. We love to discuss biblical inspiration but give much less thought to tradition. But this does not show much wisdom. Human beings are deeply affected by tradition, even when we are unaware of it, perhaps especially then. God's revelation attested to in the Scriptures continues to call forth fresh encounters in the community of faith with the Word of God. In each new situation of history, believers rediscover, reformulate, and restate in our own words the revealed Word of God that we hear. In the history of interpretation and in tradition, like so many refractions of sunlight passing through the prism, the Word of God is continually pondered, treasured, and passed on to subsequent generations. One motive of the tradition is that nothing of value should be lost and everything

be carefully preserved, while another motive wants to ensure that God's revelation remains intelligible, up-to-date, and meaningful to people. At its best then, tradition is not just something archaic and cold but the living transmission and interpretation of the Scriptures in the churches. For the Word of God lives on in the community that springs from it, and in turn sees that it is passed on. Tradition is the process of the Word of God becoming historically effective. It is a vital social reality that receives and transmits the treasure that God has given. In its tradition, the church seeks to be apostolic, rooted in the doctrine of the New Testament, and serving the gospel as the pillar and ground of the truth.

If the church should choose to go its own way and wander from the truth into error as sometimes happens, then the Scriptures serve as a corrective and as a principle of reform. They stand as the decisive counter to the church's authority and can help us arbitrate between divergent paths. The process of correction and reform through the Bible admittedly is not an easy one, but it is critical that the church be built upon the foundation of the apostles and prophets and not teach only what it happens to be thinking at any given moment.

3. God's Word also has to be experienced by the people. The individual believer is summoned to correlate his or her own personal experience with the historical experience of the faithful lodged in the tradition, interacting with the social processes of the community and embracing its memory. It would be wrong (though it is often done) to pit one's personal experience against the church's social experience. For what has been the church's experience can become one's own experience. This is what happens when one is converted and subsequently grows up into Christ. Through the teaching and preaching of the church people are enabled to enter into the faith of the community and have it authenticated in their own lives, experiencing personal transformation. Past experience, which is tradition, and present experience are both important. Evangelicals are particularly concerned that present experience not be allowed to snuff out the original message that comes to us from the past.

The integration between one's own individual feelings and the corporately remembered experience of the historic community usually takes place in worship and liturgy. There the social memory and personal feelings converge. This is only proper since personal experience is to the believer what tradition is to the church as a whole. Both are modes of receiving and pondering the Word of God that has come to us through the Scriptures, and the Spirit of God can enliven them both and wants to work down both tracks. God's truth needs to be confirmed in experience if it is to be vital and influential. The Good News has to become truth for me. But we must avoid at all costs allowing individual experience to become the autonomous source of revelation. Individual experience must not be allowed to rise up and negate the Scriptures or tradition, but it must be shaped by the Christian norms. The individual believer does not have the right to invent Christianity anew; Scripture and the traditions of the living church are the means for shaping and evaluating the experiences of individuals.

But I do not want to deny the importance of personal experience. Experience played a role in God's giving of revelation in ancient times. It was not the communication of inerrant propositions dictated to scribes. One can see when one reads the Old Testament that there was the pressure of the divine Person upon the people of Israel in their historical experiences to bring them to deeper and fuller insights into God's purpose and character. They encountered God in the context of their experience as a people and saw through to reality as God made initiatives into their history. Human experience was and is always involved. God deals with us as persons not in cold or impersonal ways.

4. God's Word is also intelligible; therefore, human reason must have a place in theological method. In this context reason performs many valuable roles. Let me take some examples: reason helps us avoid contradicting ourselves; it forces us to take account of fresh information; it helps us see the truth as a whole and not only in fragments. As Anselm said, faith seeks understanding. The mind God gave us desires intelligibility. Even revelation needs to be thought out and not left undigested. Evangelicals need to be more positive about the value of reason in theology than we usually are.

Our caution stems from the fear that reason, if it is given a role in theology, will soon assume a higher place than it should. It won't be long until it claims to be the final source and judge of all truth. How can this be avoided? By realizing that reason is not autonomous, divorced from its place in other modes of knowing God's truth. It is a human faculty and its role is a humble one. Theology should welcome its searching questions and not refuse to have its

43

own credentials examined. But reason itself is not free from captivity to culture and does not operate in a perfectly neutral manner. Therefore, it must be carefully monitored when it is employed.

These four sources of theology need to be held in creative tension for the best results. Each one is a response to the revealed Word of God. When that revelation is fixed in writing, we appropriate it amid changing historical and cultural circumstances, reflect upon it with our powers of reason, and personally discover its fresh relevance in our own experience. Just as a table stands securely on its four legs, so Christian theology works best when it enjoys a proper equilibrium given to it by its four sources.

In summary I believe that Christian theology ought to take its cues, not from what people happen to be thinking at this moment in time and place, but from the faith once delivered to the saints and passed on down to them through history. It should not accept just whatever revisions in doctrine are proposed but inquire carefully whether they emanate from the vision that grounds the church. It needs to have a defense mechanism to protect it from being swallowed up by powerful contemporary pressures. It will find this protection in the revelation of God deposited in the Scriptures.

PRESSING ISSUES FOR EVANGELICALS

I do not want the reader to think that I am unaware of difficulties in what I have been saying. Let me refer to several questions that need better answers than they usually receive from evangelicals. First, as is well known, evangelicals hold strong convictions that Christian theology should be tied to the biblical content. Theology is meant, we say, to be solidly based in Scripture, which is understood to be an infallible teacher. But is that the Bible's own intention? Is that what it was meant to be? This is the question of how we are meant to understand the role of the Bible: Is it to be thought of as a source of fixed content as orthodoxy has assumed or should it be seen to function in other more practical ways? One might choose to speak of the Bible authoring us, for example, rather than primarily teaching us. Rudolf Bultmann takes the New Testament to be issuing an existential challenge to us rather than offering us dogmas or information of any kind. Is the purpose of the Bible perhaps to transform us existentially rather than to instruct us? Perhaps it is not an either/or; maybe the Bible transforms *and* instructs us. Are the political theologians right to be seeking a liberating trajectory in the Bible or the philosophers in viewing the Bible as a source of philosophical insight in mythical terms? How should we construe the authority of the Bible? The evangelical view is under pressure today, and the search is on for alternatives that would not commit us to the cognitive authority of the Bible.

In the midst of this pressure, the evangelical chooses to stick to the ancient paths, alarmed at the implications of disregarding the teaching authority of the Bible. We understand God's revelation in Christ to involve both word and deed. We hold fast to a message that has solid content and a basic grammar not meant to be fundamentally altered. For us, whatever else it is, Christianity is a doctrinal religion.

This is surely a crux in the liberal-evangelical dialogue. We disagree over whether Christianity is tied to the truth content of Scripture or rests on a subjectivist principle. Has God communicated truth, which has been now passed on down through history to the present, or is it a question of human experience and human searching from first to last? Evangelicals believe strongly that there is a basic grammar that has created Christian community. It is the glue that holds it together and without which it cannot exist. The truth content is not something that rises from our experience; rather, it creates experience.

This emphasis is part of what gives the evangelical approach its appeal. It offers people deep meaning becaue it claims to be able to give us the solid answers to life's questions for which we yearn. This undoubtedly helps to explain the growth of the conservative churches in recent years. But the question comes: Do evangelicals want truth or only meaning? Is faith believing what we know isn't so or does it want to have its eyes open? How do evangelicals propose to make good our claims for the Bible when we know of so many strong objections to it?

Second, continuing along these lines, let me raise a related issue. Since there are many difficulties in holding to the Bible's authority as teacher, is it not naïve to stick with this model of authority? How, in the face of the problems, can evangelicals sustain our belief that theology ought to be tied to the content of the New Testament proclamation as binding on the church today?

One factor that makes us hold stubbornly to the truth content of the Christian message is our belief that the New Testament itself encourages us to do so. Saint Paul in 1 Corinthians, for example, insists that certain facts and doctrines are basic to the Christian gospel (15:1–5). This has always been the Christian understanding as the liturgy and the history of catechesis reveal so clearly. The question of how we are meant to receive the word of the gospel has not been left completely open. The church has never been hesitant to come down where evangelicals stand today.

But is it not still naïve to continue in this way of thinking now that we have come to realize how human the Bible is in many respects, now that we are aware of its diversity, its premodern prescientific ideas, its cultural limitations, including certain ethical perspectives, its many factual difficulties and so forth. How can an evangelical, who is honest and informed, continue to follow the old paths and appeal to the Bible as an infallible teacher? Do not these difficulties rule that out? Are we not forced to construe the Bible's authority differently? Don't the facts require that its authority be taken experientially not cognitively now? And don't we have to admit that the very nature of theology itself is a human enterprise based on our own fallible reflections from beginning to end? Assuming that we do not espouse blind faith, how can we ignore what reality is telling us?

I find help in what Saint Paul tells us about having "this treasure in earthen vessels" (2 Cor. 4:7 KJV). He says that God's way of revealing himself is not to knock us off our feet. God reveals himself incarnationally. If in the past evangelicals have tried to sidestep the fact of the earthly character of revelation, then we need to reform our thinking. We will need to take into account new discoveries and insights. We will need to make room for theological development in the face of man's ever-expanding horizon of scientific knowledge. But that will not require us to abandon the authority of the Bible because we find its message ever convincing and transforming.

Evangelicals often pretend that only liberals revise theology while we ourselves never do. We respond positively to James Orr's statement: "When I am asked, which of the articles of the Evangelical faith I am prepared to part with at the instance of modern thought, and in the interests of a reconstructed theology, I answer, with fullest confidence: None of them." It is true that evangelicals are not into any deep revisions of traditional theology but we would be deceiving ourselves if we denied doing any revisions at all.

Hermeneutics is a third important issue. How can evangelicals avoid the subjectivity we fear when reader bias obviously affects our interpretations as much as others'? Is it not true that Bible readers find pretty much what we want to find when we read the text? And if so, how can the Bible be said to be an objective standard for theology if its readers are socially, ecclesiastically, and historically located in our reading?

Part of the answer to this problem is to put a counter question to the skepticism implied in the objection: although it is undoubtedly true that reader presuppositions get in the way of our perceiving exactly what the Bible teaches, why conclude that the situation is hopeless? Discovering exactly what the Bible means to say remains the ideal toward which we strive, and in the fellowship of other interpreters the meaning comes to light and penetrates our darkness. Just because human perception is clouded we do not need to surrender the ideal of truth and knowledge in this or in any other area.

Recognizing the quadrilateral of sources for theology also helps us with this question. There are multiple sources to help us and not only one. Scripture, though eminent, is not the only source we have to invoke. The meaning of Scripture flows down to us through what Gadamer calls effective history, giving us the advantage of twenty centuries of experience in biblical interpretation and application. Thus, one really moves forward in interpretation by looking backward. Interpretation is not only a private exercise one does alone but takes place in a historic faith community that speaks an ancient language and sings familiar songs.

In conclusion, despite the difficulties we admit exist, we evangelicals prefer our method to the alternatives. We are not attracted to the method of liberal theology and its implications, specifically the danger of unrestricted pluralism and even at times seduction. If we were to reject the cognitive authority of the Bible in favor of a functional view of it, the locus of authority in theology would automatically shift from divine revelation coming to us from God over to human reason and religious experience already resident in us. In that case fallen humanity itself would become the ultimate court of appeal.

How, we want to ask with concern, if a theologian has only

human experience to work with, can he or she avoid an open-endedness that radically threatens doctrinal continuity and Christian identity? How then will we know what is Christian and what is not? Theological pluralism, however valid up to a point, cannot define us or give us identity. And we worry about the possibility of actual seduction. Emmanuel Hirsch, one of the theologians under Hitler, after all, wanted to update Christian concepts and keep theology contemporary by moving it in the direction of the Nazi ideology.

How will we avoid the corruption of Christian doctrine by really bad forms of cultural accommodation unless the message is fixed and normative in its core? We cannot counter ideologies that are strong, specific, and compelling with fluff. Evangelical experience shows that it is hard enough to avoid accommodation even when one does have a standard. Unless we are rooted in the faith of the historic community, we will surely be swept away. You cannot fight something with nothing. It is almost certain that we will replace the old certainties with new ones rising from modern tendencies if we abandon the foundations. Evangelicals object to the way some liberals seem to be modest in relation to historic beliefs like the Incarnation and the Trinity but are very sure indeed about the latest trendy beliefs. There seems to be a new breed of fundamentalists of the left who pursue their new causes with all the militancy formerly associated with that orthodoxy, whether it's gay rights, feminism, Nicaragua, or socialism. Evangelicals are understandably worried about the health and future of a church that operates this way. The church requires a sounder theological method than that.

The identity of the church is what is at stake here. It is a question of what we are going to teach the people. Are there not boundaries and limitations that describe the playing field of Christian discourse? Surely there always have been. Christians have always confessed that humankind is fallen and in need of salvation; that revelation has taken place in history the way the Bible witnesses; that the true God is the triune God; that Jesus is the Way, the Truth, and the Life, and so forth. Exactly what each of these statements means in detail is open for discussion. There are disputes surrounding them that have not yet been settled, and segments of the Christian community have placed peculiar con-structions upon one or another of them. Debates over such matters have even led to painful and unpleasant splits. Nevertheless, there

48

are parameters of doctrine we must not allow to dissolve. There is a framework of meaning that gives us life and hope.

> *Brown: You speak of the "basic grammar" of Christian faith. What belongs to that grammar, and in particular, how does the conservative theologian determine what in the Bible belongs to it?*

Pinnock: This is a question about the cognitive side of our Christian faith. It asks what truth claims are proper to it? The basic answer would be that Jesus' announcement of the reign of God involves many such claims, both explicitly and implicitly. These would include the existence of an infinite, personal God, the brokenness of our world, God's decisive action to put things right through the anointed one, the sending of the Spirit to save and heal, and so forth. Historically, the church has always been concerned to spell out these basic truth claims, doing this under the rubric of the rule of faith or creed. It has regularly drawn up basic summaries of faith that are believed to be at the heart of the identity of the confessing Christian community. Not systematic theology, these creedal documents offer some of the most essential intellectual conclusions to which the church is driven when required to state the implications of the rule of God. They help define the cognitive backbone of the gospel.

You are right to suspect in your question that evangelicals are often naïve about this, often supposing that the Bible itself spells out the grammar of theology in complete detail. Of course, I agree that the Scriptures present a rather clear picture of the Christian message in basic outline and in general terms. The witnesses point to many essential beliefs that we are commanded to guard and proclaim. These lay the foundation for what C. S. Lewis calls "mere Christianity," the consensus of the faith everywhere and always believed. The grammar of faith that I speak of, then, is outlined in the New Testament and has served as the language of the community over the many centuries.

But this does not settle every matter and certain questions remain. Which beliefs are essential and which nonessential? Which matters are open to opinion and which closed? Is infant baptism an essential belief or not? Is the real presence of Christ in the Eucharist

a dogma? Is predestination? Is premillennialism? Is biblical iner-
rancy? Is the everlasting conscious punishment of the wicked? Or,
on a different note, is feminism? Is religious pluralism? Is political
theology? How does one avoid arbitrariness in this area? Such
matters are the source of church divisions to this very day.
Therefore, you are right to ask me about the essential grammar.

In searching for a solution to this problem, I think it is
important to remember that we are not alone in making these
decisions and do not have to start from scratch. As hearers and
doers of the Word of God, we find ourselves situated somewhere in
the history of biblical and theological interpretation. The hermeneutical task is an ongoing one, which is never finished, and is shared
by all fellow Christians. On the other hand, I find that there is a
widespread, ecumenical agreement on the basics of belief. The
Trinity lies at the heart of a theological consensus that is ancient
and confessed by believers in vastly different cultural settings and
temporal epochs.

On the other hand, alongside this agreement are also many
disagreements. I do not wish to deny that. Certainly, there is work to
be done on those other matters of faith and order where unity still
eludes us. But even here I think the prospects are promising: when I
think of the progress in ecumenical discussions on the role of Mary;
on the significance of Peter; in the dialogue between Lutherans and
Catholics about justification by faith; and in the marvelous consensus reached in the Baptism, Eucharist, and Ministry document from
the Lima meeting of the World Council of Churches, Faith and
Order Commission.

Using the metaphor of grammar for the system of Christian
beliefs allows, I think, for both continuity and discontinuity in
theology. On the one hand, what we confess today is and ought to
be in agreement with what the early theologians confessed. It ought
to be fully grammatical with their beliefs. On the other hand, the
grammar of a living language (if we use that metaphor) is also
flexible enough to articulate many fresh insights as the need arises.
Perhaps you and I can find some common ground in this duality.

> *Brown: Reason, as you note, is not free from the danger
> of captivity to culture. But is anything—faith, biblical
> interpretation, the consensus of the church at any given
> time, a prayerful openness to God's will—free of that*

danger? Moreover, is reason not indispensable in the determination of that within the Bible that you think represents the basic grammar of faith? In sum, are not conservatives, too, bound to use the very reason of which they seem to be suspicious?

Pinnock: Reason is and has been important to the liberal experiment in theology. Hence this question. Perhaps it is inevitable that we will differ on it. Conservatives instinctively feel that humankind suffers from many limitations. This is why politically they have an aversion to utopian schemes and want to impose limits on governments. Thus in politics as well as in theology, conservatives do not exalt reason to the highest level but see it as a resource that is meant to operate in the context of other faculties without dominating them. Liberals on the other hand generally place greater faith in the creative powers of the intellect, both in theology and in politics.

At the same time, I am no fideist in matters of religion. I dislike Barth and Kierkegaard because of their depreciation of reason as much as you do. I uphold the proper, ministerial role of reason in all areas of our work. I think, for example, that we ought to deal with the questions people raise concerning the claims of faith and ought to be always ready to give a reason for the hope that is in us. I suspect that you and I stand pretty much together in the defense of reason against the Barthian veto of it. Reason comes into play in all sorts of ways in theology: in biblical interpretation, in constructing doctrinal models, in presenting the message, in defending it, and so forth.

The caution I would want to register here is the need to remember that we are affected by culture in our reason as we are in every other respect. We are historically embedded creatures and therefore need to be self-critical and suspicious of our own reasoning. It is so easy for what we suppose to be objective reasoning to turn out to be self-serving prejudice or plain gospel-denying accommodation to culture. The claims of reason are always culturally specific. It is a little ironical for me to be lecturing you on this since liberals are generally more aware of it than evangelicals usually are. Yet I believe that liberals sometimes disregard their own maxim.

51

What this means for me is that I try to do my reasoning along with the Scriptures rather than against them, and with the Christian community rather than going off on tangents of my own. I try to subject my thinking to the authority of the Bible and to the judgments of traditional theology. I do not care to follow the novel routes carved out by Enlightenment-dominated reason. I do not want to substitute the authority of a Kant or some other modern luminary for the authority of the Bible in the name of rationality. Reason ought not be allowed to vaunt itself above the claims of revelation.

I realize that it would be neater in some ways either to serve reason and take my cues from modern culture like certain modernists do, or to be wholly dogmatic and, like certain paleo-conservatives, pay no attention to what is being thought and experienced today. But I cannot accept either type of extremism. I find that reason makes a good servant but a poor master. I value reason and make a great deal of use of it in my work, but refuse to let it dictate the terms of God's truth. In that respect I look to God's self-revelation in Jesus and not to my own understanding. I suppose this means reason within the limits of religion.

To take an illustration of the ministerial role of reason, recently a number of evangelicals, including the eminent John Stott, have come to believe that the traditional doctrine of hell as endless conscious punishment is scripturally weak and morally intolerable. These evangelicals have maintained that we need to reconsider this dogma. I have no doubt that reason, both theoretical and practical, played a major role in their change of mind. But unlike liberal theologians, who would undoubtedly agree with them on the point, their decision depends on the Bible being in agreement. They are not free to make even this move unless they can be assured that it enjoys scriptural approval.

Evangelicals then do not want the freedom to invent new doctrines whenever we feel like it according to the demands of our reason. The faculty for us is on a tether and we like to have it that way. Useful as reason is in so many ways, it remains the case that God's ways are higher than our ways and his thoughts than our thoughts (Isa. 55:8–9). This means that reason for us is not the final court of appeal.

Brown: Recognizing the authority of the Bible, you maintain, is essential for the Christian faith. In my opinion, that is an important conservative insight. But, as you also observe, it is crucial to be clear about how the Bible is authoritative, and what "authority" means when applied to the Bible. Would you say more about your view of the meaning of authority?

Pinnock: Evangelicals are often naïve even about central convictions. In this case, we seem to think that, once we have secured (by whatever means) a belief in the authority of an infallible Bible, we have made it home scot-free. Evangelicals do not seem to realize that we have only just begun when we reach that point. Professing the authority of the Bible does not settle everything. It does not settle issues of interpretation nor tell us where the locus of authority rests.

The point evangelicals need to be made aware of is that the authority of the Bible means different things to different people. For some it may lie in the concepts of Scripture, but for others it may reside in its transforming effects upon readers. You yourself propose that the authority of the Bible consists in the Bible somehow authoring us. In a similar vein, others find authority in the Bible's power to occasion new moments of insight and self-transformation. Feminists, for example, locate the authority of the Bible in its ability to move us in the direction of liberating praxis and not in its literal teachings, which they often view as sexist. So it is important to ask, as you intimate, not only whether the Bible is authoritative, but where authority resides in the Bible.

Probably most evangelicals who ignore this challenge do so because it never occurred to them. The idea that the authority of the Bible might not involve commitment to the cognitive truth of the information the Bible delivers (whether historical or doctrinal) sounds alien and outrageous to them. They assume that the authority of the Bible means the truth of its content, just like the great Christian tradition tends to. They suspect that any move to deny this must be some kind of liberal plot to get out from under the obligations of believing the biblical teachings they don't particularly like. They would suspect that rebelliousness is the real reason why liberals would make the shift from an authority that

53

dictates ideas to an authority that existentially transforms. At times I share their suspicion when it seems transparent. Bultmann's denial of the miracles of Jesus or the Pauline doctrine of atonement would be a case in point.

But the question should not be sidestepped. The liberals are on to something here. We ought to ask whether cognitive authority is in fact the heart and soul of what the authority of the Bible consists of. Certainly it cannot be the only dimension of biblical authority because there is a richness to the ways in which the Bible norms and shapes us that goes far beyond mere information giving. Like a good teacher who teaches us in many different ways—formally and informally, by word and deed, in doctrine and experience—so the Bible, too, teaches us in many different ways. What we probably ought to be saying in answer to this question is that, while instructing us is one of the authoritative actions that the Bible performs, it is not the only one. It is one important function and is not something we are free to drop just because we do not always like it. The biblical writers do lay claims upon us in the realm of truth and ethics and we ought to be open to them. The historic church has always known this and evangelicals are not about to drop this emphasis.

At the same time, we do not have to exaggerate the cognitive side of biblical authority either. Just as a teacher teaches in all sorts of ways, not only by lecturing at us but in other ways, too, so the Scriptures teach us in many different ways through a rich variety of forms. Concepts and statutes are part of what the Bible authoritatively teaches us and we ought to submit to them, but they are not the whole of what it communicates. As the rule of faith, the Bible performs its function by teaching, by narrating, by exhorting, by challenging, etc. (cf. 2 Tim. 3:16). There is a rich multiplicity in its norming us.

Thus, if a Tillich, for example, should refuse to hear the Scripture when it teaches certain concepts, then he is to be condemned, for it does not lie within his power or right to lay down the decision about the way in which the Bible must function even for him. The authority of the Bible means that the Scripture instructs us in many and various ways, which implies that we ought to attend to it with unrestricted openness, even to its doctrine and ethics. While classical theologians have always known this, we believe that liberals question it for ulterior reasons that are modernity-driven. They want to do their reasoning not along with Scripture but independently of it.

In practice, the authority of the Bible is a wondrous thing, full of variety and richness. It does not enslave but sets us free. The tripartite structure of the Old Testament is a clue to this richness. In the Torah, the foundations of faith are laid for the community; in the prophets, many dynamic reinterpretations are offered to keep the ball in play; and in the writings, probing questions are posed that force the reader to think and reconsider. The authority of such a book is an easy and delightful yoke.

● Brown's Rejoinder to Pinnock

I appreciate the openness you exhibit on the subject of theological method, particularly because this has been the area of most serious dispute and misunderstanding between liberals and conservatives. We have misunderstood one another, but, more importantly, we misunderstood ourselves. That is, what we have said we are doing, as liberals or conservatives, has often been quite different from what we are in fact doing. Liberals, as I have said, have been naïve about the role of the Bible and tradition in our lives and in our theologies. In that respect (among others) we have misunderstood ourselves.

Conservatives, as you note, have been naïve about the role of the Bible, too. They have remained oblivious to what the Bible emphatically does not do. For example, it does not spell out a "grammar of theology in complete detail," as you acknowledge. If we can agree on that, and if we may legitimately differ about what is and is not essential to Christian belief, then liberals and conservatives ought to be able to converse without condemnation. That is true even with respect to your hypothetical "condemnation" of "a Tillich," because what you denounce is the refusal to "hear the Scripture," to attend to it with "unrestricted openness." Close-mindedness of any sort deserves denunciation. That is no less true when we, liberals and conservatives, close our minds to one another.

On the issue of theological method, there are two points where you and I might need to attend more closely to one another because they seem to be points where our views remain quite distinct.

One point of disagreement is the relationship of revelation and reason. Perhaps we did not adequately press one another, or ourselves, on what we mean by revelation. But whatever we each take revelation to mean precisely, we both talk throughout as though the things being discussed—revelation, interpretation, reason, tradition, modernity, etc.—are related in theology and in life. None of these is "pure" or nicely separable from its counterparts. Given that interrelationship, we should discuss further the extent to which we can distinguish revelation and reason, or tradition and its successive contemporary contexts (i.e., the "modernity" of each age).

If revelation is not sharply distinguishable from the activity of human reasoning, and if tradition always interacts with its "modernist" environment, then it is not clear to me how one *can* appeal, as you often do, to revelation and tradition against their counterparts as if they represent clearly identifiable alternatives. Moreover, if God is still active, it is not evident to me why one *should* so readily appeal to the past. Might we not learn something from God through reason and from modernity? Can that knowledge not sometimes be a corrective to the past? Do we not need to question the claims of the past, revelation and tradition, as carefully as we must question the claims of modernity and the rights of reason? These are issues I think we could profitably pursue further.

The other point where additional discussion could be fruitful has to do with the *meaning* of authority. I think you are right to insist on the importance of truth-claims in understanding the role of the Bible, and I agree with you that we ought to ask where authority resides in the Bible.

But I am not convinced that we have as yet reached clarity, in agreement or in disagreement, about *what* authority is, at least as the question pertains to the Bible. You usually speak as if the Bible's authority is its right and capacity to function as the norm of belief and action. I suspect that view of authority largely to have been an import from the Roman legal tradition (the "modernism" of the first few centuries of the common era). In any case, I do not think that view adequately accounts for the actual functioning of the Bible in Christian community. What does authority mean? What does it mean to say that the Bible is the Christian's authority? If the Bible's authority is fundamentally the fact that it continually authors our identities, then the notion that there must be *a* grammar of faith or theology that constitutes *the* essence of Christianity is dubious indeed. These, I am sure, remain issues that divide us and that deserve further consideration.

PART TWO
THE DOCTRINE OF GOD

SECTION 3

Clark Pinnock's presentation on the doctrine of God, Pinnock's answers to three questions put by Brown, and a rejoinder by Brown to Pinnock's answers.

From what I said about theological method, it follows that evangelical theology will seek to maintain biblical theism in its dynamic vividness and stay in as close a proximity to historic church doctrine as Scripture permits. Doctrine is not something that bubbles up out of human experience but a precipitate of the revelation of God in Jesus Christ. The basic style of evangelical theology on each and every topic is to draw upon God's revelation as set forth in the inspired Scriptures, and to listen to the voices of the past and appropriate any input from experience, reason, and contemporary culture that proves useful.

As regards Christian theism, evangelicals resist the contention that our ideas about God are simply human constructions, metaphors of our own experience, or subjective intuitions about the unknown Beyond. In speaking about God, we insist on operating with the models generated by divine revelation from the God who has declared himself. God has been revealing his name to the human race, and we are determined to have our experience of God shaped by that reality. Therefore, our doctrine of God attempts to be a distillation of what we believe God has told us about himself. Our calling is to worship the true and living God and not to bow down to gods we have created to suit our own liking. We deplore aspects of modernity in this regard. We regret the loss of transcendence in modern culture and we oppose the earth-bound gods of modern theology. Modernity is not normative for Christian thinking in this or in other matters.

In spite of the humanness and earthly character of revelation, which we acknowledge and which means that we do not grasp the whole of the divine mystery, we are confident that divine revelation gives us valid insight into the heart of God, disclosed to us in the divine initiatives particularly in Jesus Christ. God's essence admittedly transcends all that we can gather even from his revelation, yet we are confident that we know God as he really is even though there are realms in God which are inaccessible to us. We take comfort in the fact that, even in human relationships, insight into the soul of another person depends on voluntary disclosure; and not everything is disclosed even then.

Even though we depend on revelation for our knowledge of God, it does not follow that belief in God requires a blind leap of faith and makes no sense in terms of ordinary human experience. On the contrary, the contingencies of human life and its intrinsic limitations continually raise the basic questions of meaning and purpose that lead human beings almost inevitably to ask about and to seek God. What other way is there to handle the mysterious character of human existence that is adequate to the question it raises except to speak of God? Nothing short of transcendence can really satisfy our questions of meaning and significance, which call for answers lying beyond the horizons of the world. The experience of contingency goes a long way to explain why the human race is and always has been fundamentally religious and why secularism has been unable to eradicate it.

Belief in God is much more than an intellectual issue of course. It rises out of encounter and experience. In Christian terms, the love that flows from the Father through the incarnate Son is made personally real and vital through the witness of the Spirit in our hearts, which stimulates praises to God from within us. Eternal life, which has its origin in God the Father and has been given to us in God the Son, is made our interior possession by God the Spirit. God's breath of Pentecost fills us with praise as we contemplate the living One who is love in action and whose ways are holy. The God who made light to shine out of darkness has shone into our hearts.

The God who gives life to the dead and calls into existence things that do not exist has come to us. The God who is completely reliable and keeps his promises has blessed us. With the psalmist we say, "I will bless the Lord at all times, his praise shall continually be in my mouth." With the historic churches we sing the praises of our wonderful Lord.

THE GOD OF THE GOSPEL

Who then is God according to the gospel? What is God like? How shall we speak of God who is both near us and yet who transcends the whole world? Although the Bible does not present a systematic doctrine of God that can be easily reproduced, it provides building blocks for such a doctrine. The Scriptures bear a rich witness to the variegated encounters his people have enjoyed with God in a variety of situations. In the Old Testament, Israel experienced God as living and gracious, as the One who by his intervention in human affairs creates hope for humankind. And the New Testament confirms this experience of God and adds detail and clarity to the picture it creates. There we learn that the God who intervened in history under the old covenant is none other than the Father of Jesus Christ and the Savior of the whole world. The New Testament presents in an even more radical way God's coming near to save us.

Evangelical theology delights in the majesty of God. It entertains a glorious vision of the living God, maker of heaven and earth. It does not lack paradoxes in speaking of God as the One whose power, though it is unlimited, is the power that is used to save sinners. The God who transcends all creation stoops to save sinners. The God who is not bound to the world nevertheless identifies with the sufferings of people. The God of holiness is also the God of love who does not keep his anger forever. God, though he is a jealous God and is intolerant of sin, yet embraces sinners. Evangelical theology confesses God as the creator of the world and our own personal being, the source of all that has value, the foundation of all meaning, the Lord who gives hope to all, who is always present in our midst, whose plan is to restore the whole creation and transfigure it. This God alone deserves our praise. Let every knee bow to him. Like the apostle Paul on Mars Hill, our spirits are provoked within us; and we feel jealous for God's honor, too, when we see cities full of idols and people worshiping false gods. The chief motive of world mission is to proclaim his name, which rightly deserves humanity's praise.

Adoration of the triune God lies at the heart of evangelical theism. Christians hold to this mysterious doctrine, not only because it has been the confession of the historic churches, but because it is commended to us by New Testament teaching, which presents a triune pattern of divine working for our salvation. The gospel speaks of the Father, Son, and Holy Spirit working together in a relational pattern to save humanity. In John 15:26 the Son promises to send the Paraclete to us from the Father. The divine Trinity is surely a divine mystery without parallel. Three persons within God interrelate to bring about the salvation of the human race. God is not a single person, but a society of three distinct but closely associated persons.

This doctrine makes a good deal of practical sense. For one thing, it sanctifies our social relationships on earth. The way we relate to one another in family, church, and society reflects God's own social nature and matter ultimately. To be bound together in love and harmony in human relationships mirrors the divine Society. The doctrine also indicates that the deity is not a superdictator kind of God but the essence of other-regarding love. It also gives depth to the meaning of our baptism in that we are baptized into a family on earth that is destined to be joined in union with the fellowship of the triune God (Jn. 17:23). And when Christians pray, we do not invoke one solitary listener, but enjoy three divine persons in attendance at our petitions. Even as we pray, the Son intercedes for us with the Father, while the Spirit helps our infirmities, praying for us and in us with groanings that cannot be uttered. The Trinity is a doctrine with many practical implications.

But does the doctrine make any rational sense? People often give the impression that they think it does not. Admitting that it is a mystery, I would contend that the doctrine is rational, too, in many ways. Once we think of God as personal, loving, and communicative, we are on our way to thinking of God in social terms. For if God is personal, loving, and communicative, as Christians want to say he is, how else except on the basis of the Trinity can God be like this, unless we posit an everlasting creation alongside him? If God is personal, does he need to depend on a creation to exercise personality? Or, if God is love, does he have to depend on a creation to express his love? Or, if it is God's nature to communicate, does he have to depend on a creation in order to converse? In terms of intelligibility, it would seem that the Trinitarian model has some advantages over the unitarian view. So, although the doctrine is not rationally derived but based upon God's revelation in history, I would never admit the charge that the doctrine is irrational. On the contrary, it seems to possess a superior rationality compared with the alternatives.

In terms of the attributes of God, one should call attention to the striking balance of transcendence and immanence in the biblical presentation. God is the One who surpasses all that we know and yet at the same time stoops to be with us. In relation to God's transcendence, we affirm God's infinity. By that we mean God is neither just outside the universe nor inside it. He is simply not limited by the universe, which does not contain him. God is not just a created thing, only much bigger. "We live and move and have our being in God." Therefore, God is not aloof or distant even in his transcendence.

We confess God the Lord to be the creator of the world, which he called into existence by his word and an act of his own freedom. The Bible says that what God made was good, which means that creating things was a worthwhile thing for God to do. It means that the world is an expression of God's workmanship. In love, God made the decision to posit and then to live along with a finite reality outside himself, a reality of a different order with relative autonomy. For this reason we experience life as worthwhile and significant.

God is a person with purposes to fulfill. It is God's purpose that the world should be here. The world gives God the opportunity to enter into relationship with another and let it share aspects of his own glory and being. In creating a significant world, God stooped down, limited himself, and made room for the other, room enough even for it to rebel against him and reject his plans.

The God of the Bible is also One who acts. We should not put him into a box or narrow down what he can do. We have actively to resist the pressure of the Western cultural paradigm, which demands a form of Christianity without power. It wants us to be functional atheists. Much modern theology has gone along with this, but evangelicals have to break the habit of not believing God for his ongoing mighty works. The church has to be converted in mind and behavior to the condition of kingdom normalcy displayed by Jesus.

God is also immanent and near to us. He comes down to our level and gives himself to us to enrich our lives. God can easily become abstract and aloof in our thinking if we forget that "from him and through him and to him are all things." God does not exist in splendid isolation from the world but is in the midst of history and active in the becoming of the world. God's free and unnecessitated love comes down from the higher to the lower plane as God gives himself to humanity. At the same time, God is holy love and wants us to belong to him alone and not to any other powers. He would be our God and our God alone.

God is very different from the gods of the nations. Among them there exists an almost universal stereotype of God as One who is high above the world but who has little real interest in or concern for it. The God of the gospel of Christ is significantly different. Though all-powerful, God lets man take away his own initiative to some extent. The One who cannot be resisted in his almighty being is yet longsuffering and patient with us. He is willing to let man become his competitor, if he will not be his partner. God's glory is revealed supremely on a slave's cross, while at the same time he is Lord and ruler of all. We could call him the defenseless superior power.

As individuals who relate to the world, we can speak, too, of God's changeable faithfulness. God lets the world be. He invites us to enter into dynamic relationship with himself. He lets things affect and even change him. He is not revealed as the God who cannot experience any kind of change but as a God who wills to be our covenant partner through history with all of its surprises and fluctuations. God is involved with us in the drama of life and salvation. Though unchanging in his character and person, God's knowledge changes concerning the things that become actual through our decisions.

Root metaphors for God are very influential. These are the basic portrayals of God which affect how we view and relate to him. Many evangelicals entertain a root metaphor in which God is absolutely sovereign, as planning everything, as never being defeated, as always getting his way. Others like me find it more biblical and better in other ways as well to think of God as a loving parent, not determining all things, but allowing a good deal of freedom, as someone who is involved in our lives and open to our input, not overruling our contributions. In the early development of Christian theism, there was a strong tendency to posit a God high and lifted up, in opposition to the changeable deities of the Hellenistic world. But in recent years there has been a shift to a greater emphasis on God as near and involved in our lives. The root metaphor we use is important because it affects a great deal in both theology and life. If God is genuinely responsive to his creatures and not in total control of what they do, this will affect the way we understand the image of God, the providence of God, the action of God in creating the world, the nature of sin, the strategy of atonement, the humanity of Christ, the nature of election and so forth.

These remarks expose a debate among evangelicals. The powerful influence of the Reformation upon us has meant that we have been strongly influenced by a model of God who manipulates his creatures. It is important today to challenge this root metaphor and liberate evangelical understanding in the direction of a free-will theism.

BIBLICAL THEISM AS RATIONAL THEISM

A major evangelical concern in the area of the doctrine of God is the ebbing of theistic belief in a world influenced by secularism. As believers in a God who actually exists, we dislike the shift we see away from belief in a God who exists outside of ourselves and on whom we all depend to the idea that God is a construct of the human soul. In Western culture the decline of belief in the objective God rose from the impact and influence of such thinkers as Darwin, Marx, Freud, and Nietzsche. Modernistic theologians who take their cues from the dominant Western currents moved in the direction of religious volunteerism. This trend toward the interiorization of faith where Christianity becomes an ideal of life rather than a truth claim about an objective God beyond the natural world is something we deplore. Evangelicals stand with all those who contend that God exists truly and objectively as the rewarder of those that diligently seek him. Belief in God is not just a projection or function of the human psyche but exists in a realist sense as the source and power of the world. This we believe is both a biblical and a rational conviction to hold.

67

Kant bears a good deal of the responsibility for this sad state of affairs. His skepticism about the possibility of knowing reality in itself undercut the Christian conviction. He claimed that we can know things only as they appear but cannot know the ultimate nature of things. That means the human self becomes the source of what reality ultimately is. It means that belief in God is not a claim to reality but only an expressivist ideal or a belief projected out from our own experience.

It is important that we not go along with Kant. We must refuse to set out down that path that leads to the idea that humans are the sole source of knowing what reality is. The world is accessible to human knowledge as both everyday experience and the sciences prove, and it is reasonable on that basis to conclude that there is a God who reaches out to humanity. The world of our everyday experience is a structured reality of determinate nature that exists outside of ourselves. It is not wholly pliable to our manipulations of it. Christians need to speak up on behalf of the independent reality of the everyday world in which we find ourselves and affirm the possibility of our knowing truth and God.

Modern theology has followed these trends into serious reduction in the area of the doctrine of God. There has been a strong tendency to reduce the picture of God as revealed in the gospel and to confine him to much too narrow a space. This is due in large part to the shift to human experience as the real basis for grounding theological concepts. For if human experience is the sole basis for meaningful concepts of God and the human subject is the sole seat of authority in matters pertaining to truth, Scripture and tradition being radically questioned, the outlook for the doctrine of God is very bleak.

The problem of God in contemporary theology can be indicated by some illustrations. Kant was led to reduce God to an ethical postulation. Schleiermacher reduced God to the whence of one's feeling of absolute dependence. Hegel reduced God to the energy that causes the upward surge of evolution. Many modern theologians deny God the freedom to act in special providences in his world. Some make God a function of the world and not its sovereign creator. Others limit God to watching and suffering, or they take their leave of God altogether and speak of his death. There is a monism at the heart of liberal theology where reality is seen as basically one realm, one process, one structure of activity.

Continuity exists between the world and God, and God is viewed as the immanent spirit at work in history.

THE POWER DIMENSION

Another reduction in the doctrine of God today is in the area of God's power. The God of the Bible is the God of Elijah but this is rarely so in modern theology, liberal or evangelical. Theologians in the West have tried to edge God out of his world, as if reality were solely material and natural. They have made large concessions to Enlightenment thinking. They have overtly or covertly demythologized the New Testament proclamation. How many today believe in the power of God to do signs and wonders? How many are open to demonstrations of God's power? Western theology may have some great strengths in the area of fairness, critical thinking, toleration, scholarship, rationality, etc., but it is heavily influenced by the Western paradigm in its materialism, naturalism, humanism, and individualism. Our theology, both liberal and evangelical, has tended to become rationalistic, naturalistic, humanistic, and individualistic. Much of the time we propogate a Christianity without power. We all need to get over a bad case of cultural accommodation and experience freedom in God's Spirit.

Such reductions as these do not exalt the God who has revealed himself in Jesus Christ. They do not present the God who has been worshiped by the historic churches. They are not religiously adequate for people today. Evangelicals are aware of some of these problems and see the need to make changes.

SOME TASKS AND CHALLENGES

At the same time, liberals have a right to expect evangelicals to grapple with some of the issues that brought about and perhaps necessitated these revisions in the doctrine of God. After all, they did not come out of nowhere and for no reason. It is reasonable to ask how evangelicals are responding to some of the challenges that account for this situation. What about modern scientific understanding, the evolution of the universe, the fact of human freedom, the sense of historical relativity, etc.? Liberals do not reformulate Christian doctrine just for the fun of it and without good reasons. It does impress when it appears that evangelicals avoid the necessity of theological reformulations largely by ignoring the problems that make rethinking necessary in the first place.

For example, what about the relation between divine sovereignty and human freedom? Classical theism has been committed to a strong doctrine of God's sovereignty that does not leave much room for genuine human freedom. There has been resistance to granting to the creature effective freedom for fear that he would then become self-sufficient in his mind and detract from the glory and power of God. God, many have felt, would not be God unless he had total control over everything that happens. This desire to protect the divine freedom by suppressing human freedom came to fruition in double predestination, according to which God simply condemns a portion of the human race whom he decided should not be saved. Although there is an attempt to place the blame on man himself, Calvin admits that finally God excludes them because he wills to do so and for no other reason. Calvin calls this the dreadful decree.

Obviously, there has to be a corrective to this way of thinking, if human freedom is not to be eclipsed and God's reputation is not to be destroyed. There must be a better way of reading the Bible than that. My inclination is to think that we would be much wiser to speak of free-will theism, according to which God approaches his image bearers and they respond to him in freedom. We need to cultivate the idea that God can be sovereign and still encourage other beings to be energetic, creative, and free themselves. For God to be God he does not have to be a despot. God according to the Bible has given to us a creaturely form of freedom that enables us to respond to God and live responsibly before God. God's omnipotence and human freedom go agreeably together. God is a free personal agent and able to bring into existence any kind of creature he wants to in order to realize some value. He can then, if he chooses, make creatures who are free to shape their own destinies. Though omnipotent, God can decide to limit the exercise of his power and not force us to do things against our will. His power remains unlimited and is restrained only by his choice. God chose to actualize a world in which the future would rest partly in the hands of the creature. God could have predetermined it all if he had wanted to, but he did not want to.

To be fair I should add that this idea of God limiting his power is a modern proposal and could fairly be called a revision in theology. It is an understanding that we now find convincing because of our experience of modernity in its dynamism and its sense of temporality. At the same time it lifts up biblical truth in a fresh and faithful way. What it shows is that evangelical theology is far from static and unchanging.

What about miracles in an age of science? How can evangelicals make good on this claim of ours? We would say that God's creation of the world means on the one hand that it is also open to surprises and changes. God's creation means both natural causality and still there is room for miracles. God uses all that he has created and set in place (he is the God of secondary causes), but he is also free to give signs of the kingdom that call attention to what God is doing. He is also free to break through into our lives and open them up to the future. We should not think of any of this as contrary to nature, but only as contrary to what we usually think of as nature. God has made an open, ungraspable universe. This means natural causality but leaves room for miracles as well.

At the same time, evangelicals cannot be smug. We too have conceded the influence of modern science in our interpretations of some of the biblical materials where previously we saw miracles of greater proportion. One need only read some evangelicals' comments on the meaning of the Creation and the Fall, what some think about the extent of the Flood, the plagues of Egypt, or the long day of Joshua. Evangelicals have also accommodated Western science in not expecting God's power to accompany his Word today, while insisting on miracles accrediting the apostles. This is inconsistent and makes us look much like liberals in this regard. Evangelicals, too, it seems, want religion to be safe, predictable, refined, and tidy. A revival with its disorderly vitality and remarkable manifestations would not be all that welcome even among us.

Nevertheless, we all believe that God invites and answers prayer, even though some would expect more in the way of special divine actions than others do. Because evangelicals believe in prayer, we also experience the failure of God to act when it seems it would be appropriate. We have to ask, for example, in the tragic death of a loved one: Why did this have to happen? Why didn't God prevent it, if he could have prevented it? One might be tempted at this point just to say that God couldn't have done so because he lacks the power to do so. But we evangelicals cannot bring ourselves to say that. We can get angry with God like Job, but we cannot conclude that God lacked the power to do anything about it. For to say that would deny a central tenet of biblical theism. Instead we resort to the more awkward solution by invoking the mystery of God's will.

What about inclusive God-language? Here the influence of theological method on evangelicals is very clear. We feel obliged, since for Jesus "father" was the central address that he used in his own prayers, to continue to use the same language. This illustrates powerfully the fact that authority for us resides in the content of the Scripture and the revelation we attest to rather than in modern experience and ideology. We lean strongly in favor of the ancient grammar and the authority of the Christian past. We do not think so important an element in the gospel can be explained as a mere cultural influence but accept it as God's own decision how to represent himself. Evangelicals assume that father is what God must have wanted to be called because of the content of this very language. Although we can permit feminine images for God because they are employed by the inspired writers, we would resist inserting "mother" alongside "father" in the Lord's Prayer, for example, because it would carry nuances that Jesus did not intend.

In principle, evangelicals are opposed to the liberal position that declines to identify biblical images with the Word of God, but tends to see them as rising out of human experience and as human construction. We resist this way of thinking. For us the biblical images are not merely humanly generated ciphers of transcendence but inspired teachings that give us a true knowledge of God. Those teachings do not give us merely a symbolic awareness of ultimate reality, tentative and exploratory but never final or definitive. Our position is that the foundational symbols of the Bible cannot be replaced, though they may be supplemented and interpreted. The symbols cannot be replaced because they are not based upon cultural experience but on a divine intrusion into history. They root in a revelation of God that does not originate in us but that comes to us from beyond us. We do not feel entitled to resymbolize Christian theology to suit ourselves, based in the ostensive authority of human experience.

In conclusion, then, evangelicals want to sustain the biblical portrait of God and the classical tradition as much as possible. We certainly feel many of the same pressures that have led liberal theologians to make major revisions in their theology. But we do not want to follow liberals along this route and are now trying to respond to challenges to what we believe is a more God-honoring way.

> *Brown: You argue that if God is personal, loving, and communicative, then either God must be triune or else there must be an everlasting creation to which God is related. While a Trinitarian concept of God may be defensible on other grounds, would this particular argument not lead you to affirm an everlasting creation? To appeal to the Trinity here would require that God be self-related, self-communicating, self-loving. Does the New Testament ever speak in this way, especially about God's love? If it does not, is your position viable for an evangelical?*

Pinnock: This question offers an illustration of the dangers reason can pose to theology, in this case not to a liberal theology but to my own. For the question suggests that in seeking to render the doctrine of the Trinity more intelligible, I may have transgressed a basic scriptural notion—specifically, its concept of the divine love. Thus we have the nice irony in which Brown calls me to task for thinking sub-biblically at this point. Is this true? There is even a second twist to it. Doesn't my argument backfire and cause me to fall almost into process theology, something that the argument was meant to protect me from and not lead me into? If the Trinity does not supply what is needed here, then the natural alternative to look to might be process theology.

First let me say that the argument did not pretend to be the basis of my doctrine of the Trinity. The doctrine rests on other grounds, namely on biblical foundations. It rises out of reflection on the Incarnation and Pentecost. My argument was only the attempt at a useful apologetic excursion in defense of biblical truth. If it fails, let it be banished and nothing be lost.

But I am not sure it does fail. The thought was that God's self-sufficiency is well safeguarded by the social Trinity, wherein love goes on everlastingly within the Godhead itself and the creation of the world can then be seen as an overflow not out of necessity. I saw the social Trinity as picturing God free of any necessary metaphysical dependency on the world. God is love in the depths of his own being and does not require a creation in order to express it. I am agreeing with the Cappadocians that there are three distinct subjects of the divine life that know, love, relate, and communicate together.

I was drawing upon Augustine's famous analogy of the divine life, which was later used by Richard of St. Victor. It focuses on the three of the Trinity: the lover, the beloved, and love itself. In this model, the Father gives himself to the Son, who in turn responds to the gift of love, with the Spirit as the bond of that love. Thus the divine life is like a circle or a dance. By the Spirit the circle is completed but not closed in upon itself. For the Spirit not only perfects the divine love but is the opening of the divine love outward to the world and communicating with it. It draws upon a manner of thinking about God that stresses the abundance and the overflow of love and grace.

One could say that God is like a human family. The love of two parents overflows in a child and then beyond the family into the world. The love of my wife, my daughter, and myself which we reciprocally enjoy in communion and communication within the family unit also overflows its banks to others. I see God as a community of selves, not an absolute single self, and the divine love, which is always flowing at the highest of levels, also flows out and down to the creaturely levels. God is a relational and communicative being both within his own life and in relation to us. In both cases it is other-directed love, though admittedly in a different way. God the Trinity is an open structure, desiring but not needing to create.

In relation to process theism I would say that like it the social Trinity recognizes internal differentiations and relations within God, but unlike it the doctrine has more scriptural substance and intrinsic worshipability.

> *Brown: I see how your "free-will theism" escapes some of the problems of classical theism, but I cannot understand how it addresses the theodicy issue. If God has freely chosen to restrict the divine power, can God not also freely choose to restore that power at times in order to prevent gross, unnecessary and unproductive*

evil? If in your view such evil exists, why does God not prevent it?

Pinnock: The problem of evil is a large and intractable one for human reason to cope with and explain. It is likely that a perfectly satisfactory rational solution to it in its entirety cannot be found this side of heaven. It is a problem that is beyond our human intellectual powers and it belongs to the mystery of God (Rom. 11:33–36). Liberals are less eager to admit to mystery than evangelicals, but this itself is a little unreasonable. At the same time, for my part I do not intend to take refuge in fideism. So let me speak to the issue.

You are essentially correct in stating what I believe. First, I think that God limits his power in order to let the world exist with its own integrity. According to the Bible, God has willed a significant universe with free creatures in it and does not wish to overpower it. In this respect Scripture says what our experience confirms. On this I believe we are in considerable agreement, although you do not think this is so much a voluntary limitation on God's part but a necessary one.

Second, because it is a voluntary decision, I believe that God could at any time exercise his power to prevent some particular evil from occurring (e.g., an earthquake) or cause some miracle to take place (e.g., the Resurrection of Jesus). A finite god would not be able to do this, but the God of the Bible can do so.

But if I believe these things, then I have the very problem you identify. If God can intervene in history to bring about his purposes (positively and negatively), why doesn't he do this more often and to greater effect? If God could have prevented Auschwitz, for example, why didn't he do so? Do not such evils constitute the main objection to an otherwise compelling case for Christian theism? Even if God's mystery must ultimately be invoked, doesn't there need to be a decent attempt to explain this absurdity?

I have three components in my attempt to produce a theodicy. First, personal life cannot develop and function except in a law-abiding and stable environment. This places a limitation upon the number of times God will want to intervene in history. There is a price to be paid for intervention. Second, much of the suffering that rises from the structures of the world can be redemptive because it serves a purpose and need not be removed. God can use for the good in terms of character formation or soul-making the evils that result from the misuse of human freedom. Third, ultimately there must be a final reckoning and vindication. Unless there is everlasting life, justice cannot be fully realized.

This framework means that divine interventions may occur but not always in the way we might wish at the moment. God has to think about how they would serve his general plan as well. At the same time the future is open and God is free. I would recognize, then, certain limitations on providential activity, which are imposed by present structures of creation. But I also see room for divine action in the world when it is appropriate. God is constantly at work in and through the created structures, drawing the threads of human history and individual lives into providential patterns. He is also free to stretch forth his hand in mighty acts when the time is right.

> *Brown: Why does the fact that Jesus used the term "abba" bind evangelicals to refer to God in exclusively male terms? Doesn't Jesus' use of "abba" point more to intimacy with God than to God's maleness. But even if Jesus had used "father" in our sense of that term, why would that usage constitute a part of the "basic grammar" of the Bible? Finally, is your view faithful to the New Testament in which Jesus' parables use feminine imagery to refer to God, and his actions radically challenge patriarchal custom? In short, even in terms of your own methodology, do we have the right through our language to associate God more closely with males than with females?*

Pinnock: This question brings up an issue that is disturbing many churches today. Some may refuse to sing the doxology or repeat the Lord's Prayer, while others get peeved at those who refuse. Some are upset at those who are busily rewriting the hymns and cleansing the Bible of sexist language, even in the area of God language. Is this not a good example of modern ideology demanding satisfaction? Why is that when feminists say, "Jump," it is the liberals who ask, "How high?"

The reason evangelicals have such strong feelings about keeping God-the-Father language and not replacing it with God-the-Parent or God-the-Mother is the belief that it belongs to foundational symbolic language. We do not see calling God Father as quite the same thing as calling God a rock and a fortress. "God the Father of our Lord Jesus Christ" seems to belong to the original language of Christianity. We believe that such a foundational symbol may need to be explained but is not something that can be dropped or replaced. Underlying this would be the conviction that it is ultimately based not on the cultural experience of early Christians but on divine revelation through Jesus Christ. God chose this way of speaking of himself and as such it belongs to revelation that originated not in time but in eternity. Just as the noun "God" itself can be explained by words like transcendence or mystery but not replaced by them, so it is with the term "father." If God declares his name, whether YHWH, Lord, or Father, that is not something we can change at will. Father, Son, and Spirit are the Christian names of God, and God's name is important.

At the same time I freely grant that feminine images are also used of God in the Bible, making it perfectly proper for us to use them, too. God is compared to a woman caring for her child (Isa. 49:15) and described as the One who gave birth to Israel (Deut. 32:18; Isa. 42:13ff). Maternal images are certainly biblically appropriate. But they need to be kept in proportion. Masculine images are common and in the case of "Father" fundamental. We have no right to turn the Bible on its head. The female imagery cannot be used to supplant the controlling symbols.

At issue is the authority of the Bible. For many feminists it is an androcentric book that deserves their condemnation. They read it in overtly biased ways and accord infallibility to their own experience instead. This places them firmly outside the mainstream Christian community.

Is there any reason though, why the Bible adopts father- rather than mother-language as the controlling image or is it just arbitrary or even sexist? I think there are some good reasons why it does so. First, the religion of the goddess is heretical from the biblical point of view because it is pantheistic in direction. It simply undercuts the otherness of God. This is why mother-god language is rejected in the Bible. It is still true today—mother-goddess language portrays God as the matrix of the world, not its Creator. In principle we could speak of the divine motherhood because God acts like a mother, too, but in the light of the dangers evangelicals will not choose to. It is naïve to think that one can simply exchange one metaphor for another and end up with the same thing.

Second, I think masculine imagery was chosen because of the connotations it always carries: leadership, respect, and authority. In virtually all human cultures, males are associated with leadership roles more than females are. Therefore, if one wants to make the point that God is the Lord of the universe, masculine language will communicate that best in human speech cross-culturally even today. Female language does not convey ideas of leading, protecting, and providing quite so well. Therefore, female imagery is useful in qualifying the sense in which God is Lord. He is not an oppressive kind of king. It comes in as a secondary language for God. The Bible prefers masculine imagery for God who is beyond sexuality because it works better.

What about Brown's point about "abba" meaning "daddy" and not so much a male term as one denoting closeness and intimacy? It might be that when Jesus called God his Father he was really saying that God is like a loving caring woman, thus practically his mother. I do not think this will work. Despite Jeremias, "abba" is a term of respect not sentimentality. Neither father nor child is romanticized in the New Testament as they are among us. A child is one who lacks status, and a father is one who deserves respect. As James Barr has written, "Abba isn't daddy."

● Brown's Rejoinder to Pinnock

I am attracted to the tentative and exploratory style of your answers to the first two questions. In the same spirit I can only admit that I find the answers themselves to be unsatisfactory. It remains unclear to me how God can always be agape (unmerited love, love as an expression of grace) if there is not always something other than God, that is, a world of some kind, to which this agape is directed. Nor do I quite understand your answer on the theodicy issue. To take but one point, I do see why, on your view, God cannot be expected to intervene in history to the point of disrupting the stability of our environments. It is not clear to me, however, that the number of divine disruptions is as yet very close to this danger point. At least one more intervention—say, the prevention of the holocaust—would seem to have been permissible, especially since something like a heart attack that retired the young Hitler to a quiet

German nursing home would never have been identified as a disruption of natural causality.

With respect to the debate about inclusive language, I want to ask why we should believe that those who defend egalitarian language are being "ideological" and those who defend patriarchal language are not? Why represent the defense of inclusive language as a mindless one—"when the feminists say 'jump,' the liberals ask 'how high?'"

To take the case of one liberal, I began thinking about this issue before I had ever heard the term "inclusive language" and before I had ever read any feminist literature. My wife and I were sitting in church with our oldest two daughters, then five and four years of age. The girls were coloring. The minister was praying extemporaneously. As I listened and watched our girls, it seemed to me that almost every other utterance in the minister's prayer made reference to God as "Father" or alluded to God as male. I grew increasingly uncomfortable. I looked first at the girls' mother, and then at our daughters who could someday grow up to be mothers but who could never become fathers. I experienced, vividly and powerfully, what I later came to think of as a kind of ontological embarrassment. I was horrified that the minister's prayer uniquely associated my gender with deity, the standard of perfection in our tradition. I was angry that his language separated my wife and daughters from me and from God. I shuddered to realize that some Sunday our daughters would stop coloring long enough to listen to what the minister said—to his special equation of God, maleness, fatherhood, and me—and to think about what this implies about them and their mother, my wife. I thought of Paul's injunction that we should not do anything that might make others stumble. That injunction seemed to me especially appropriate with respect to children in the years when their self-image and self-esteem are being formed.

Perhaps it is inappropriate to cite such a personal experience in theological discussion. I allow it, however, in order to insist as emphatically as possible that concern about inclusive language, and sexism generally, should not be dismissed as ideology or a knee-jerk acceptance of modernity. It can be, and often is, a conviction that grows out of immediate personal relationships—the same place, I dare say, wherein God most powerfully challenges slavery, classism, sexism, and other forms of oppression.

The important point, however, is not that opponents on this issue should take each other seriously, as important as that is. The crucial point is to ask whether we have a right through our language to divide the human race and to give one group, the males, a privileged proximity to God. For the liberal, the resolute answer is that we do not. The arguments for male arrogation are patently self-serving; the arguments against it, from every quarter of modern understanding, are overwhelming.

Is the answer not the same, with the same resolve, for the conservative? Are your own "biblical feminists" not undeniably correct in arguing that, yes, the expressions of racism, classism, and sexism typical of the first century are indeed vividly present in the biblical text, but the way they are criticized and radically undermined in that same text, even while remaining evident, is truly remarkable?

Is not that logic of equality undeniably there in the Bible? Is it not a gift that conservative Christians, above all, have the right to claim and proclaim?

SECTION 4

Delwin Brown's presentation on the doctrine of God, Brown's answers to three questions put by Pinnock, and a rejoinder by Pinnock to Brown's answers.

Liberal Christianity allows for various concepts of God, but there are common elements in the way liberals approach this topic. Fundamental to the approach, as I have indicated, is the conviction that what is said about God ought to be defensible in terms of the other conclusions of modern knowledge. To be defensible, liberal Christians assume, a concept of God must be consistent with the best that is known about the rest of the world.

There is an obvious and well-taken objection to this assumption. "Surely your head must be swimming," the evangelical might well say, "because the judgments of modern knowledge change so terribly fast. You can never be sure from day to day what you are entitled to believe if everything you affirm must fit the intellectual fashion of the times."

Clearly, the demand for consistency cannot be stated quite so baldly as I put it at first. But before I seek to clarify this assumption let me ask, what is the alternative?

Suppose we resolve to follow the teaching of the past, allowing that to determine what we should believe with respect to God. That wisdom, in the case of our Christian past, has been severely tested over two thousand years of human struggle, reflection, and experience. Is it not saner, maybe even more "scientific," to accept the tried and true over that which is constantly changing?

When the question is put that way, the answer is "yes, of course." But the question so stated simply assumes what we all want to know. Almost every view of God is tried, but what is true?

First, we must acknowledge that there is not one past, there are many. The teachings of some religious traditions have been tested many more years, with at least as much intensity as have the teachings of Christianity. These traditions, too, have transformed lives, attested to the wondrous and inexplicable, and, at their best, brought great benefit to the human race. If we are going to be intellectually serious, to say nothing of being faithful in the quest for truth, we cannot merely assume that classical Christian teaching about God is to be preferred over all these other teachings about ultimate reality. These views, too, are entitled to a hearing. Where will they be heard and assessed except in the arenas of our contemporary discussion?

Second, even if for some reason we limit our consideration to the Christian past and even more specifically to the New Testament, it does not present us with a theology, a single systematic view of God's nature. There probably is greater homogeneity in what New Testament writings say about God than what they say about numerous other theological topics, such as the place of Torah, the role of Christ, and the nature of salvation. Even so, what is said there is less a systematic conception of God than it is a witness of faith expressed in terms of what the first-century world thought to be possible. We today should no more absolutize the first-century worldview on the topic of God than on women's roles, monarchy, and slavery. For conservatives as well as for liberals, the issues are inescapable. What is the essence of the gospel? How do we decide? What are the proper criteria? Is there an essence for all time, or is there instead a central Christian witness for one time and somewhat different witnesses for other times and places?

These are, in a sense, pre-theological issues that can be productively discussed only on a neutral turf where everyone's assumptions are subject to the same scrutiny and where everyone's conclusions must answer to the rest of what we responsibly affirm to be true. That, as I understand it, is the essence of the contemporary quest for knowledge. That, at least, is the liberal view. Liberalism holds that a view of God must in each age be reevaluated and reconceived in light of our best views about the world. The Christian concept of God must cohere with the rest of modern knowledge.

To say this, however, is not to absolutize modern knowledge. At least this should not be its meaning even though liberalism sometimes makes this mistake. The point is simply that a concept of God must be defended in the arenas of modern discourse, taking the criteria of each arena with sufficient seriousness either to accept them, improve them, or replace them with others developed in continuity with previous discussion.

The liberal is as free, and as obligated, to be the critic of modern assumptions as of ancient assumptions. The liberal's theological vision must give an account of itself in terms which modernity might be able to understand even if modernity cannot accept it. But that, of course, is simply the general procedure by which modernity seeks to correct itself, whether in history, philosophy, science, or whatever. Christian liberalism belongs to this situation and works within it although liberalism's purpose often is to go beyond it. Thus we may say that liberal theology is "revisionary" theology. It examines the past in light of present insights and the present in the light of the past, seeking always from this encounter a revised perspective that is more adequate.

While this approach is characteristic of liberalism, no particular outcome of this approach defines *the* liberal view of God. Thus what follows in this discussion about the nature of God must be seen as one liberal's point of view, representative, perhaps, but certainly not definitive of liberal Christianity.

In evaluating the classical view of God, one can distinguish between the dominant elements of classical piety, on the one hand, and the conceptuality in terms of which that piety was expressed, on the other. Several elements of classical piety are compelling. God is experienced as the source and ground of our lives and the life of the world, and so is spoken of as "creator." God is intuited as a power at work affecting the direction of things, personal and historical, and therefore is spoken of as "lord." Classical references to God as "judge" convey a sense that God stands for moral order, for justice. Talk of God as "redeemer" reflects that notion that God somehow is that which makes for right, is the guarantor of ultimate rectification. But of course there are also numerous metaphors, both in the Bible and in the subsequent Christian tradition, that refer to this same creator, lord, judge, etc., as a personal presence, a friend and guide. This unique blend of the personal and suprapersonal, emphasizing always the positive in each, made it natural also to speak of God in terms that convey a sense of ultimate worth.

Classical Christian theology sought to bring this rich and complex piety together into a consistent, believable conceptuality. It did so using the best resources available to it, the philosophical categories inherited from the Greeks. That categorial scheme was not neutral, of course. None ever is. The Greek categories harbored within them fundamental assumptions about the nature of "perfection," for example, that profoundly affected the expression of Christian piety. That which is perfect, the Greeks contended, is absolutely independent of all else in every way. Thus when the concept of God was developed systematically using Greek categories the result was a wholly unchanging deity, absolute in power, who is literally unrelated to the world and literally unaffected by it.

That is surely an odd way to portray the God who, according to the Christian witness, was in Jesus Christ so utterly related as to become incarnate in humanity and so utterly affected as to die on a cross. It does not follow, however, that the "Greek strategy" should never have been tried, or that we today should eschew all alliances between piety and the reflective categories of our times, or that we even can. Nor does it follow that piety is always innocent and reflection always the villain. Classical piety contained much that is reprehensible, such as sexism and racism, and Greek philosophy made positive contributions as well as negative ones. Greek modes of thought, for example, enabled the development of a theory of Trinitarian relationships that would be utterly revolutionary were we today to view human relatedness in the same egalitarian, holistic, and dynamic terms.

The lesson to be learned from the ancient affiliation of Christian piety and Greek philosophy is that neither partner in such an association is infallible, that such associations are useful as well as dangerous, that they should always be tentative, and that, whether conscious or unconscious, they probably are inescapable. That, at least, is the lesson liberalism draws. The consequence is that liberalism again and again seeks to dwell at the intersection between the sensibilities of the historic faith and the best intellectual resources of its own time, relating them as critically and creatively as possible. This is especially evident in contemporary liberal Christian thinking about God.

Just as classical theology emerged out of, seeking to give systematic expression to, what I have called classical Christian piety, so a viable modern or neo-classical theology expresses the elements of a modern Christian piety, that is, our intuitive sense of the world today. This piety includes, for example, the judgment that vulnerability is intrinsic to strength of character. True, there is a macho mentality within many of us that continues to equate perfection with imperviousness, but on reflection we judge this mentality to be a destructive illness. Today, the whole or healthy person is thought to be one who is open and sensitive to others, strong enough to put him or herself at risk in real, not merely superficial, relationships. If we think of God within this framework we will think of God's perfection as being somehow supremely open and supremely inclusive of the experiences and aspirations of others.

Feminist thinkers in particular, however, have taught us that a healthy openness can come only from an abiding, if dynamic, inner identity. We need to know who we are and what we are for. Thus God cannot be simply vulnerable, simply open; God will also have an abiding identity, a stable character impervious to the whims of our history. This is what we mean by God's essence. In our theologies, then, we need to hold together these changing (dependent) and unchanging (independent) elements of God's life. Hence today we are likely to speak of God as interdependent with the world. Not wholly dependent, to be sure, but not wholly independent either, as Greek sensibilities prompted classical Christian theologians to conclude.

Another aspect of the experience of contemporary Christians is a sense of contingency, the unsettledness of outcomes. For better or worse, the future is open. Modern Christian hymnody expresses this. Whereas Christians once gained comfort from singing about a God who controls the future, the hymns we find more credible today speak of God's dependable love for us and presence to us whatever the uncertainties of the future. If God is genuinely related to, and thus affected by, a contingent historic process, then there will be real contingency, even uncertainty, in the divine life. In a world of freedom, chance, and unpredictability, a God who really is with us and for us can hardly be conceived apart from the contingency that characterizes our lives. This must mean that in some important way the realization of God's own goals in and for the world are themselves uncertain. There is genuine risk in the life of God.

Related to this are our modern notions of power. The traditional idea of absolute power is a vestige of the monarchical worldview in which the power of the ruler was multiplied to infinity and assigned to deity. Today this seems indefensible. For one thing, an absolutely powerful being would necessarily exist alone, in absolute isolation. That would not be an enviable position for any God; it is not a possible position for a God who is loving. A loving God is necessarily a related God. It is impossible, then, to hold that the Christian God is all-powerful. More than that, it is undesirable, indeed intolerable. There is so much pointless, unnecessary evil in the world that we find it very, very difficult to believe this world to be governed by an omnipotent deity, at least if this God is good. Far from the remote, all-powerful deity of classical thought, a God accessible to modern Christian piety would be always incarnate in the world, accepting the risk of that involvement, bearing the world's sorrows and sharing its joys. Thus, God would be supremely powerful, but not omnipotent.

Finally, modern piety has largely outgrown the antipathy for temporality and human embodiedness that characterized the ancient world. In its potential at least, this world is good. Thus, whatever self-identity ("transcendence" in a sense) God must have in order to be at all, a viable God will also be a this-worldly deity. God's being and purposes will be inclusive of the created world. This is really not an additional point. It is already implied in what we have said about God's vulnerability, God's relatedness to the world. But it has only recently become apparent to us that this means unmistakably that God works in this world for a just economic order, political equality, and a wholesome environment for all living things. The God who made *this* world in its entirety seeks to save this world in its entirety—at every level, what we call "physical" as much as what we call "spiritual."

If these are the main elements of a modern or neo-classical Christian piety, then the liberal might well view God as an essentially relational reality, supremely powerful but not omnipotent, whose knowledge is circumscribed by chance and human freedom, and whose aims include the redemption of the entire created order from all forms of brokenness and alienation. God's being is intertwined with that of the world. God works for right without a guarantee of ultimate or total triumph. If faith affirms the victory of God's purposes, the affirmation is indeed one of faith, not of knowledge, for both God and those who respond in service to God's aims.

My own way of formulating this conception of God draws upon the categories of the process philosophy of Alfred North Whitehead. In this framework it is possible to think of God as a reality who is personal in a sense strictly analogous to human personhood. God is constant in character—always just and loving, for example—but changing in the divine experience and changing, too, in the application of the abiding divine values to the concrete world. God's power is supreme in the sense that God enjoys all the power consistent with the real freedom of the creatures, but God is not and could not be "all-powerful" in the traditional sense of that term. God knows the actual world as actual, but the possible world, that is, the future, is known to God only in terms of greater and lesser degrees of probability. "God" and "world" are interdependent terms. There is no world without the God who is always at work creative-ly/redemptively within it, and there is no God who is not always related creatively/redemptively to some world or other. God is, God is loving, and God is saving.

Other liberal views of God are possible, of course, some of them even less traditional, less "personalistic" than the view I have outlined. God might stand for the mysteriousness of things, whether of origins or of endings. God might represent what is deemed to be the most redemptive element in the cosmic process, such as creativity or love. God might refer to the power of human ideals. Some liberal Christians argue—curiously, along classical Lutheran lines—that we neither can nor should say anything at all about God except as God is represented in the biblical portrayal of Jesus. Thus they contend that Jesus is the meaning of God for us.

What will unite all of these views is the obligation to defend talk about God in relation to contemporary knowledge and in terms of contemporary criteria of adequacy. Therefore, liberal theologies will be inclined to speak of God's relatedness to the world in relation to contemporary physics, and God's creative involvement in the world in relation to current biological theory. The status of the concept of God will be developed in the context of the sociology of knowledge and theories of language. The nature of God will be considered in relation to modern understandings of personhood.

This does not necessarily represent a capitulation to the whims of modernity. It does take the world seriously enough to speak of God within it, to it, on its own terms. It seeks to join the modern world and to participate in its own self-criticism. Christian liberals, thus, often find themselves recalling the insights of the Christian past as a means of bringing about contemporary self-criticism and re-formation. This is not surprising. Not only does liberalism refuse to kneel obeisantly before every secular doctrine *and* every ancient mandate, it also is a product of the Christian past *and* a full participant in the present age.

The liberal position is not fence-sitting nor is it indecision. The betwixt and between status of liberalism is simply historical realism. The neo-classical piety of the Christian liberal cannot be set sharply over against historic Christian sensibilities. Modern Christianity, after all, is but the present development of the full range of Christian history. In some ways modern piety is relatively unique; in many more ways, however, it is an outcome of the Christian past, manifesting now what has long been latent within it or what has been there explicitly but without the benefit of adequate conceptual support. Between ancient and modern, or classical and neo-classical, piety there is a complex relationship involving continuity and discontinuity, and there is little hope of our knowing precisely where the one ends and the other begins.

However that may be, to the extent that we are distinctively Christian, our sensibilities have themselves been "authored" by the Christian past in the context of the present age. Christian belief in God, for the liberal, is not a replication of past Christian belief; it is a belief about what is ultimately real and ultimately worthwhile that emerges when the power of the Christian past is efficacious within the givenness of modernity.

Liberal Christians need not be dismayed by the fact that their particular views of God will probably have staying power only for their own generation and perhaps inspire new and somewhat different ideas in the next. The best evidences of modernity will be different for those of the next generation. That evidence must be heeded there by them. Apparently that is how God is made known.

But the witness of evangelicals has much to teach us as well. Above all it re-presents the witness of the past. It is our failing as liberals—a betrayal of our own liberalism—that we sometimes close our ears to ancient voices. Conservative criticism reminds us that "modernism," too, can be parochial and that ancient views of God deserve, and rightly demand, a hearing in the contemporary debate. Too often we have been enamored of the new simply because it is new. Too often it fails us.

No doubt we, or our heirs, will someday discover failings in the notion of a relational and processive deity. In thinking about God the Christian is called to be faithful—to be sensitive to the past, responsible to the present, open to the future. We are not called to be correct for all time.

> *Pinnock: I hear you referring to piety as the source of the doctrine of God and contrasting that with concepts that were developed in the history of doctrine. Do the Scriptures themselves not present strong outlines of a vigorous kind of theism and do these not provide us with rather firm guidelines for our own reflection?*

Brown: Your question prompts me to correct the impression I must have left, that I sharply distinguish piety and conceptuality. There is no pure piety, uninterpreted by concepts, just as there is no "pure experience" if that means that we can first have experiences and then interpret them. Experience is always interpreted experience, and therefore what I mean by piety, or the life of faith, is always experience in interaction with some level of reflection and interpretation.

What I wanted to say, however, is that the life of faith as it manifests itself in the biblical tradition is in considerable tension with the technical theological structures that evolved in later traditions of reflective Christian thought. And just as these later theological structures existed in interaction with the more intuitive, less reflective dimensions of experience, so also throughout the earlier biblical period forms of piety interacted with contemporaneous conceptual structures. Thus, as you suggest, the Scriptures do communicate conceptual frameworks, including conceptual frameworks about God, whether implicitly through expressions of piety or explicitly in the more didactic portions of the Bible.

Do these conceptual frameworks constitute "strong outlines of a vigorous kind of theism"? The answer, I should think, depends to some extent on the comparative context of the question. If the comparison is with the notion of ultimate reality implied in the Buddhist doctrine of nirvana, then the biblical perspective does indeed present a seemingly univocal alternative about what is ultimate. Considered internally, however, there is considerable variation in biblical theism. Is God omnipotent and omniscient? I don't think the biblical tradition is univocal on either of these issues. Is God personal, changeless, and transcendent? The answer, I think, is "yes, in some senses," but in what senses God is each is not so clear.

This variability and even ambiguity in the biblical view of God notwithstanding, however, I should still want to say with you that the Bible gives us the "strong outlines of a vigorous kind of theism." But the point is that "strong" does not mean uniform in every important respect and "vigorous" does not mean intolerant of alternatives. A recent novel by a Latin American writer has a powerful message about solitude, but the message (like the meaning of "solitude" itself in the book) is not univocal. A part of the book's strength is the rich play of the subtly contrasting meanings that it contains. Nor is the book's judgment about solitude a singular judgment. The vigor of the book resides partly in what it communicates precisely by its contrasting judgments, aesthetically conveyed. As a reader of the book, however, I do not simply reside unreflectively in this tensive richness of meaning. I try to sort things out, however, tentatively and temporarily. I try to make sense of my life and my relationships by seeing myself and solitude in this way or that, though I do not expect ever to fix on one final way of self-understanding that will put an end to all further reflection.

This, I believe, is analogous to the strength and vigor of the biblical witness regarding the nature of God. What do we learn from the claim that God is creator when, for example, it is coupled with the contrasting affirmation that God incarnate was born in a manger? Surely the contrast of these visions—God as cosmic lord, and God as child—is powerful, but it is not uniform. In fact, this portrayal of God "authors" us, and our self-understanding in relation to God, precisely because it does have this richness, a complexity that refuses reduction simply to one way of seeing things or another. Still, our obligation to love God with our minds means trying to understand God and God's relationship to the world in this way or that. These efforts are always tentative and, in retrospect, they seem always to be temporary. But the efforts continue to be created within us by the richness of the biblical witness as it encounters us in our everyday lives.

Does the Bible present us with "firm guidelines for our own reflection"? The power of the biblical witness is presented in its complexity and contrast. In itself the biblical witness is too plurivocal to be viewed very helpfully as presenting a "firm guideline." It is firm and it is a guide, but the strength, the power to guide, lies partly in the diversity with which it speaks of God and God's ways in the world. If we need a clear guideline to end dispute and diversity once and for all, the Bible is not what we need. If we require a strong and vigorous author of Christian identity, then I think we shall find what we need in the multiple voices of the Hebrew and Christian Scriptures.

Pinnock: Obviously I am concerned lest, in orienting ourselves too closely to people's intuitions about God, we may miss the distinctly Christian revelation of God's identity and actually remake God in our own image. Help us understand how you deal with this potential danger.

Brown: There is always a danger that we will miss what is distinctive about God's identity as portrayed in Christian revelation, and especially that we will, as you put it, remake God in our own image. These are indeed dangers to be guarded against, and I'll come back to them. But there are opposite dangers of which we should be conscious, too.

There is the danger of trying *too* diligently to fix on some one distinctive thing that is *the* Christian this or *the* Christian that, with the consequence that we reduce the richness of Christianity to an outline of the latest "intellectual" or "spiritual" fad, be it liberal or conservative. I am most certainly not opposed to trying to see things theologically in a single, coherent fashion. But I am opposed to so hypostacizing our conclusions, and then privileging them with the mantle of "Christian revelation," that we close ourselves to hearing the alternative motifs within the Christian portrayal of things.

There is, in addition, the danger of so fearing that we will remake God to suit ourselves that we end up stultifying the intellect and disdaining the imagination. That, too, is a liberal as well as a conservative danger (though liberals want desperately to believe that it is only conservatives who run the risk of shriveled minds!). This fear is dangerously close to "works righteousness," that is, the supposition that we will be lost unless somehow we "get it right" (in this case) theologically. We won't get it right! All of our views will be to some degree reductions, exaggerations, distortions of one sort or another; that, after all, is the practical meaning of saying that "God's thoughts are not our thoughts." And that, the ancient rabbis claimed, is one reason why there must be generations to come! It should be enough that our intellectual stewardship in this generation might enrich the explorations of the next and that we might leave for those who follow something worth learning, even from our mistakes. We need not fear to explore.

But your concerns, too, are wise ones. The risks of becoming blind to what is there in the Christian witness, and of distorting it and the God of which it speaks, are very real, too. How do I think we deal with these dangers?

I do not think resolving to be a steadfast conservative or an unswerving liberal is any safeguard at all against the dangers we are discussing. Neither provides special protection; neither position is a privileged haven. Each, the conservative mood and the liberal mood, has over time taken multiple opportunities to blind itself to what our history has given us and to bend this history to suit its immediate purposes. Like all human projects, liberalism and conservatism are sometimes strategies of insight and sometimes strategies of self-deception. Being faithfully one or the other guarantees nothing of importance.

I think the most reliable safeguard against the dangers you noted, as well as the opposite dangers that I mentioned, is a sustained and reflective openness to the views of, and the criticisms from, others within and outside of the Christian community. Whether the issue is the doctrine of God or abortion or church polity, we are most likely to persist in our own comfortable distortions if we remain closed within our own circles of comfortable agreement. One implication of the Christian doctrine of the Incarnation, I think, is the confidence that in the sometimes hard and (one hopes) caring criticism we hear from others we also hear the judgment of God. God's judgment can be manifest in the judgment of others upon us, our views, and our ways. To the extent that we believe this, we will develop contexts for dialogue across the boundaries that divide us. This would mean that we will seek critical, caring discussions between Christians and non-Christians, and within Christianity between conservatives and liberals, Catholics and Protestants, Western and Eastern Christians, etc. It would mean, too, that we pursue these dialogues not as occasional forays prompted by curiosity or as strategic public relations ploys, but in sustained ways as an enduring obligation of our intellectual stewardship as Christians.

> Pinnock: The God of the Bible is a living Agent who acts in history and responds to the prayers of his people. I am worried that modern God concepts often seem to reduce God to a dimension of the world itself and do little justice to God's transcendence. Does this concern you, too?

Brown: Your concern is fully justified, but I think your way of stating that concern is only half right!

Is it only "modern God concepts" that run the risk of compromising God's transcendence? What of the ways in which conservative Christianity has, in recent United States history especially, reduced God to a champion of the interests of a particular class, race, economic system, etc.? It is difficult for me to imagine a more worrisome attempt to exploit the Christian God than one finds in current equations of God's will with American foreign policy, capitalist economics, patriarchal social policies, racist illusions, and a few other favorite themes of conservative sermonizing. Politics, economics, racial distinctions, and social structures are each a "dimension of the world itself"; and their various forms reflect greater or lesser degrees of justice. But each is always ambiguous. From listening to some conservative apologists, however, one gets the impression that "God's will" and "Christian" are just names for whatever happens to be the conservative crusade of the moment.

My point is that reductionism is everybody's problem. Its forms may tend to differ somewhat for liberals and conservatives, but reductionism is not unique to those who champion "modern God concepts." Still, you are right—it is also a problem for those of us liberals who do explore such concepts. Why?

One of the liberal Christian's continuing concerns has been to show the compatibility of Christian faith and the most credible conclusions of modern knowledge. This concern has been especially prominent in relation to the sciences. Occasionally we have been so anxious to justify Christian teachings to the scientific mind that we have simplistically equated each scientific hypothesis that comes along with some element of the Christian worldview, for example, "some call it evolution, others call it God." If truth is one, then the underlying concern of liberalism—about the compatibility of science and religion—is a sound concern. But the simplistic way that liberalism has sometimes sought to accomplish its goal is clearly not sound.

Liberal Christianity is much less enamored of science today than it has been in the past. Indeed, liberalism has played no small part in criticizing the adulation of science in the modern period. This, as much as anything, may explain why liberal theology today adopts a more "revisionist" stance. On this view, as I indicated in my statement on theological method, we are no more entitled automatically to accredit the latest in modern knowledge than the earliest in ancient wisdom. Instead, the Christian's obligation is to enable each—the claims of the past and the claims of the present—to illumine, test, and correct the other.

Will this revisionist conception of the theologian's vocation keep the liberal from reductionism? Will we now no longer be tempted to equate God with the ultimate principle of our favorite system? Well, we liberals should now be less inclined to assume that our favorite system is itself ultimate, and thus we should be more tentative in our reflective conclusions. But you and I both know that we, liberal theologians, will continue to find ways to exaggerate what we can be certain of and to baptize the hypotheses we hold dearest. But I hope we both think, too, that conservative theologians will just as easily fall prey to comparable illusions of finality.

From a human point of view the "solution," as I said in answer to the preceding question, is greater openness to the views of others, especially an openness between liberals and conservatives. We need one another, as compassionate but candid critics.

Yet from a theological viewpoint there is another, though related, kind of solution. It is the conviction that God is indeed a "living Agent" and therefore that God can take care of preserving the truth. Liberals, I am sure, have a parallel weakness, but it seems to me that conservatives are a bit too worried about heresy, minutely measuring every theological proposal for fatal mistakes as if it has been left to us alone to protect God from misrepresentation. Can we not count on God to do that? Our minds, certainly, are too fallible to do it very reliably.

● Pinnock's Rejoinder to Brown

Once again I am impressed by your penetrating answers to my queries. You do not take offense at a possible impertinence on my part or reply in a defensive way to my probing. But you patiently explain your meaning in most helpful ways. I say this not to be nice but to admit that a liberal like you can get through to an evangelical like me. So I hope you will keep trying to communicate with evangelicals, frustrating though it must often be for you.

I am also positive, not only to the manner, but also to the substance of what you have to say. I see two important points of agreement here. First, I take it that we both want to defend what I would call objective theism, against the subjectivists or constructivists of modern theology who present God as a symbol of our human values, as little more than a poetic expression of our own ideals. I think that we both oppose that. I understand process theists like you to be saying that God is real in an unqualified and objective sense; as Schubert Ogden has said, God is the ground in reality itself of our confidence in the final worth of our existence. In embracing metaphysical theory (even if it is Whiteheadian!), I hear you to be saying much more than those who construe God as a human construct in the face of an objectively meaningless world. I am in agreement; God is definitely more than that, thank God!

Second, we both criticize classical theism in much the same ways. As my own presentation has shown, we both oppose certain Hellenistic influences on patristic thinking about the deity that push the doctrine of God in the direction of strict immutability, seriously threatening the dynamic theism of the Bible. The Greek notion of perfection (I agree) is not very helpful for rendering the incomparable One of the Scriptures.

My anxiety about your view arises in relation to an important point of detail in the doctrine of God. I worry that the process deity you and others describe is much too passive; always receiving influences from the world, but not taking much initiative in promoting the kingdom. I like the way God in your view is really related to the world and to history, the way God has inner sympathy with his creatures and derives pleasure from our lives. I say amen to that. But I do not think it is quite enough to assign God the role of experiencing and remembering everything, to make God the final organizer of what comes to him from the world. According to the biblical message, God takes the initiative in the history of salvation. So even though I, too, want to replace a static view of God with a dynamic view, it cannot just be any dynamic view but must be the dynamic theism of the scriptural witness.

I worry that liberals listen to modern voices too much. I see your process theism allowing the Bible's picture of God as dynamic agent to slip. The modern worldview, after all, is naturalistic; and even when God is believed to exist this belief can be vague and God's actions very much constrained. Westerners think and act as if God has little to do with everyday affairs. They tend to be practicing deists. Captivity to the secularist paradigm has got to change.

PART THREE

THE DOCTRINE OF HUMAN NATURE AND SIN

SECTION 5

> *Delwin Brown's presentation on human nature and sin, Brown's answers to three questions put by Pinnock, and a rejoinder by Pinnock to Brown's answers.*

Liberal Christians assume that what Christianity says theologically deals with what ordinary people think about, whether or not they are Christian, whenever they think about life seriously. The theological reason for this assumption is the doctrine of the Incarnation, to be discussed in the next chapter. For now I can simply report that liberals insist there is a continuity between what Christian faith affirms and what is most important to people simply because they are human. This continuity may be easiest to show in Christian talk about human nature and sin. Moreover, it seems to liberals that Christian faith *must* be illuminating here. Who are we truly? How is it that we so distort our lives? And why? These are not simply Christian questions; these are *human* questions. They, above all, are the questions Christian faith must confront insightfully if it is to be credible for our time.

Christianity has a very general conception of human nature and the ways it is distorted. This general conception has taken many forms in biblical and post-biblical history. One of the ways it has been formulated, stemming mainly from Paul and Hebraic thought before him, is in terms of the contrast between "nature" and "spirit."

In recent Christian theology, especially, the term nature has denoted the physical, worldly, and relational side of being human. The other term, spirit, has referred to that which distinguishes humanity from the other animals. This concept of spirit is sometimes developed in terms of human transcendence—our ability to reflect on ourselves, to step "outside" of our actions and examine them. Sometimes it refers to our human agency—our ability to act, to be intentional causes affecting other things. Always, however, spirit also refers to that in us which is somehow reflective of, or connected to, God.

This way of understanding humans can be marvelously illuminating, particularly if it is interpreted in the context of what we might call biblical holism. For the biblical tradition generally it is probably most nearly accurate to say that nature and spirit refer to two different dimensions of the whole person. At least it is clear that nature and spirit are not separable sides of personhood. That organic way of thinking about selfhood stands in brilliant contrast to the narrowness we see in many secular ideas of the person. Secular views seem always inclined to separate the self and to focus on one side to the exclusion of the other. Existentialist philosophies, self-actualization psychologies, and capitalist economics tend to focus on spirit, interpreted in a particular way. Behaviorism, Freudianism, and orthodox communism focus on some understanding of "nature."

The holistic vision of personhood predominant in the Bible is not right because it is biblical. If we judge it to be right, we do so because again and again its holistic notion of selfhood exposes the shallowness of attending to one side only, nature or spirit, and thereby it tells us what we need to know in order to live life more profoundly. It proves itself to us, often when we would prefer not to heed its claims. More than that, it proves itself to us in unexpected forms. In fact, the biblical vision of the person is hardly a particular concept or theory. It is more like a family of related ideas, or, as the rabbis used to say of Torah, it is like a precious gem with many facets; as we slowly turn it in the light of changing human experience each facet provides some unexpected brilliance that illuminates our self-understanding in quite new ways.

I should point out here, parenthetically, that this way of

understanding Christian anthropology is a liberal approach, reflecting liberal presuppositions. First, I am assuming that there is no one Christian, or, for that matter, biblical doctrine of human nature, even if there is clearly a biblical orientation. This orientation is a complexity of interrelated voices that offers itself to us as a provocative guide in our own personal explorations of what it means to be a self. In isolation these voices—what Paul says about the place of women, for example—are not always right, and in their collective diversity they could not possibly all be right. But precisely in their multiplicity, in their contrasts with each other, and in the reflective struggles they generate in us, they continually author our own sense of what it means to be a person.

Second, what the Bible says about personhood is not true because it is in the Bible. We do not attend to this view of the person because it is in a book with an honorific title. We attend to it because it has proved itself to us as partner—friend, guide, and often adversary—in our continuing search for a reliable sense of selfhood. But, is the biblical perspective on personhood true? For me that question means, do we find it a reliable guide in this search? The answer must be determined, as I indicated in previous chapters, as it is tested in experience, personal and collective, and assessed in the arenas of our contemporary discourse. Does this not mean that we set human experience and human reason above the Bible? No, but neither do we set the Bible in a protected place above the tests of experience and the scrutiny of reason. Instead, we assume that the biblical voices can take care of themselves. To seek protection for the Bible, to ask that we assume its truth at the outset, reflects, it seems to me, a weak view of the Bible.

Liberal Christians in the twentieth century have found the biblical vision of selfhood to be a definitive resource for, and judge of, modern anthropologies. Reinhold Niebuhr has been the most effective interpreter of this vision, especially as his work has been critiqued and corrected by feminist theologians. My own way of learning from their appropriation of the biblical tradition must be summarized briefly so that its implications for a couple of liberal/conservative debates can also be addressed.

The important thing, as I see it, is to begin with the holistic conception of selfhood that seems so fundamental to biblical sensibilities. Spirit and nature are complementary. For biblical thought, the human spirit reflects God's own nature. God the creator brings this world into being, and God continuously is at work in the world to make plain its destructive elements, nourish its goodness, and bring the world to greater wholeness. To speak of human spirit, then, is to speak of our capacity to serve God's continuing creation. Spirit refers to our "transcendence." This term means that we have the ability to stand outside ourselves and see who and what we are even as we are engaged in being and doing. Thus transcendence also means that we are responsible. We are not blind cogs in God's cosmic machine. Being able to stand outside ourselves, we are able to do other than what we do, and thus we are rightly held accountable for the kind of life we form through our actions.

Being spirit also means that we are "agents," that we have the capacity to make a difference. Just as God made a difference by bringing this world into being and continues to make a difference within the world, so we, who image or mirror God in ourselves, make a difference in the world. We are called to be co-creators with God, to serve God's redemptive aims in the world. We can be called to this task precisely because, as spirit, we are agents.

A story in Genesis 2 represents the task of co-creation in its most radical form. There God tells Adam to "name" the animals. In the biblical worldview to give names to people or things is not simply to label them. It is to decide their places in the nature of things, to determine their meaning. The point is that "Adam" (or humanity) is not given a blueprint for creation to which we must conform. The ongoing creation is not a paint-by-numbers process. It is a work of artistic creativity. As Christians, we believe that this work is preeminently the artistry of God. But, like those who served a master painter such as Leonardo de Vinci, we are called to be God's artisans. Our task is sensitively to explore the evolving pattern of life, and to take responsibility for helping to create in our own time and place those particular life forms that will best serve God's general aims for the world.

Clearly, then, the concept of spirit denotes a distinctive connection between humanity and God. The point to be emphasized here is that we mirror God's own nature in our capacity to be responsible, creative agents of judgment and redemption in the world.

If we are faithful to the biblical way of portraying humanness, however, we will be just as emphatic in emphasizing "nature" as part of our being.

Unlike the views of other ancient traditions, the Bible's view of the created order is positive. God created the world and pronounced it good! The concrete world is not to be suspicioned or disdained. The natural world, natural processes, natural needs are the worthy creation of a good God. More than that, these things that form the context of our lives are in fact a part of our lives, a part of us. We are body or nature as well as spirit. That is why the New Testament does not, with the Greeks, speak of the immortality of the isolatable, spiritual soul. Instead it speaks, as it must, of the resurrection of the entire embodied self. That is why Paul, in Romans 8, does not, with Plato, portray salvation as escape from the physical creation. Instead, he understands that the whole creation, and not only we ourselves, will somehow be set free from bondage to decay and death.

Long before it was "discovered" by modern thought, then, the Bible knew that to be a self is to be both spirit and body. We are both agents and recipients, both individuated and related, both creators and "createds." This means, for one thing, that our embodiedness, like our agency, is fundamentally good. The sins of the "flesh" are not natural needs and bodily desires; they are destructions of nature or body and of mind. They are modes of life lived in "hostility to God" and thus to God's creative aims in the world. Nature is as much God's good creation as is spirit. But second, to affirm "nature" as a part of our selfhood is to break down the absolute wall between humans and the rest of creation. We are at home in the world, at least in the world as God intends it. Nature, too, is a cherished creation of God, and it, too, is the object of God's redemptive activity. According to the divine pronouncement in Genesis 1, nature, too, is good; it, too, has intrinsic worth.

With this sketchy interpretation of the nature of personhood as a background, we can now ask, even more briefly, about the nature of sin. If sin is viewed as the destruction of personhood, then we may say, with classical Christianity, that sin is the manifold way that we deny or distort ourselves as a part of spirit or as a part of nature. Sin is a denial of ourselves as God created us—as spirit-and-nature, as nature-and-spirit.

In classical theology there were two main types of sin, referred to most often as "pride" and "sensuality." (Today "arrogance," and "irresponsibility" or "laziness" are perhaps better terms.) Pride, as understood in the classical tradition, is pretending that we are pure spirit, free of nature, independent of context and its graciousness. It is the denial of our indebtedness, receptivity, relationality—the illusion that we are absolutely free. Sensuality, in its classical meaning, is pretending that we are pure nature, devoid of spirit, unable to name who and what we are. It is the denial of our responsibility, agency, influence—the illusion that we are absolutely bound. Pride and sensuality, or arrogance and laziness, are sins against God because they are distortions of what God has made us to be.

If we conclude, as I do, that this general understanding of personhood and its distortions, sin, acquits itself successfully in comparison to alternative anthropologies, then we begin the difficult task of trying to discern what this suggests about the manifestations of sin in our own time and place. This is hard not only because we are fallible, but also, and especially, because, as Paul suggests in Romans 1, we are so adept at deceiving ourselves about the very distortions that we ourselves perpetrate upon ourselves! That is why Christian wisdom has been content to leave final judgment to God, taking for itself only the obligation to try to discern in admittedly imperfect ways the forms that sin takes here and now. We seek to learn from the discernments of the biblical and post-biblical past. We seek to learn from other Christians in contemporary debate. We try to learn from our secular critics and people of other faiths who sometimes see through our pretenses with embarrassing ease. And we attempt to be open to God's own leading presence in these and other places.

It is difficult to speak of sin, as I say, but it is possible. Liberals have not always remembered that. Any time we accept some normative vision of selfhood, however, we already have an implicit standard by which to judge what are and are not the distortions of selfhood that twist and destroy our lives. Moreover, any time we tie that normative vision of selfhood to the will and workings of God in the world, then we can and must say that sin, whatever else it is, is emphatically also sin against God.

Not only can we speak of sin, we must. Whatever the difficulty of identifying the sin in our lives, and however tentative that endeavor must be, it is just as necessary as it is difficult to speak of sin concretely if Christian faith is indeed relevant to ordinary life in our times.

I will not attempt a systematic discussion here. Instead, I will focus on one way of distorting our selfhood, namely in sexism. I do not mean to suggest that concern about sexism is a specifically liberal concern, but I do think this is one issue where the conservative method tends to inhibit a redemptive openness.

Christian feminists have helped us to begin to see that sexism is not simply the repression of women; it is a distortion of personhood, female and male. If humans are indeed both spirit and nature, and if both are truly good, then their integration must characterize all humans. Historically males have attempted to embody the spirit, or agential, side of personhood. We have made that normative. In fact, the discerning reader may have noted above that, according to traditional Christian thought, human "spirit" images or mirrors God's own being. Nothing comparable is said about nature.

Why not say that humans as nature or embodiedness, no less than humans as spirit, image God's own reality? The initial answer may be that nature, after all, is visible, and no one has seen God. That answer is inadequate, of course. A great deal of the nature—known scientifically (atoms, black holes) or known ordinarily (love, memory)—is not seen either. More importantly, as I indicated earlier, the basic meaning of saying that humans are "nature" is to say that we are embedded in concrete and dynamic relationships. Who we are involves always those to whom and that to which we are related. But this is also true, and preeminently true, of the God of Christian faith and witness. A God who is essentially agape is also essentially relational and receptive. It follows that we image God in our receptivity and relationality just as we mirror God in our agency!

I believe the failure of traditional theology to see that we image God both in spirit (our agential side) *and* in nature (our relational side) is a theological root of sexism among Christians. It has blinded us, in theology, to the correlative character of nature and spirit, to the fact that each implies the other and transforms the meaning of the other, in ourselves as in the God whom we mirror. This has been disastrous in our lives. Pretending that they can be separated, we have assigned nature to femaleness, spirit to maleness, and—erroneously, from a Christian theological standpoint—we have taken spirit to be normative. The result is a distortion of women and men. We have denied to women the agential role that "spirit" connotes, to men the relational role that we indicate by our term "nature," and to both the essential interconnection of nature and spirit in the individual life.

The long process even of understanding, to say nothing of finally eradicating, this distortion of selfhood will surely occupy Christians for generations to come because it has controlled us for so long. This patriarchal distortion of personhood, after all, is evident in the Bible itself. It was strengthened and perpetuated by church structures, economic interests, social practices, and, as we have seen, theology. This distortion, this sinfulness, remains ensconced even in our piety.

Consider, for example, the insistence of many Christians that God can be referred to only as if God is male. No Christian, probably, thinks God is actually male. But that makes the insistence all the more bizarre. If all of us acknowledge that God is literally beyond gender distinctions, why the insistence that the terms proper to one gender, but not the other, be applied to God? The answer, I think, is to be found not in logic but in sin. The sexist distortion of selfhood has become deeply ingrained in our personal and cultural relationships. It is perhaps even more deeply ingrained in our consciousness, so deeply in fact that it manifests itself in our language about God!

At this point some conservatives—by no means all—may appeal to the fact that Jesus in the New Testament refers to God as Father. That strategy, however, is no more compelling than it would be to appeal to Jesus' tacit acceptance of slavery as a defense of slavery. More importantly, I think the temptation to employ this kind of strategy (whatever it says about sexism) reveals a danger in the conservative approach to the Bible. What is wrong, in my view, is not that conservatives hallow the past, approaching the Bible with the humble expectation of learning in their encounter with it what they need to know. That attitude is perfectly defensible, one liberals need to emulate. What is wrong is that conservatives reduce the Christian, and especially the biblical, past to a normative set of allegedly consistent specifics. I do not think that is an accurate understanding of the biblical text. More than that, it hinders the Bible's creative power. Reducing the Bible to one thing, and supposing that we grasp it now, does not lead one to expect that the biblical witness will speak in new ways the word of judgment and healing that must be heard in every age.

Sin, however, is not primarily a matter of mistaken methodology, conservative or liberal! It is rooted in the mystery of the human will. This means, undoubtedly, that sin is first of all personal. Conservatives have witnessed to this fact most persistently, and we liberals must acknowledge its truth. Fundamentally, sin is individuals doing those things that we ought not do and individuals not doing what we should. Left here, however, a view of sin is inadequate.

For one thing, as indicated above, Paul speaks all too truly when he speaks of the "ungodliness . . . . of men [and women] who by their own wickedness suppress the truth." Although "what can be known about God is plain to them," he says, "they [become] futile in their thinking and their senseless minds [are] darkened" (Rom. 1:18–19, 21–22 RSV). We cannot, then, speak of sin simply in terms of the individual's conscious failings, for the problem of sin is precisely that we so neatly hide it from ourselves within ourselves. We suppress the knowledge of our sin, removing it to the obscure recesses of our hearts. This means that we ought never to rely on the tidy calculus of innocence that we invent at a conscious level in order to exonerate ourselves. It means that we ought ever more intently to listen to the strange words of biblical judgment that persistently search through the failings of all of our Christian traditions. And it means that we ought to listen carefully to the criticisms of our brothers and sisters in these other Christian traditions, as well as in communities outside the Christian faith, conceding—no, hoping desperately—that from them, too, we might learn what we need to know.

But an individualized notion of sin is inadequate also because it overlooks the social nature of personhood. If the human self is relational or social, then so, too, are the distortions of the self. Sin assumes proportions larger than individual choices and actions. It infects our social systems, as racism, sexism, and classism prove so destructively. It is expressed in widespread habits of mind that denigrate as less than adequately human those whose natural sexual preferences differ from the statistical norm. It emerges in the reduction of Christianity to nationalist self-righteousness and triumphalism. It appears as the baptism of greed, the glorification of war, the celebration of force. Sin corrupts our language systems, cultural self-understandings, and social customs. In the words of Edna St. Vincent Millay, "evil upon evil laminate through layers uncountable as leaves in coal."

Sin takes on the kind of corporate character that Paul indicated when he spoke of "principalities and powers" that dominate our lives. If Paul's elucidation of these powers seems mythological to us, the realities to which his words point are real. Liberals have been more faithful in their witness to the collective reality of sin. Conservatives have more adequately attested to its individual character. In understanding what sin means, we need one another.

> *Pinnock: Religious liberals like yourself now take sin more seriously than they did a century ago. Is this just because the cultural mood has shifted in its favor or is it a return to the authority of biblical teachings or perhaps both? How do we arrive at a doctrine of the human— through our own insight or in the light of divine revelation?*

Brown: This question is as much about theological method as it is about the doctrine of human nature, and for good reason since they are intimately related issues. But I will separate them for purposes of discussion.

You ask, do we arrive at a doctrine of what it means to be human through our own insight or through divine revelation? Your distinction between insight and revelation is legitimate in the abstract. Just as there is "what I say" as well as "your insight into, or interpretation of, what I say," so also abstractly it makes perfectly good sense to speak of what God reveals in distinction from our human interpretations of this revelation. Practically, however, you can never get around or beyond your own successive interpretations of me in order to check what it is that I "really" say. In a similar way, it seems to me misleading to distinguish sharply human insight and divine revelation in matters of practical interpretation since we can never get beyond our interpretation in order to get at what God "really" revealed or reveals apart from human interpretation. Whatever "revelation" can and must mean in Christian theology, I think it cannot be juxtaposed to human modes of knowing in the way that one frequently finds in conservative thinking.

With respect to the substantive anthropological question, I agree that liberal Christians now take sin more seriously than they did some decades ago. My guess is that this has something to do with the cultural mood; I cannot imagine that liberals are not influenced by the contemporary setting on this issue, as I think we all are on every issue to some extent. But this cannot be the whole explanation, since if Western culture generally now has a sense of sin, it nevertheless seems not to have a very strong sense that sin is terribly inappropriate! Culture cannot be the whole reason. Neither do I think liberals now take sin seriously because the Bible says they should. The Bible says a lot of things—about monarchy, divorce, slavery, homosexuality, etc., that liberals (and many conservatives, too, judging from their practice) do not find especially adequate.

I think liberals take biblical assessments of sin so seriously today because these ways of viewing the human condition make sense out of the traumas of personal and social existence in the twentieth century. The persistent admixture within us of virtue and vice, the recalcitrance of destruction in our lives, the shrewdness with which we deceive ourselves, the intertwining of the personal and the social dimensions of sin, the ambiguous relationship of fate and freedom—these realities seem to many of us surely grasped and courageously named in the biblical tradition.

The Christian liberalism of earlier times (particularly in its popular form) had become much too optimistic, rationalistic, and individualistic in thinking about human nature. It trivialized sin, thought sin could be neatly sorted out, and believed it could be willed away by individual or collective resolve. Life together since World War I exploded these illusions, and when liberal Christians sought to comprehend what was left we found that the Hebraic-Pauline tradition of anthropological understanding provided a compelling way of doing so.

Thus, while I would not say in your words that we "return[ed] to the authority of biblical teachings," I would say that the authority, the authoring power, of the Bible reasserted itself in our living and thinking. I do not think anyone should ever believe anything simply because it is in the Bible. That, in my view, is an abdication of our responsibility as Christians to love God with our minds. But if we believe in accord with elements of the biblical witness, that is because in our continuing conversation with this canon, in the midst of our contemporary affairs, this biblical way of seeing things demonstrates its perspicacity.

But sometimes what is authored by our continuing struggle with Scripture are conclusions that do not correspond to the Bible. That this happens is, in my judgment, the most vivid mark of the Bible's authority. What this means practically for the topic at hand, however, is that we cannot settle uncritically into an acceptance of the Hebraic-Pauline view of human nature and sin. Whatever the enduring gifts of insight it offers us, questions should and do emerge. Is this tradition of reflection, however illuminating, fully adequate? Does it remain anthropocentric, hierarchical, and patriarchal in ways that are at odds with other important elements of a viable Christian vision?

My point is that the quest for adequate theological understanding is never completed, not even when we find ourselves more or less at one with some key element of the biblical witness. Because experience is so manifold, because our minds are so fallible, and especially because the Bible keeps opening within us new ways of seeing things, Christian theological reflection is a continuing process of intellectual stewardship. It is never a finished achievement.

> *Pinnock: You refer to sexism as an example of a sin of the present day. The apostle Paul identifies homosexual behavior as an example of the wickedness that elicits God's wrath (Rom. 1:26–27). How do you handle this issue and his ethic in the present context?*

Brown: I think the liberal and the conservative might say very much the same thing about Paul's view on this issue, yet, though what we say is the same, we would be doing two quite different things. What both the conservative and the liberal (myself included) might say is something like the following:

Paul makes a number of comments about behavioral issues, both personal and social, that reflect the wisdom and situation of his day. In his own reasoning he tacitly accepts the legitimacy of monarch and slavery, and with the rabbis of his time he explicitly elevates men above women and condemns homosexual relationships.

110

As farfetched as these Pauline views might seem to some of us today, they are never unworthy of examination and disputation. They always merit struggle, and sometimes in Paul's case, especially, this is so because Paul himself struggles so admirably and insightfully with difficult issues. Take the issue of male and female relationships. As the evangelical scholars Paul K. Jewett and Virginia Mollenkott have noted, Saint Paul works with two antithetical notions, one being the subordination of women to men within a hierarchical worldview, and the other being the remarkable egalitarian vision enunciated in Galatians 3:28. Paul moves back and forth between these ideas, sometimes ingeniously and sometimes inconsistently. The result, one could argue, tends to favor the rhetoric of a patriarchal hierarchy while at the same time fatally undermining it and moving it in a more egalitarian direction.

In listening to Paul struggle with the ambiguities of his day, we hear implicitly the claim that we should do the same with the same sense of freedom and responsibility in our own time. We also witness a splendid model of inquiry, and, of course, we learn something from Paul about particular issues along the way.

With regard to homosexuality, Paul did not struggle very much. There would in fact be little reason for him to struggle, given both his theological vision and the kind of homosexual relationships that he is likely to have known about in the ancient world. Theologically, Paul traded very heavily on the category of what is "natural." This is a much more problematic category today (as I believe a usually careful thinker like Paul would readily concede), and, in any case, what genuinely seems to be natural in the twentieth century differs markedly from what seemed so in the ancient world. At the very least, one must admit that to assert at the outset that heterosexuality alone is "natural" simply begs the question at issue. Frankly, I think certain forms of homosexual relationships are "natural" for some people. By that I mean that they are wholesome, enriching to the participants, committed, and consistent with God's will for their lives.

From what we know about the ancient world, homosexual relationships, especially among males, were frequently terribly exploitive. The predominant model of homosexuality in these cases was the relationship between a boy and a man, who simply used the child for his, the man's sexual gratification. While there are also adult homosexual relationships, of course, they too were viewed as

111

exploitive, as Paul seems to imply in Romans 1:27. It is clear, in any case, that such relationships were not encompassed within, or expressions of, a free and enduring commitment and deep personal caring.

The particular kind of homosexual relationships that Paul evidently had most in mind are most vigorously to be condemned. The logic of Paul's condemnation, however, should apply to all sexual relationships! All sexual relationships, including heterosexual relationships within marriage, that occur apart from a free and enduring commitment of personal care are exploitive, demeaning of the participants, and are therefore wrong. Sexual expression that is uplifting, caring, and committed is good and, in my view, Christian. There are some people for whom, quite inescapably, this Christian quality of sexual expression can take place only with members of the same sex.

The foregoing is what many liberals and conservatives alike might say in response to Paul's condemnation of homosexuality. But in saying this the liberal and conservative will be doing two quite different things. The former, maintaining that the Bible is that which authors our belief and practice in so far as they are authentically Christian, will be struggling with and learning from Paul as Paul himself struggles with the issue at hand. The conservative, maintaining that Scripture is that to which authentically Christian belief and practice must conform, will be showing why Paul's judgment regarding homosexuality is applicable only to a particular kind of homosexuality and not to all homosexual expression. The conservative sees Paul's views and the Bible generally as normative for the Christian. The liberal sees Paul's views and the Bible generally as formative for the Christian; it is that in relation to which one's identity as Christian is continuously created and sustained.

> *Pinnock: As you know, evangelicals charge liberals with the sin of rebellious reason. They think that liberals refuse the light of divine revelation and prefer to follow their own inner light. Are we wrong to think of this as sin?*

Brown: You have characterized "rebellious reason" rather specifically here as opting for one's own inner light (I would not call it that, but I will use your term) over divine revelation. You are not wrong to think of the liberal method as sin, if (a) this sharp distinction between divine revelation and one's inner light can be sustained in practice, and if (b) sin is defined as opting for the latter rather than the former. At the least, however, I think you ought to acknowledge that the liberal—carefully, honestly, and as the consequence of what may well be a Christianly motivated quest—does not believe we have been given a divine revelation in the Bible that either can, or was intended to, function as a norm distinguishable from our human experience and reflection in the way you seem to assume in posing this question.

From a liberal point of view, it is essential to see the Bible as it is, and this means, we think, recognizing the diversity of voices and teachings within it. The liberals will hold that this diversity is "the divine pedagogy," to use your own term in another context, and with you will go on to conclude that:

> God must want to force us to think as mature people. . . .
> The Bible in the form that it comes to us is the kind of teacher that draws us into the process of learning and helps us learn to think theologically and ethically in new situations. God seems to instruct us in this way in order to bring us to greater maturity. (*The Scripture Principle*, 194)

Given this view of the Bible and its function in Christian life, the liberal thinks it a bit "rebellious" for the conservative then to call for "scriptural submission." At least it ought to follow that truly to submit oneself to this kind of scripture is to think responsibly for oneself. (I think the conservative properly reminds the liberal that responsible thinking is formed continuously by the past. I think the liberal properly reminds the conservative that responsible thinking is normed by fallible, communal criteria in the present.) In any case, what might seem to be "rebellious" reasoning for some can be, for the liberal, one's obligation as a Christian. The liberal believes that reason is a divine gift, and that the Bible, properly understood, fosters the careful, tentative (i.e., the "reasonable") use of reason, not its denial or its diminution.

I have tried to respond to your question as you formulated it. If I may now use the term "rebellious reason" more broadly, I would say that I do not think it is a useful charge for conservatives to make against liberals. It seems inappropriate to me, not so much because it is untrue, but because it is too frequently true across the board of theological thinking, liberal and conservative. Within all theological positions one finds examples of thinking that seem to operate with self-serving disregard for important evidence and an arrogant disdain for the contribution of others past and present. If this kind of reasoning sometimes present in liberal theology condemns liberal theology as a whole, conservative theology fares no better.

Finally, however, I think the attribution of rebelliousness to anyone, liberal or conservative, obscures the real questions. Liberals rather commonly dismiss the writings of conservatives with the judgment that their works are obscurantist, legalistic, and downright meanspirited. Even if this judgment is true, however, it still leaves open the important questions: However motivated, whatever its underlying spirit, is the argument of this conservative text valid in important ways? What elements are and what are not? And what in this text, however emotionally charged and poorly motivated, helpfully calls into question the adequacy of my own view as a liberal? The converse is also true. Whether or not this or that instance of liberal scholarship might be driven by a rebellious spirit, the question ought to be: Is this liberal's argument valid, insightful in important ways, worthy of the conservative reader's reflection?

● Pinnock's Rejoinder to Brown

I appreciate the way you end your essay with the appeal that we liberals and evangelicals need each other in order to understand what sin means for our time. I agree that sin has many dark facets and we seldom manage to do justice to them all by ourselves alone. We can help each other.

Evangelicals particularly need to realize that sin identifies a resistance to God that is larger than merely the decisions of individuals. There is, according to the Bible and our own experience, a deeper social and demonic dimension to it, which we need to pay more attention to. Sin is a power, larger than human beings, that attempts to bring the whole creation under the power of death. From Jesus we learn that sin is a demonic force that becomes operative among human beings when we strive after other gods of power, wealth, or security and is a sort of collective energy uniting

114

peoples and even institutions against the kingdom of God. So I sincerely appreciate your point.

The main difference between us in this section, as you point out, is chiefly one of theological method and the priority we assign to the sources, Scripture and experience. Clearly it matters primarily to me that our doctrine of human nature correspond to biblical norms, and to you it matters greatly that one's position ring true to what we know about human life from experience. But the opposite is also true: I care a lot about the power of the biblical teaching to illuminate our experience, and you are not indifferent to biblical teachings but take them with utmost seriousness. So even though our view of the Bible differs significantly, I sense a degree of complementarity in our remarks and commend it.

My concern is a methodological one of course, as you anticipated it would be. Though I am happy to see how your reading of the human situation today meshes with the general tenor of biblical teaching, I am also troubled by the distinct possibility that one day it will not mesh, and when it does not you will have to opt for the witness of experience. We will see repeated the tragedy of nineteenth-century liberalism, which opted for an unbiblical position, as you yourself admit. Working from an optimistic reading of the human condition, it did not tell the truth about our desperate need of salvation. Liberal theology's problem was methodological: it did not work from the authoritative biblical message over to the human situation but the other way round, and because it worked backward, God's truth about the human condition was suppressed when the culture found itself moving in a different direction. This can happen again unless there is some anchor in theology to resist it.

Make no mistake, I am happy that your analysis agrees with the Bible; I am only concerned about what liberals (not necessarily you as an individual) will teach if and when the analysis does not line up with the Bible. Should not Christian theology speak darkly of sin in whatever cultural context it exists? Does it need a world war to convince it to do so? My problem with liberal theology never changes: it needs to be better anchored in God's Word and to be less open-ended, less kaleidoscopic, and less relativistic.

I can't resist picking up on the two evangelical names you threw at me (Jewett and Mollenkott). You should understand that a writer may be evangelical in terms of theological method or just in relation to a subculture. In his book on gender, most evangelicals

115

would agree that Jewett slipped into liberal methodology. He read into the Bible the up-to-date egalitarian model he deeply wanted and pronounced the category of male leadership erroneous wherever he found it. Jewett, ordinarily an orthodox stalwart, blinked. Similarly, when she writes about feminism and homosexuality, Mollenkott performs the same trick, reading into the Bible the standard liberal ideologies on these subjects. My point is that, although these two belong to the subculture we call evangelical, in these instances they are not functioning as evangelicals. They are not employing an evangelical theological method that puts the canonical Scriptures first, and are in these instances therefore evangelicals only in the sense of belonging to a certain subculture. Evangelical would refer primarily to the way they network rather than the way they think about these particular subjects.

SECTION 6

Clark Pinnock's presentation on human nature and sin, Pinnock's answers to three questions put by Brown, and a rejoinder by Brown to Pinnock's answers.

The modern world puts the human first. There is a turn to the human, a shift from the object known to the knowing subject. This means there is more attention given to the doctrine by theologians (particularly liberal theologians) than previously. In line with their method in theology, evangelicals aim to develop a doctrine of the human that reflects biblical paradigms and relates effectively in the world.

At the same time they realize, along with liberals, that people will not believe the Christian message only on the basis of an abstract proof of its credibility, but will want to know whether it can illuminate and transform their lives. So our theology must be intrinsically as well as extrinsically credible. People will find it difficult to accept an idea as true unless it corresponds in some way to something they have already thought or experienced. The fact that it is biblical will not be enough for many of them.

It is surely a paradox that, although we have never known more about the human by way of its physiology and psychology, or its place in history and society than we do today, we are really no closer to a common understanding about what being human

117

signifies and is. Evangelicals believe the reason for this paradox is that the human can be understood only in relation to God and interpreted in the light of revelation.

The turn to the human in modern thinking holds apologetic promise out to us. For at the point of the human, theology engages the world very directly. All people are acquainted with what it means to be human and are greatly concerned with it. Life is their existential project. So if our doctrine of humanity can be shown to have applicability in the real world of their experience, if our doctrine of the human can correlate with what people at large know human existence to be like through observation and experience, then we will have a means of proving its validity in the realm of human transformation.

Modern thought of course abounds in alternative anthropologies (Freud, Darwin, Marx, Skinner, Sartre, etc.), and these can be used in Christian theology where it seems appropriate so long as they do not dictate the terms. These paradigms have much to offer theology, while theology has much to offer them. It is valuable to study the human being as biological, as political, as psychological, as philosophical, as religious. Are human beings only higher animals? Are they flawed by some defect? Are they determined by their genes or the environment or both? Is there a fixed human nature? Is death the end? Man is a mystery to himself. The present uncertainty whether to treat man as an animal (reductionism) or a god (deification) gives theology a golden opportunity to enter into the discussion with its own insights.

WHAT THEN IS MAN?

The Bible understands why man would be a mystery to himself. Psalm 8:4 asks, "What is man that thou art mindful of him and the son of man that thou dost care for him?" (RSV). The central problem of modern thought turns out to be the question posed by the Bible. What can explain the paradox Pascal noted of the greatness and the misery of man?

Evangelicals are certain about one thing, that man will never know himself if he ignores the light of God's revelation that falls over his life. As Calvin said, our knowledge of the self will not be possible if isolated from the knowledge of God. To understand himself, man must look into the face of God. The person who tries to construct a picture of the human without the light of revelation will not be able to achieve an understanding in which the true significance of the human is seen.

At the same time, there must be something about man that makes such a revelation possible. He must have been made capable of relationship with God, a relationship that therefore also fulfills him. He must be a creature open not only to other human beings, but also to God, able to transcend its finiteness to the ground of its being in God. Humankind must be naturally able to know God and in knowing God come to know itself. It must be capable of dialogue with God and able to receive or to reject his Word. Such a concept is found in the biblical understanding of the human.

How then are we to understand the human? On a large canvas, one can view the biblical paradigm of the human in terms of three aspects: the human being as God meant it to be in creation; human beings as they actually exist in the condition of sin; and humans as they can become under the conditions of salvation by the grace of God in Christ. Such a model would allow for a full treatment of the subject and has guided many studies.

From another angle, one could pick up on the dialectic presented to us in Genesis 1 and 2. In the former chapter we were led to think about the unique dignity and high status of humanity created in the image of God, sharing something of the divine glory, while in the second chapter we encountered the creatureliness of the human—frail, dependent, weak, perishable dust—two important and complementary aspects.

Another way, perhaps the best, to get at the biblical doctrine of the human is to consider the category of the image of God in humans. It is a broad concept and must not be given a narrow meaning if it is to embrace the fulness of the biblical understanding of the human. Three aspects are prominent and important in this category.

First, one way in which our being human reflects God resides in the fact that we are personal agents as God is—not just in the faculty of reason that we share, but in all of that which enables us to be persons: including our spirituality, morality, creativity, and even embodiedness. Being in God's image in this basic sense is inalienable. Being human is something we possess and cannot lose. Image is then not just an ideal or a goal in the process of

119

becoming. One must first *be* a self in order to *become* a self. The image in us makes both relationship and development possible. The image at this level then is substantive not merely relational. We are the created likeness of God, while the eternal Son of God is the uncreated likeness. Christo-formity was the aim of creation even as it is the goal of redemption.

This gives us a solid basis for personal self-esteem. It helps to explain the value Jesus placed on human life. It stands as a corrective over against the careless language of total depravity in evangelical (mostly Calvinistic) theology, as if sin had obliterated the image of God in man. Due to this mistake, religion has all too frequently been associated with a denunciation of self-worth and has fostered a low self-image with debilitating implications. Over against that, there is a basis in the Bible for the importance, worth, and potential of every human self, which in right relationship with God can be tapped and realized to the fullest. Being made in God's image gives us the basis for respecting life, including that of the unborn, which is unquestionably human. In every way evangelicals want to celebrate life and rejoice in the dignity God has bestowed upon us.

A second dimension of the image is relational. As persons, we are capable of relating to God, as God's covenant partners. To be human is to be spirit, to be able partially to transcend the world, to enter into fellowship with God. We were made for relationship, made for love, made free. Knowing God is the destiny of humankind. God did not make us to be static beings but dynamic, growing, changing, and responsible persons. Open to transcendence, we were made to encounter God and respond to his Word, to reach out beyond the finite horizon and reach toward transcendence. The human is a being oriented toward God and always having to do with God, whether he thinks about it or not, whether he accepts it or not.

Third, as persons open to God we are summoned to exercise stewardly dominion over the world. Openness to the world and the future is basic to our humanity. We are called to be co-workers with God in the creation of history. Thus our identity in that sense lies out in front of us. God has called a creature into existence that can dream of salvation and wholeness with God and devote himself/herself to implementing this glorious vision.

God acted in the making of the world and now continues to

develop and draw out its potential in history. We are historical creatures in partnership with God. We are made by history as finite beings and also make it as agents. I make myself through my decisions: we create one another as we interact; we are in turn affected by the decisions of the past that impinge on us. Thus we are both destined and free. There is a context for our lives that is given to us, and that is what supplies the setting for the exercise of our finite freedom. We are beings in process, coming from a distant past and moving toward a hidden future. We move from a significant past, through the creative present, into a meaningful future. I would call this the openness of man, called to steward the environment. It is both our dignity and our danger. The openness means that we ever tend beyond the present into the future and ultimately the consummation of history. We live in hope of sharing fellowship with God and with others beyond death in the resurrection of the dead.

OTHER ISSUES FOR THEOLOGICAL ANTHROPOLOGY

1. Biblically, we must speak of corporate personality and human solidarity. In the Bible there is an oscillation between the individual and the group or nation. Humanity is like a tree, with a life of its own, of which individual selves are a part. The ancestor is like the root and the descendants are like the branches. The whole forms an organic unity that transcends time and place and may be described as a collective personality. Thus Paul views Adam and Christ as representing other people and can think of the human race as participating in the disobedience of Adam and in the obedience of Christ. As Paul says, in Adam we all die but in Christ we die and rise to newness of life. Central to Pauline soteriology, in Christ a new humanity is raised up from death and believers become members of the body of Christ.

Obviously this poses something of a problem for modern interpreters to make sense of this idea in a period of individual rights (political liberalism). But there are ways to make this biblical idea intelligible. People even today constantly feel the effects of the actions of others. Life is profoundly social both in creation and in redemption. Collectivity is part of our experience, too. Granted, such a notion requires an adjustment in our ordinary thinking about individual responsibility since we tend to construe it in such highly

121

individualistic terms. But it is possible and desirable to make that adjustment. Human society is such that individuals are always suffering for moral defects that belong to others and not to themselves. Parents are held responsible for the actions of their children up to a certain age. No one commits sin in complete isolation from the social structures of which one is a part. So the idea of corporate solidarity is not a strange vestige of Hebrew thinking but something profound about human nature.

2. Was Adam a historical figure according to evangelical theology? Often this is a point of clear distinction between it and liberal theology. Liberals no longer take seriously the Creation and Fall account in Genesis as a historically informative text so Adam and Eve are not seen as historical figures who lived once upon a time somewhere in Mesopotamia. The accounts are thought to be mythical, though they contain existential truths essential to Christian theology. Evangelicals on the other hand usually still try to find historical information in Genesis despite difficulties both exegetical and historical.

Nowadays the antithesis is not so sharp as it used to be. Many evangelicals accept some form of evolutionary theory as compatible with their doctrine of creation. They have become more comfortable with the idea that evolution might be God's way of gradual, continuous creation. Some are now willing to accept the possibility that Genesis presents a highly symbolic and theological account of creation and the fall into sin that is operating on a different level of truth than science does and that can be positively related to modern scientific and historical research without necessarily coming into conflict with them. For example, I would say that Eden was a place on the map I know not where, and the Fall was a date in history I know not when. Any warfare between religion and science on such details as time and place is folly. Theology and science both delve into the mysteries of God's handiwork, and we should be as critical of theology in its limited ability to fathom the unsearchable judgments of God as we are of science in its limited ability to penetrate the ultimate mysteries of God's creation.

3. Is human nature static or dynamic? One thing that was involved in the turn to the subject was a shift in the understanding of human nature as something fixed. An orientation to the human as dynamic subject rather than fixed essence became common. In classical thought the human being was thought of as a substance

with its own nature or essence, as an entity composed of soul and body as a distinct form of life in the hierarchy of being. But in modern times there was a shift toward thinking about man as a center of consciousness and action, not so much as a being with a unique essence as a subject with a structure of consciousness shaped by history and decision making. We tend to see humans now as individuals dizzy in our freedom who have to make decisions in the context of objective uncertainty.

There is truth here both in relation to biblical categories and human experience. But it should not be taken too far. For there are constraints on what humans can become, constraints that rise from the natural limits that hem us in. Although rational thinking has enriched substance thinking about human nature, I do not think it can altogether replace it. We need both categories to account for human nature. Even in Kierkegaard, who emphasized the relational, one finds the balancing insight that one must first be a self in order to become more fully a self. We should say that there is a natural human self rising out of God's creative activity that has a future. A human being is both an entity and an achievement. We are created persons but as yet incomplete and possessing future possibilities. To actualize these possibilities is what it means to be a person in relationship with God. We are called to become what we are, both in creation and in redemption. We are persons and our call is to become persons. We are created in God's image and called to become like Christ his Son.

4. What about man as male and female? God made us male and female in his image, perhaps reflecting the social Trinity that God is. We reflect God in our complemetarity of gender. We are equal partners in creation and in redemption. Women are certainly not inferior to men, even if they have different roles. On this point, as we all know, evangelicals are less likely than liberals to assume that this means the roles of males and females will be interchangeable. Although granting an equality in dignity and freedom, we often accept the idea that gender differences project social patterns in which males and females fall naturally into roles that are different and complementary. Evangelicals notice that fathers are not mothers in more ways than one and vice versa. We see these roles as created realities that cannot be fundamentally changed, though there is much that is variable. Therefore, we do not so readily assume as liberals would that patriarchy, defined as males tending

to occupy the majority of leadership roles, is automatically an evil arrangement rather than a creational or natural pattern. Liberals are much more likely than evangelicals to accept feminist ideology on these matters as gospel truth. What this reveals, I think, is a higher degree of resistance on the part of evangelicals to current cultural pressures like feminism as a general rule. Let me hasten to add that there are, of course, evangelical feminists. But these tend to be moderate feminists, and they are not meeting with great success whenever they try to implement their convictions.

Let me refer also to the familiar evangelical attitude toward homosexuality. Evangelicals believe that the Scriptures teach and experience confirms that God's positive will for human beings is heterosexuality and that homosexuality of any sort (whether inversion or perversion, whether exploitive or nonexploitive) falls outside his express will. Some would, however, be prepared (with Thielicke) to recognize a moral distinction between faithful relationships between consenting adults and exploitive sodomy so characteristic of the gay scene. Again, we meet the principle in evangelical thinking of constraints upon what is possible by way of reshaping human nature due to patterns created by God.

HUMAN SINFULNESS

How do evangelicals understand sin? In the past we have often placed emphasis on sin as a failure to keep God's law and on God as an outraged lawgiver. I see a tendency now to understand sin as saying no to relationship rather than simply falling short of a legal mark. Sin is taking flight from God and hiding from God. God says as much through Isaiah, "Sons I have reared but they have rebelled against me" (1:2 RSV). Jesus implies it in his parable of the Pharisee and the publican who was a perfect scoundrel, a collaborator with Rome, an undoubted swindler; yet he was justified by God. Why? Because he was sorry for his sins and accepted full responsibility. He was repentant and wanted to be reconciled with God. Or recall the parable of the prodigal son in which the wayward boy considers the folly of his actions and returns home only to find his father eagerly awaiting him and desiring a restoration of relationship. Sin is a refusal to love, a saying no to relationship, a seeking of salvation and worship elsewhere than in God. Sin is whoring after other gods, after other lovers.

124

Sin can also be related to the three points in the image of God. Sin is denying one's being as the reflection of God's personhood. It is the refusal to relate to God in our freedom. It is the refusal to exercise stewardly dominion over the earth and history. Or in regard to human creatureliness, sin can be either exalting the animality (nature) or denying the lowliness in pride (spirit).

Sin can also be taken as a comprehensive term symbolizing the conflict, injustice, estrangement, and suffering that humans bring on themselves by their foolish and perverse choices. God set us on a path toward fulfillment, and we have refused to travel along it. Even though we may be weak and vulnerable to temptation, in the last analysis we are responsible for our deeds. Sin may not be an act of sheer perversity, utterly unconditioned by mitigating circumstances, but neither does it follow from necessity or from causes too powerful for the weak will of tempted humans to resist.

What is the source of sin? Evangelicals take the clue offered in Genesis 3 and see the problem rooted in a misuse of our creaturely freedom. Augustine saw it that way, though it really implies a stronger definition of human freedom than he and many evangelicals today have to work with. We cannot really put the blame for sin on man if it turns out that man himself is manipulated by God!

But how did a creature with such great dignity and potential become existentially sinful? How did the awful gap between man as he ought to be and man as he actually is arise? I see that creating human beings with freedom was a risky undertaking on God's part. For it would always be possible for the creature to refuse to love God and love something else instead. Adam could always say no to God. According to the Bible, this possibility became an awful reality that characterizes the current human situation. Sin then does not properly belong to created reality; it is something unnatural that has become natural.

We were intended by creation to live our lives in the love of God and to find our security in him. In sinning we express a refusal to find our anchor there and our decision to find it elsewhere. Human beings in their freedom have deviated from the divine purpose for themselves with the result that tensions have appeared in the historical process, leading to a struggle of cross purposes. We have become sinners even though it was not a necessary consequence of our nature. Sin has become a structural feature of human existence. A cycle has been set in motion of cumulative degeneration with disastrous consequences for everyone. And it is all rooted in the primeval decision we call the fall of Adam, which has continued to affect history down to the present. The fall of Adam was an event, even if told pictorially, that is the silent presupposition of human history.

How did the Fall actually happen? Scripture helps us with this question because in telling the story it includes us in it. In Adam we all sinned and we all die. Paul refers to a time in his life when he experienced this personally (Rom. 7:9, "I died"). The Fall narrative, then, is something the dynamics of which we have all taken part in and understand. We can understand. We can understand the Fall inasmuch as we can understand our own freedom to turn against God.

While affirming the fall into sin as an historical event, we should not exaggerate the role of Adam, which, after all, is not much emphasized in Scripture. The story notes that sin began with him, but there is little speculation beyond that. Nothing is made of the primeval pair elsewhere in the Old Testament, for example. Much more is said there about sin rising out of our own perversity than from his. Sin is that which we ought not to have done. Here we see human solidarity playing a role. "The fathers have eaten sour grapes and the children's teeth are set on edge" (Jer. 31:29 RSV). Sin is both universal and inevitable. All of us together are in a condition of rebellion and disobedience. Yet there is a level on which sin is freely chosen. By saying that the circumstances that surround our choices make sinful decisions overwhelmingly probable and the necessity of divine initiative in salvation absolutely urgent, we are not denying individual responsibility in sin.

Can we come up with an analysis of what sin is actually like? Yes, we can try. As finite, historical agents, human beings naturally experience anxiety. It would be fine, if we were not finite and limited but more godlike, or if we were not so historical and responsible but more animal-like. Our big problem stems from the fact that we are both finite and historical, limited and yet creative and free. Humans are semi-transcendent beings and therefore experience the temptation on the one hand to be gods and act like gods (hubris) or on the other hand to be just animals and to give up on life (sloth). God's call, however, invites us to be free, finite creatures and to trust in him, living our lives in the context of God's purpose for the world. He calls us to live in finite freedom but without fear. Humans cannot escape this calling to relate to God and make history, but they are cut off from God and feel anxious about it. To make the situation tolerable they move in one of two directions: either creating another god out of some finite reality like money, sex, or power or else withdrawing from the struggle of existence and retreating from life itself. In such ways as these we try to make up for what has gone wrong and in so doing create a terrible mess of things. Thus God's image-bearers move toward self-destruction and slavery. There is no way to avoid the problem and no solution to it either unless God provides one, for we exercise our selfhood in a situation codetermined by shared guilt.

ORIGINAL SIN

Augustine stated the classical doctrine in opposition to Pelagius. Perfect man, he said, sinning out of his pride, and becoming disordered and corrupt, passed sin on down to us all through sexuality, rendering us all doomed and worthy of hell. The Fall corrupted Adam's nature and that corrupt nature gets passed on to subsequent generations through the carnal pleasure that accompanies conception. And humanity is made incapable of doing good or remedying its fallen condition. Every child born into the world is born into a mass of perdition with a corrupt nature and inherits guilt from the primal parents.

This bleak view was corrected and modified at the Council of Orange in 529 A.D. where it was denied that we are predestined to sin and that grace is irresistible. This move brought the Western church more into line with Eastern Orthodoxy, which had never thought of sin in this way in the first place. But Augustine's doctrine was resurrected in its awful purity by the Reformers who sought to eliminate all such semi-Augustinian tendencies. They placed powerful emphasis on man's total depravity in order to underline the absolute necessity of God's sovereign grace in salvation. The move led them practically to deny the image of God in sinners.

Wesley began to move in a better direction. He took original sin to mean that man is indeed enclosed in himself and cannot break through the walls of his prison, and that only if God takes the initiative in his love and breaks through to man can he experience liberation. But he taught that the grace of God is available to all sinners and that the natural propensity to sin can be conquered by

God's grace, which is at hand. Sin is indeed a power in our lives from which we need to be set free, but we are not puppets or creatures of fate or unable to call upon God for mercy. Wesley recognized as we should that there is inherited corruption, but he denied inherited guilt. There is no guilt for ancestral sins according to the Bible. Where there is no law, there is no sin. In this way evangelical thinking has been developing in positive directions.

But evangelicals stand together in opposition to any modern inclination to believe in the goodness, automatic progress, or perfectibility of man. Those Pelagian views were revived by liberalism in the context of the secular optimism of the nineteenth century, but were given a jolt by the catastrophes of the twentieth century. Liberalism was challenged on the point by the neo-orthodox school, and the point has registered with liberal theologians who reveal much more respect now for the darker dimensions of the evangelical position. Liberal theology has undergone a fruitful change, and now there is a much deeper appreciation of the magnitude of both sin and grace. This fact brings liberals and evangelicals much closer together than previously, at least on this topic.

Our consideration of human sinfulness leads us on to the next topic because it points to the desperate need for God to break into the situation and to set in motion a countervailing movement that will heal and restore humankind. Obviously, we need a power to save us, which is not going to rise out of the twisted human situation but must come to us from beyond it.

> *Brown: I appreciate your insistence that we are called to be coworkers with God in the making of history. Does this not imply that the human contribution is crucial to the achievement of God's aims in the historical process? If so, could God's effort in history fail without human cooperation? If not, isn't our human contribution really superficial to the divine working in history? In short, what is the human role as "co-worker" with God and what is its importance in the divine economy?*

Pinnock: As you say, I believe that humans are co-workers together with God as Paul wrote (2 Cor. 6:1). Our being created in God's image refers in part to our ability as persons to set purposes, to decide for ourselves, and to transform the historical process. We have been called to shape history together with God. I see this as an important part of what the image of God means.

But this freedom of ours, which issues in a history-shaping activity, also takes place in the presence of God, making us responsible to him in this obligation. God has made us to live before him and in relationship with him. Our liberty, then, is not autonomous but is exercised under the directing hand of divine providence. I would say that we have been made created co-creators. The circle of our freedom exists within the larger circle of God's freedom. God makes us his partners and allows himself to be limited by what we decide, but this does not mean that God loses his grip on the world. God remains active even when he is refused. Because we are created beings, we are dependent. Nevertheless, we do have a measure of creaturely power to shape history and form the future. Thus we do indeed participate with God in the ongoing creative process.

This certainly means that God's purposes for individual people can fail if they repudiate those purposes for themselves (Luke 7:30). Surely the reality of hell signifies this. God desires to save all persons but may not be able to do so if they decline to be saved. God is not willing that any should perish, but that does not mean such will not happen. The many passages on the divine judgment strongly imply that some people will say no finally and decisively to God. God takes the human response seriously. Augustine thought that no plan of God's can fail. But he was wrong. Certain of God's micro-purposes can and will fail when people reject God's will for their lives.

On the other hand, the Scriptures also tell us that Israel's refusal of God's purposes for them will not in fact derail his purposes either for them or the world as a whole (Rom. 9–11). God can draw straight with crooked lines. He operates with a wisdom that the rulers of this age are ignorant of (1 Cor. 2:8; Acts 2:23). I think of him as a master chess player in this regard. Divine sovereignty linked to the divine wisdom is still very real, even if limited to a degree by delegated human freedom. God can even cause the wrath and unbelief of man to praise him. There is always a counterplan to what man has foolishly chosen. If God were incompetent, I suppose his purposes might fail badly. But obviously they do not.

The choice then is not between total significance and no significance at all. It is the significance proper to finite agents operating within the sovereign yet flexible purposes of a mysterious and sovereign God. God is not surprised by what any of his creatures decide to do. He can take actions that are appropriate to every such circumstance. Nothing can happen that God is not prepared for and that in his wisdom he cannot handle. His anticipation of future contingencies is perfect.

> *Brown: Evangelicals have recently spoken with great conviction about the social, as well as the personal, character of sin. Before the Civil War in the United States, evangelicals were even more insistent in their proclamation of the social side of sin and salvation. They were courageous leaders in the fight against slavery, champions of equal rights for women, and defenders of the poor. Why did evangelicalism lose this sense of the social dimension of the gospel?*

Pinnock: Timothy Smith has documented the passion for social reform that existed among evangelicals in the nineteenth century in America. More broadly one thinks of Wesley, the Clapham Sect, the Salvation Army, and Charles Finney. Smith also refers to the decline in such involvement after 1910 as the great reversal. For some reason, as you point out, evangelicals ceased to care as much about social and economic reforms as we did before.

Why is this? I can identify several contributing factors. First, there was a reaction against religious liberalism and its social gospel. Evangelicals saw the gospel reduced to a form of religious humanism and to a program for reforming society and this encouraged us to stay clear of all social and political involvement. Second, there was a cultural shift in the direction of pessimism after World War I. People began to wonder whether reform of society was possible and worth working at. Third, a pessimistic premillennial eschatology came into prominence, further discouraging social reform. Evangelicals wondered why they should polish the brass on a sinking ship. Fourth, much church growth occurred among middle-class people who had a certain vested interest in the status quo.

But this has also been changing in recent years. Evangelicals in all of the churches of North America are waking out of our slumber and becoming involved again. There is a new engagement in social issues. Across the whole ecclesiastical spectrum one can see a remarkable convergence: in the Protestant mainline, in the Roman Catholic Church, among the evangelicals, and even the fundamentalists, ethics is back at the center of Christian theology where it belongs.

Some anxiety goes along with this of course. There is the fear lest the Christian message be interpreted in solely historical terms, as a political impulse and not the message of redemption and conversion. Evangelicals fear a secularized and political gospel. Ours is a religious mission that makes social engagement possible but is not replaced by it. What evangelicals fear we also see embodied in much of the political theology adopted by the bureaucracies of the mainline Protestant denominations. So much of it resembles a religious version of the Left, a new orthodoxy that defines what it means to be socially concerned by an alignment in politically correct ways. Evangelicals find considerable agreement with the Roman pontiff in favor of the religious mission of the church and in opposition to any reduction of the gospel to social and political liberation, which ironically seems to liberate no one.

Regarding Christian social involvement in the 90s, I would see one obligation for us in the West as giving support to political structures that enhance life and promote justice—such conditions as respect for human rights, religious freedom, limitations on the power of the state, freedom of the press, an independent judiciary, and the like. I would consider such arrangements as sanctified social structures and expect the churches to support them. We should deplore the critics of Western liberal societies among us (e.g., Noam Chomsky) for failing to appreciate the institutions that give us the right to speak out, and to praise uncritically regimes that never grant their people these benefits.

The other major obligation I would see is the role Christians need to play in the moral and cultural sector. Christians make an enormous contribution to society when we witness to values that transcend the world and when we inject them into the naked public

131

square. To function humanely, free societies need the moral texture of life that Christians build and strengthen by their lives and witness. Christians should foster good habits of the heart in the culture and help prevent liberal societies from falling into the abyss of moral license and the death of decency.

> *Brown: You note with approval that many evangelicals now interpret the Genesis creation stories in a manner that is informed by modern science and modern historiography. However, you seem resistant to the "feminist" idea that women are as entitled as men to take leadership roles in society. Its patriarchalism notwithstanding, there is much in the Bible that, for its time, is shockingly critical of gender-defined roles. Why, on the one hand, do you resist this feminist critique, which has an explicit grounding in Scripture, when, on the other hand, you approve of modern ideas about evolution and the symbolic character of Genesis that have little if any warrant in the Bible?*

Pinnock: This question brings two things together in a way I find misleading. Let me try to clarify my position on these matters. I do not think I am being inconsistent.

First, in regard to my handling of the creation texts you are just plain wrong. I do not interpret them at the beck and call of modern science as liberals do. Here is how I think about it. Initially, I notice that the idea of seeking a concordance between modern science and Genesis is a rather anachronistic thing to be attempting and that it would make better sense to interpret Genesis from within the setting of its own time, that is the second millennium B.C. When I do, I find that the biblical text addresses issues raised in the polytheistic cultures surrounding Israel: for example, are the sun and moon gods to be worshiped? Did God have to fight with a chaos monster to create the world? Thus the thrust of the Bible is not really in the direction of what Darwin is speaking about, at least not in specific ways. Now I would admit that modern science may have led me to raise these questions and look in this direction. If one thought that the world is only six thousand years old, he or she would not likely be inquiring into the length of the days of Creation. But that does not mean that science has dictated my interpretation of the Bible to me. I think it drove me back to the original intention of the writer of Genesis.

Now on the second issue that you raise, the matter of feminism, I approach it as the modern ideology that it certainly is. Feminism is historically located in modern Western society and rose within that context. It is arrogant and ethnocentric to suggest that it is the only way an intelligent and decent person can think about gender. Most people (men and women) in the world do not in fact think in feminist ways. Its future even in North America is in some doubt today. So naturally I approach feminism as I would approach Marxism or existentialism, listening to what people are claiming and not jumping on their bandwagon. I compare what they claim with my Christian worldview before making up my mind on the subject. I won't be bullied. Ideologies however popular do not determine what I think, not if I can help it anyway.

In the case of feminism, I notice initially the different types of feminism that there are and I listen to what they say. Then I consult the Scriptures and the accumulated Christian wisdom of the tradition. Analogous to my creation hermeneutic, I let feminism suggest new questions to me to take to the Bible, much as science suggests questions for me to take, with fruitful results. I then try to read the Bible in a fresh way to see what God's truth may mean in the presence of this new horizon. But in neither case do I look for answers in the culture. I stand beneath the Word of God.

I should add that evangelicals are not all in agreement about these issues. There is in fact a movement called biblical feminism, which espouses egalitarianism. Others support a partnership of the sexes in which the male and female roles differ. I struggle over which position to adopt, sometimes preferring one, sometimes the other. I am especially influenced by what I see as certain patterns of gender that favor the traditional, nonfeminist patterns. They lead me to believe that men have a benevolent responsibility to lead and protect women, while women have the disposition to receive the leadership of worthy men. This is at any rate the position many evangelicals hold based in the Bible and in their perceptions of what it means to be human.

● Brown's Rejoinder to Pinnock

You already know well what my response is to the substantive side of your answer on feminism and biblical interpretation. With respect to method, however, I did not intend to suggest that you interpret Genesis at the "beck and call of modern science," but only that you seem to be perfectly comfortable allowing science to "inform" your view of Genesis. You clarify the kind of relationship you affirm between modernity in its varied aspects and the biblical witness when you say that you allow feminism and science to suggest questions for you, and then you "try to read the Bible in a fresh way to see what God's truth may mean in the presence of this new horizon."

I affirm that mode of relationship, too. I do not, however, understand how you can claim to look for questions, but not answers, in modern culture. I should think that our answers themselves are partially formed by our questions and the way we ask these questions. If that is so, then the culture that is a source of questions is also, willy-nilly, a source of answers. I do not understand why that should be a problem for the Christian. If, with Barth, we recognize God's freedom to be God, then this radical freedom means that God can choose to speak to us through modern culture, even to give us answers through feminism, science, philosophy, etc. Is it not possible that the Christian who looks for answers in the Bible might learn from it to look elsewhere for answers, too?

On a quite different issue, related to the first two questions, I am not clear about your view of the personal and the social. You say, for example, that God's will for individuals can ultimately fail, but God's will for the social/historical realm cannot forever be frustrated because God's anticipation of the contingencies of this process is perfect. I am unsure why God can so effectively manage the collective process, but not the personal processes that we are as individuals. More importantly, however, I do not understand how the personal and the social can be distinguished in this way.

This same kind of distinction reappears in your answer to the second question. There you separate the Christian's "religious mission," which deals with "redemption and conversion," from what you call "social engagement," which relates to politics. Is this kind of distinction not still too much caught up in the individualism that we have inherited from the Enlightenment? I believe we all, liberals and conservatives together, must struggle to find ways of thinking that will allow us to take seriously the redemption of the "entire creation" and not only of "we ourselves" (Rom. 8). Many developments in modern thought (anthropology, psychology, philosophy, physics) suggest that this ancient vision ought to be viewed as more than quaint ancient symbolism. Learning how to do this is a task we can undertake together.

PART FOUR
THE DOCTRINE OF CHRIST

SECTION 7

Clark Pinnock's presentation on the doctrine of Christ,
Pinnock's answers to three questions put by Brown,
and a rejoinder by Brown to Pinnock's answers.

Now we reach at the heart of Christian theology in the doctrine of the Mediator. Against the dark backdrop of sin, Christ stands between God and humanity, pointing us to God and bringing God to us. Christ is the Mediator who stands between us and brings about reconciliation (1 Tim. 2:5–6). Christology is the hinge on which the Christian system turns. Although all doctrines relate to one another, there is a sense in which Christology is the focal point of Christian truth. For the distinctive meaning of all our concepts is derived from the Incarnation and the kingdom of God. Christianity *is* Christ in a way in which Buddhism is not Buddha and Islam is not Mohammed. According to the Gospel God was in Christ reconciling the world to himself.

Because of this mediation, the dual pattern characteristic of Christology emerges—Christ is human and divine, one person in two natures. He is the wisdom and power of God, providing us with the knowledge as well as the power of God. Through his threefold office, he restores humanity to a right relationship with God by standing between God and humanity. As the go-between, Christ brings God to us and presents us to God. He is the unique medium through which truth and grace, illumination and healing appear. The challenge for theology is to explain, if it can, how this happens.

It is not an easy task. First, because the Christology of the New Testament is complex not simple. Different models are used by the various witnesses. What Luke has to say is not exactly the same as what Paul says. Hebrews speaks in a different accent from John. Therefore, we are forced to make judgments about what the overall understanding of Christ should be. Second, it is difficult because the Incarnation is intrinsically mysterious. How could the One who was rich become poor for our sakes? What is it about God that would make such a thing possible?

Evangelical theology and piety are necessarily centered on Jesus the Christ in whom the whole fullness of the Godhead dwells bodily. By his obedience on the cross we proclaim justification and life for all people. The heart of the gospel is that Jesus Christ died in our place by his sacrifice on the cross and through his resurrection delivers us from sin and death. God saves us, not by the works of righteousness which we have done, but by his mercy to us in Christ. Salvation is through grace and by faith alone. We preach the unsearchable riches of Christ and announce Good News of great joy to all people because unto us is born a Savior who is Christ the Lord.

Besides being the heart of what the Bible teaches, Christology makes sense to the human condition. Just as the doctrine of God makes sense in relation to our experience of the contingency of human life, so the doctrine of Christ makes sense in relation to the equally human experience of brokenness and estrangement. For there is something dark and destructive in and around us that needs to be healed, the reality of which confronts us everywhere we turn. The good news is that in Christ, God has come forth to seek and to save that which was lost. He has brought his kingdom near. He has stooped even to the point of participating in our creaturely life and sharing in its suffering. God has acted in order to extend his love and grace to all sinners and won a victory over the powers of the evil ranged against us.

Why, we might ask, should an historical event be so important to the Christian faith? Why can we not just become creative and sensitive (saved) people, expressing our gifts and caring for one another through our own efforts? Why can we not just reach out and grasp authentic existence with our own hands? We do not do so because we cannot do so. We do not have the power, but Jesus Christ incarnates a divine power that makes it possible. Through his death and resurrection on our behalf, the power of transformation is available in history. In him God has entered into the world to save humanity. The ideal possibility can become real through the power of the Spirit of Jesus. According to the New Testament actual salvation depends on the act of God in Christ, upon historical truth and metaphysical reality. We have not found it possible to become healed from what afflicts us by our own efforts. If God had not done something about the problem of sin, salvation would remain an impossible dream. One is saved by the power of God or not at all. Sin had to be dealt with and death had to be conquered. This could not happen by chance or through human effort.

THE PERSON OF CHRIST

Jesus' identity has to be understood in the context of the kingdom of God, which was the way he himself understood it. Too often the person of Christ is considered in isolation from the central category Jesus employed. But that cannot be right. Jesus came preaching the kingdom, not the two natures. In him, the future kingdom of God was brought forward into the present. The timetable of the Old Testament hope was fulfilled and God broke into the world in power. The presence of the kingdom of God in the power of the Spirit is the proper context in which to think about the person and work of Christ. It provides the appropriate matrix and the conceptual framework and should not be neglected. Jesus came preaching the kingdom and in that framework spoke about his identity and role as the agent, instrument, and personification of God's gracious rule.

Approaching the two-sidedness of Christology, let me again begin with the human dimension as the Gospels themselves do. All of them present his public ministry, which culminates in the cross and resurrection, and raise questions of his identity in this narrative context. It was the ministry of Jesus from Nazareth that caused people to ask, "Who is this man?" Even the term "messiah" refers to a function and is not an ontological title. The ontology comes later. Theology may finish up with but does not start with Chalcedon. To know Christ initially is to know his benefits; later the believer goes on to try to understand the two natures in the mode of

141

incarnation. I think evangelical Christology has belabored the deity and relatively neglected the humanity of Christ. It is time to right the balance.

Jesus did not appear on the earth out of the blue as an isolated epiphany. He did not drop down from heaven. One must try to make sense of him first in the context of his own people. Jesus came at a decisive point in God's dealing with Israel, the people whom he had chosen. The Christ event occurs on the horizontal line of the divine activity in history. God's saving power had entered history long before, and Christ came in fulfillment of the divine promise and in the wake of its failure in Israel's case. It was to be a turning point.

In the human dimension, Jesus was revealed to be God's Son in the Old Testament redemptive-historical and nonmetaphysical sense. Peter sums it up: "God anointed Jesus of Nazareth with the Holy Spirit and with power; . . .he went about doing good and healing all that were oppressed with the devil, for God was with him" (Acts 10:38 RSV). Jesus was and functioned as God's covenant partner, the last Adam, the archetype of humanity, humanity as God had meant it to be, Israel as God meant her to be. He was a man filled with the Spirit who embodied a new way of human existence that was pleasing to God. Jesus set out to fulfill the purposes of God in his creation of humankind. As the ideal Son of God, he knew God to be his Father, the One with whom he enjoyed perfect fellowship. And through Jesus we, too, can know God as our Father and become God's sons and daughters by grace and adoption.

To avoid minunderstanding, let me add by way of explanation that the title "God's Son" is used both redemptive-historically and ontologically in the New Testament. I am laying emphasis on the former meaning because evangelicals almost always ignore it in favor of the latter usage. But later on I will refer to the metaphysically stronger sense of Jesus' sonship, claims that are also part of the New Testament witness.

Jesus' life therefore reveals to us what sonship means. It is a mode of existence in which love for the Father also puts the human neighbor to the forefront. Such a life is the goal God has for us all, the goal of our own sanctification. It is what Paul refers to when he writes, "[We are] predestined to be conformed to the image of his son" (Rom. 8:29 RSV). Too often evangelical Christology treats the humanity of Christ in an abstract way, in a way oriented to the

Atonement, and has not bothered to talk about the human path Jesus actually followed. This unfortunate decision slights a major reason for the Incarnation and conceals the goal of our own Christian path. Sonship denotes the messianic likeness which will be ours in the end.

Christ's life in this mode of sonship led to his death and rejection. People were invited to the feast Jesus preached, but many refused to come. They did not see any room for this kingdom of his in the world. It was not long before it became apparent to Jesus that blood would have to be shed if a new covenant was to be established. He realized that the representative of Israel and of all humanity would have to die. There was no other way to break the impasse. But God raised him up, vindicating his cause and validating his claims. The tomb was found empty and the Lord appeared to many after his death. In raising up Jesus our representative, God raised humanity up in him and made them sit at God's right hand. Too often evangelicals recognize an apologetic function in the resurrection but disregard the soteriological meaning whereupon the breath of God was poured out and history itself turned a corner. The first fruits of salvation that were glimpsed in the ministry of Jesus can now become a worldwide experience, "God making all things new." The renewal of the human race is underway. The age of mission has begun; the peoples of the world can be gathered. Christ has become a life-giving spirit to all flesh.

Turning now to the divine side of Christology, Jesus is also more than mere man. He is God's Son in a more exalted and ontological sense. He is also the eternal Son who was with the Father before all ages and became flesh. Sonship in this ontological sense should not be seen as an idea that evolved out of the simpler functional usage but rather as an idea that was always there alongside and implicit in it. For there was a transcendence in Jesus' identity that had already surfaced in his life in the Jewish context. He had called people to put their faith in him. He had placed himself in a strategic position as far as man's relationship with God was concerned. He had made himself central to all God was doing and was about to do. He had presented himself and his message as the fulfillment of what had gone on before in the covenant with Israel. In short, Jesus made tremendous and unparalleled claims that cannot be swept aside. The very earliest Christians reverenced Jesus as a divine figure and worshiped him. Later the Christology of the

143

Catholic church chose to continue along this high road and intended by "son" a metaphysical and not merely an eschatological sonship. Both forms of Jesus' sonship are of course both biblical and important.

In all strata of New Testament teaching, Jesus is more than just a good human example or anointed prophet. He is also a new creation, a fresh beginning, an act of God. The claims that he made, the filial relationship with God that he enjoyed all point to a transcendent dimension in and about him. Jesus was God's agent in the world. He is all that we are meant to be; he is all that God is for us. Jesus was God expressed in a human life. In him God came radically and almost unbearably near. Indeed as Paul said, "in Christ God was reconciling the world to himself" (2 Cor. 5:18 RSV).

Classical Christians have always thought that the image of incarnation describes it best. Saint John's language has become the preferred way of speaking in the Christian tradition, even though it is not the only way of speaking about Jesus in the New Testament. John's image of Jesus as the logos who was in the beginning with the Father has triumphed; the logos that was one with the Father and yet less than the Father. He was God the Son, only begotten, become flesh, the fullness of the Godhead bodily to whom worship is appropriate and world mission the natural outcome. Certainly this language goes beyond what Jesus himself normally said and probably thought. Only in the fourth gospel is there any indication that he thought of himself as having preexisted with God before his birth. But our Christian claims for Jesus are not limited to what he may have said about himself. After his resurrection the church's reflection on his significance shed light upon the meaning of the whole event.

Thus Christians have been taught to speak of one person in two natures as the pattern of their Christology and to hold both the human and the divine as true and valid. For us Jesus not only assumes humanity; Jesus is truly man. Jesus not only reveals God; Jesus is truly God. Humanity and divinity are objectively and ontologically present in Christ. As such, he rules over all things and will be the eschatological king and redeemer, one Lord for all humanity to worship and in whom to find our unity.

Orthodox Christians like evangelicals have a strong basis for their Christology. There is much to support it exegetically in the biblical witness and much precedent historically in terms of the grammar of the historic churches. Confession of the Incarnation in the full sense enjoys a strong measure of continuity with historic Christianity. It amounts to a defining characteristic of the authentic Christian community, a central belief that has come down to us in the tradition and in the liturgy to shape our experience of God fundamentally.

CHALLENGES TO CLASSICAL CHRISTOLOGY

Liberal theologians do not usually wish to speak in these terms. They do not want to attribute divinity literally to Jesus so overtly because of the many difficulties they see in it. They hope that they can find equivalent expressions that will be close to what the church has historically confessed but not involve a literal incarnation. However, this is not easy to accomplish and creates a problem. The substitute language after all has to sound similar to the Incarnation language or else it will evoke a protest from the people who are accustomed to a continuity of content and not just a continuity of piety on this point.

So there have been a great many efforts to come up with a substitute. Schleiermacher reduced Jesus' divinity to his God-consciousness. Ritschl spoke of Jesus revealing the will and character of God. Tillich located the divinity in Jesus' overcoming of the estrangement. Niebuhr saw Jesus on the cross as the perfect symbol of love. Baillie suggested that God was fully present in Jesus' life. For process people, Jesus is normative revelation when he fully actualized the special aim that God had placed before him. All such Christologies have something in common. They seek a functional equivalent of Chalcedon by finding in the human life of Jesus a unique divine presence, a normative divine revelation, a decisive saving action. But none of them wishes to say that Jesus is God in the ontological sense that orthodoxy has demanded. They will go only as far as functional categories.

Of course there are reasons why liberals are skeptical of classical Christology. There are difficulties that evangelicals need to respond to. Liberals do not undertake their revisions in Christology just for fun. They are asking important questions. Does the New Testament actually teach a doctrine of incarnation as a metaphysical singularity? Was it not perhaps a Hellenistic development, which came about later on? The evangelical would say in reply that the

New Testament does appear to teach the Incarnation. Not perhaps in quite the straightforward way we may have assumed in precritical days, but truly. The fact remains that in the days after Jesus' resurrection, the community worshiped him and ascribed to him the highest possible praise. Can we do less?

But, liberals ask, can sense be made out of claiming that Jesus is both God and man? How can God with his attributes be incarnate in man with his attributes? Is it not a logical contradiction to say that? In relation to this question I find it helpful to employ the category of kenosis. The eternal Son in his incarnation by a voluntary act limited himself to a historical human consciousness and to human faculties of knowledge and action. Kenotic theory is, I think, the most important fresh contribution to Christology since the early centuries. It helps to explain how Jesus could be a human like us, one who grew in wisdom and knowledge, was limited in time and place, and who depended on the Spirit for his effectiveness. As Charles Wesley would put it: "[Jesus] emptied himself of all but love and died for Adam's helpless race."

But how could the Son of God have done this? First, we can say that if something exists, it must be possible. I mean, no one is in a position to say what it is possible for God to do with his own freedom. There is bound to be mystery here and we cannot be ashamed to admit it. Second, we have to remember that Jesus became man and not something else. He took on the nature of the creature who was made in God's image and likeness, who was in effect a facsimile of the divine original. We could say that the human is a structure that is capable of receiving the divine logos and of being a vehicle of the divine presence. And, third, we have to recognize that many of the problems with the rationality of the Incarnation originate in problems with the rationality of the divine attributes themselves. If, after all, we say that God cannot change or suffer at all, then of course the logos cannot become flesh and die. The difficulty would really lie with our theism not with our Christology. So we would have to go back to our doctrine of God and clear up the difficulties with it first. Or, if we already would understand that God limits his power in order to let a significant creation exist, how hard is it to accept God going even further in the same direction with the Word becoming flesh? Does not the revelation of God in Christ tell us that it is God's very nature to give himself away in love for the sake of others? I believe that a kenotic

Christology raises the intelligibility of orthodoxy and robs its critics of much of their ammunition against the doctrine of the incarnation.

Also, incarnation is a problem for liberal theology because it spells miracle and the supernatural. Their Western mindset raises problems for liberals at this point. But surely this is a case of cultural accommodation that we should try to get over. A person who is oriented to the kingdom as Jesus proclaimed it would not reject the Incarnation for such a reason. If God's kingdom is breaking into history, there is no problem thinking of incarnation as a mode of its intrusion.

A recent difficulty raised in connection with the Incarnation relates to a supposed exclusivity of salvation. The way to avoid it is to adopt an inspiration Christology. But wait just a minute. There is another possibility. Just because God is at work decisively in Jesus to bring about salvation, it does not follow that God is nowhere else active in the world. Abraham was saved by God even though he did not know about Christ. A high Christology simply does not automatically entail the exclusivity of salvation as the Second Vatican Council proves.

THE WORK OF CHRIST

The work of Christ or the functions he performed as the Mediator is also a rich and complex subject. Calvin gave it a fine representation when he spoke of his threefold office: Christ as prophet, priest, and king. He viewed Christ's work not as a single, undifferentiated thing but as something rich, complex, and embracing. Yet evangelicals regularly give the impression of narrowness here probably because of our struggle with liberalism. Evangelicals seem to be so eager to focus attention on the atoning sacrifice of Jesus in particular, not just because it is important in itself but because it is so often minimized by religious liberals. We should try not to be so polemically driven because we give the impression that we think the work of Christ to be a narrow thing when it is not.

At the same time, given the context of the larger vision of the total work of Christ, evangelicals should continue to point to the reconciling act that Jesus' death on the cross was and effected. God gave him up for us all and made him to be sin for us. Jesus died as a Passover sacrifice, and there is expiation for our sins

147

through his blood. Jesus came to give his life a ransom for many. He was put to death for our transgressions. We have been reconciled to God by the death of his Son. The judge has been judged in our place in a marvelous exchange. To this truth evangelicals wish to testify.

Let me now attempt to clarify a few points along these lines. First, we must keep the Cross and Resurrection together and jointly prominent. Evangelical theology has been biblically deficient in its treatment of the resurrection of Christ. It treats the Cross soteriologically but seldom the Resurrection. It is a remarkable omission in evangelical theology. It can see the apologetic but seldom the soteriological significance of the Resurrection. Yet Saint Paul says, "We were reconciled to God by the death of his Son; now that we are reconciled, we shall be saved by his life" (cf. Rom. 5:10 RSV). Obviously, Jesus saves us through his resurrection existence as the life-giver, yet evangelicals rarely speak about it.

Second, there is also work to be done on the evangelical doctrine of atonement, which has focused on penal substitution in altogether too crude and exclusive a manner. I am not surprised that liberals have turned away from it sometimes in disgust. For example, when people suggest that Jesus appeased the Father to make him willing to be merciful to sinners, they are on very shaky ground. They make it sound as though God really hates sinners and has to be persuaded/placated to love them through an innocent victim. We must try to be clearer concerning the relation between the Father and the Son in the atoning event.

Evangelicals make a valid point biblically and psychologically when we highlight the removal of our guilt through the death of Christ. But we are not on solid ground when we suppress the other biblical pictures of atonement in favor of substitution and when we depreciate other offices of Christ than the priestly. Nor do Evangelicals impress when we show ourselves woefully ignorant of the history of doctrine in the matter of atonement and forget the lack of ecumenical consensus around this particular topic.

Another troubling aspect of evangelical theology is its emphasis on substitution. We give the impression that all that interests us is the justification of individual sinners and not their sanctification or the institution of the church or the sanctification of the world. One suspects that the narrow focus on substitution has a reason. It is oriented to a one-sided vertical definition of salvation itself.

Obviously, there are several areas where evangelical theology likes to speak but where it needs to pull up its socks.

Third, evangelicals really need to wrestle with what we think the effect on God was of the work of Christ on the cross. For one sometimes receives the impression that evangelicals think God hated sinners before the Cross but was persuaded to love them when Christ actually died. Evangelicals seem to think that, until the Cross, the divide had not been bridged, as if the Cross actually changed God in A.D. 32. Do we mean that there was no salvific will of God before that moment? Do we actually think that the Cross changed God's wrath into love rather than its being the gift of his love? Evangelicals' way of thinking about substitution seems to lead us into this way of thinking.

Surely it would be better to say that God is love, everywhere and always, and that what we needed from Christ was a decisive presentation of it in history. What we needed once and for all was a representative act on the part of the Messiah that would deal with something in the holiness of God's nature that would open up the perfectly satisfactory basis of reconciliation. Jesus' death then should not be seen as the cause of God's love but the final and irreversible expression of what God has always been like and has always been doing in history, which had until the time of the Cross been inadequately seen. On the cross Jesus clears up the ambiguity and became the sacrament of the salvation of the world. The grace and love that were always there come into their fullness in him.

Fourth, perhaps we need to be less rationalistic in our thinking about the work of Christ. We need to go slowly in manufacturing rational theories out of the word pictures of the Bible that are colored by images drawn from alien contexts like the feudal realm or the modern courtroom. What we want to say does not require us to do this. In an act of limitless love and obedience to God, Jesus went to his death, not because he deserved to die, but because as the representative of his people and of all humanity he was determined to make a gesture that would accomplish several things at the same time. It would expose man's injustice while revealing the righteousness of God. It would overcome the powers of darkness while delivering humankind from them. It would reveal God's heart definitively. As for the substitution, only God really understands the Atonement in its godward side and why it was necessary.

Brown: Many liberals will agree with your insistence that first there was the experience of Christ as Messiah, then the witnesses to Christ's full divinity and full humanity, and finally the particular ontological theories (those of Nicea and Chalcedon) about what divinity and humanity are and how they are related. I understand why, given your assumptions, the experience and the witnesses are held to be normative. But are the theories of the fathers, dependent on Greek metaphysics, also normative for you? Can we not speak about the divinity and humanity of Christ more adequately today in the language of some modern metaphysics?

Pinnock: Let me begin by saying that there is a presupposition in your question that I do not accept, which trades upon a dubious distinction. I would not want to characterize what the first witnesses had as only an experience without truth and ideas as well. This might lead one to suppose that the Christology of the creeds is something entirely different from what the New Testament says when really it is not. The language of the creeds may be Greek, but the substance of them is biblical. A wedge cannot be driven so easily between the New Testament and the creeds. "Consubstantial," for example, is certainly a Greek word, but it expresses something that the New Testament itself is saying. I do not see the church's Christology as a theory that came later. Dogmatic formulations come later but not the ideas they express. They rest firmly upon truth claims of the apostles that Jesus was the Son of God incarnate. The creeds try to safeguard that claim and do little more than that.

The idea floated by Adolf Harnack that the functional Christology of the Bible got Hellenized and transformed into alien Greek metaphysical categories is wide of the mark. If one wants to see the Hellenization of doctrine, one gets greater satisfaction looking at the heresies than at the creeds. It is there that one finds the amalgamation of biblical and pagan ideas. It is in the creeds that we find the demand made on humankind by the person of Christ undiminished by syncretism.

You ask about the possibility of stating what we believe about Christ in modern terminology. Of course it is possible to state the truth about the person of Jesus in modern terms. The only requirement would be that we say the same thing in the new formula and not something different. For example, speaking of Jesus as an avatar in Hindu terms would be misleading because the connotations of this idea and the underlying view of transcendence are so different. Such a translation would probably fail. Obviously, the biblical claim could not be stated in monistic metaphysical terms either because it would distort the New Testament claim, which implies theism. The challenge would not be the language used but the question of truth and reality expressed by it. The problem with liberal theology is not that it offers a new translation of biblical doctrines but that it doesn't. What it proposes are so often denials and replacements.

The Chalcedon statement itself is not an end but a beginning, as Rahner has said. What we have in these early documents concerning the person of Jesus Christ is the attempt to be faithful to the gospel proclamation of Jesus Christ, the Son of God and bringer of salvation to all mankind. The technical terms that were developed in the early discussions have served a useful purpose to the community of faith in that they have kept alive the claim of Christ upon us all and have not allowed them to be weakened by dubious interpretations. They tell us that in Jesus the living God entered history and achieved the salvation of our race. They offer us an understanding of the faith, which in no way diminished the mystery of the gospel but lifted it up. We should be profoundly grateful for that, and if we wish to go beyond these statements, let us do it in a way that discloses more of the fullness and not less.

> *Brown: You make a number of claims about Jesus and the faith of the earliest Christians. Are you able, theologically, to consider on purely historical grounds the claims of some scholars that much of what the New Testament says Jesus said and did was a product of the later witness of faith. Some liberal scholars have claimed, for example, that the historical Jesus called people to put their faith in God, not in himself, and that Jesus probably understood himself as the forerunner of the Messiah, not the Messiah. Regardless of your judgment about these particular claims, do you think*

> *this kind of claim should be evaluated solely on the*
> *basis of the historical evidence?*

Pinnock: My answer to your question about biblical critical issues is affirmative. As I have already made clear, I do not adopt a fideistic approach to Christianity. Some evangelicals, I admit, like the coziness of self-authenticating faith, and fear the chill blasts of criticism that cool their blood and makes them want to find shelter. But I am not one of them, and I rise to your question with zest. Historical critical work, so long as it harbors no naturalistic bias, holds no terrors for me. I trust and do not fear the truth.

Christians should not want to believe fairy tales, if that is what they are. If it were the case, for example, that Jesus made no claims for himself, then we might as well know that. If Christianity is false and the resurrection of Jesus only a legend, then (as Paul said) our faith is vain and there is no point remaining Christian. So, if a skeptical case can be made, let us hear it. Let the critics speak and we will judge what they say. Why would we want to escape from history, if the Word was made flesh?

But the knife cuts both ways. Are the liberals also willing to abide by historical reality? If Jesus did in fact make exalted claims for himself, can we expect liberals to stop denying and begin to affirm these things along with the rest of us? It is not only fair technically to put the question the other way around, it is also relevant because the New Testament documents are early and the claims by and for Jesus very high and very widely distributed through all the strata of the literature. The reader should not have the impression that evangelicals are the only ones on the defensive when it is actually a daunting task that liberals have set themselves in trying to get rid of the proposition that Jesus made exalted claims for himself, even as the apostles did for him following the resurrection.

Without going into much detail, let me indicate the problem liberals have with critical historiography at this point. Reading the Gospels, it is exceedingly difficult to miss the fact that Jesus placed himself in a most strategic place as far as the relationship between God and humanity is concerned. He called people to follow him and thus to enter into a relationship with God his Father. He claimed to be the fulfillment of what the prophets foretold and what the Torah intended. He revealed a remarkable sense of mission and authority. His penetration of moral and religious issues is well known. His unique relationship with God the Father is everywhere apparent. He knew himself to be God's chosen servant to whom heaven's secrets were open. And then there is the Resurrection and the worship of Christ.

How did this all happen? The whole phenomenon becomes coherent on the assumption that Jesus made unparalleled claims for himself and God vindicated him. Things are very mysterious if this is not true. All the documents present the uniqueness of Jesus repeatedly and in a variety of ways. He speaks and acts as no rabbi could. He interprets the law with amazing authority that causes consternation. He proclaims the kingdom of God as present in his person and ministry. Jesus is central to his own teachings. We confront in him a person who assumes an authority without parallel and who places himself in a central position in relation to the fulfillment of God's purposes. All in all, I do not find that this question causes me any special difficulty as distinct from the problem it creates for you.

In addition, I should enter a couple of caveats. For one thing, evangelicals read the New Testament along with the historic community, which has recognized Jesus' claims for well-nigh two thousand years. So the idea that some hotshot biblical scholars are going to be able to overthrow a conviction of this antiquity and power is unlikely even if it were plausible. And there is a second reason why it is unlikely. The question presupposes a foundationalist rationality. It imagines neutral scholars picking through the data and coming up with a revolutionary revisionist hypothesis that will cause orthodox Christianity to crumble. I suppose it could happen but I wouldn't suggest holding your breath.

> *Brown: Liberals generally are troubled by the exclusivist claims that conservatives usually make about the Incarnation of God in Jesus. But you say that Jesus is the decisive re-presentation of a divine love everywhere and always present in history, that Jesus' death is the finally adequate expression of a divine grace that was always there, and that this grace and love can be adequate to salvation even apart from an explicit acceptance of the proclamation that Christ is Savior.*

Does your view reflect historic Christian conservatism?
Is it not closer to most of twentieth-century liberalsim?

Pinnock: If you find some of my ideas more liberal than evangelical, then I will take that as a compliment. Not all conservative traditions are ideal in my view, and liberals sometimes adopt positions that seem superior in truth value. Particularly in the area of the universality of the grace of God, traditionalists have been consistently too niggardly about the accessibility of salvation for those who have never heard the Gospel. In this case liberals (and Vatican II) have reached back to the more inclusive ideas to be found in the book of Acts and in some of the Greek fathers and made a positive contribution to the churches. I admit that.

On the other hand, I would want to add that it is possible to distort these lenient traditions of orthodoxy. Justin Martyr, for example, was not praising other religions as vehicles of salvation or denying the deity and finality of Christ as modern pluralists do. Lenient orthodoxy is one thing; relativist liberalism is something quite different. My own position ought to be understood as falling within lenient orthodoxy.

Let me spell out my thinking a little more clearly. John tells us that God so loved the world that he gave us his only Son. Thus the gift of Christ came from the heart of God. The Cross happened because of the love of God. It is scripturally wrong and nearly blasphemous to think of Christ's death as changing God's mind from hate to love. It is appalling to realize that some evangelicals talk that way. Whatever happened in that great substitution on the cross (and it was surely a great mystery), it was not a propitiation to persuade a reluctant God to love sinners as if he did not love them already. One does not have to be a liberal to affirm that God's grace was given to us before the world began (2 Tim. 1:9; Eph. 1:9). Abraham two thousand years before Christ was saved by the same grace that saved us. This grace did not begin to exist in 32 A.D. If I am introducing a change into evangelical thinking as you know it, then it's about time.

Paul speaks to this issue and tells us more about it (cf. Rom. 3:24–26 RSV): "In the past God was patient and overlooked people's sins; but in the present time he deals with their sins in order to demonstrate his righteousness." Plainly, God's grace was always present in history, even though the reconciling act itself had not yet occurred. Paul tells us something else about it as well. "God overlooked the times when people did not know him, but now he commands all of them everywhere to turn away from their evil ways" (Acts 17:30 RSV). Again he says, "In the past God allowed all people to go their own way" but now calls them to Christ (Acts 14:16 RSV). Evidently God takes into account the fact that many people have not had an opportunity to know God's grace in the way we can know him through Christ. And being the just and merciful God that he is and the judge of the earth who does only what is right, he deals graciously with them, too.

I'm glad that you like my way of thinking more than that of other evangelicals you have known. But I would also caution you not to misinterpret what I am saying. The main point I am making is that a belief in the uniqueness of God's act in Jesus Christ does not have to imply that God is not at work anywhere else in the world or that those who through no fault of their own are prevented from learning about it suffer loss on that account.

● Brown's Rejoinder to Pinnock

You are right. My initial question does suggest as a presupposition something that I, too, do not accept, that is, that there can be experiences free of interpretive ideas. My question, then, ought to have been more clear about the relationship of the interpreted experiences of the early Christians (which by all means imply truth claims) and the Christological theories of the fathers. Your reply, I believe, hinges on the assumption that what the fathers said through the use of the categories of Greek metaphysics can be the "same thing" as what was intended in the early Christians' witnesses to the meaning of Jesus.

I would respond, first, that there is in the New Testament a richness of meanings, a "plurivocity," that no Christological theories, including those of the fathers, could possibly reproduce. As useful as theories are, they always abstract; they can never say the "same thing" as the concrete realities from which they abstract. Second, if, as linguists suggest, it is impossible to say precisely the same thing in, say, English and German, then I would doubt that the Greek metaphysical language of later Christian creeds could be so thoroughly equated with the manifold affirmations of the earlier biblical witness as you seem to hold. My point, then, is that I do not see how one can give normative status to the theories of the Christological councils if, at the same time, one wishes to affirm the normative character of the biblical witness. If I understand your view correctly, this is a point where we emphatically disagree.

With respect to your comments on biblical scholarship, I certainly agree with you that the historical critical study of the Bible cuts both ways. Liberals have acknowledged that fact since the late nineteenth century when they admitted that the Jesus uncovered by their historical research did not conform to the Jesus of their liberal predilections. This, as well as comparable admissions from some recent conservative New Testament scholars, suggests to me that biblical scholarship, liberal and conservative, is in the main a serious and self-critical discipline. Its conclusions are made tentative but they are not undermined by the fact that they are never produced by "neutral scholars." (I doubt, by the way, that historical conclusions should be thought less tentative simply because they are in accord with nearly two thousand years of Christian theology.)

Just as in biblical scholarship the terms "liberal" and "conservative" represent approximate ends of a rough continuum rather than inflexible divisions, so also in theology. That is wonderfully illustrated in your spirited response to my question on evangelical exclusivism. It is a good sign that, increasingly, conservatives can espouse customarily liberal views on some issues, and liberals can espouse customarily conservative ones, without embarrassment or accusations of betrayal from colleagues. It means that serious and open theological inquiry is more important than the purity of party labels.

SECTION 8

Delwin Brown's presentation on the doctrine of Christ, Brown's answers to three questions put by Pinnock, and a rejoinder by Pinnock to Brown's answers.

Although most disputes between liberals and conservatives are ostensibly about the Bible, the roots of our differences are probably about Jesus. We have markedly different views of Jesus, what can be known about him, and what it means to say that Jesus is the Christ. These differences capsulize the problem and, I think, the promise of conservative/liberal dialogue. The problems will become obvious in the exchange that lies ahead. The promise is that on this difficult and intense issue we might genuinely understand one another, not only in the sense of knowing what the other has said, but also in coming to see both the conceptual integrity of the other's point of view and the kind of piety that motivates it.

Perhaps it would help at the beginning to describe what I see to be caricatures of our Christological positions. Conservatives think that liberals have become so immersed in modernity and its secularism and therefore so shallow of spirit, that we do not, and as liberals probably cannot, have the capacity to recognize the uniqueness of Jesus as God incarnate and relate ourselves to him personally. Liberals think that conservatives have become so immune to the requirements of critical reflection, in matters of religion at least, that they have beliefs and attitudes about Jesus which are irresponsible, humanly speaking, and are antithetical to the Christian meaning of Jesus. If these are apt caricatures, then they represent to some degree the reality of each view. But they also badly distort. It would be a major achievement, of benefit to both parties, if we could move beyond the distortion in order genuinely to understand the other's point of view.

I shall start with a general observation. It is helpful, I think, to view liberal Christianity as an attempt to carry the doctrine of the incarnation to its logical conclusion. We take that doctrine to mean that God has become one with us and our history in its full humanness and naturalness. A God who is thus radically incarnate, it seems to us, is a God whose being and activity will *properly* be described in terms continuous with our descriptions of ordinary reality. Thus we find it entirely appropriate and, indeed, essential that in the first century Christians should have spoken of God in terms then commonly employed to describe the way the world seemed to be. We today, following the same incarnational logic, find it equally appropriate and equally essential to speak of God and God's activities in the terms of our modern knowledge.

Liberals today, therefore, are compelled to talk about God, and in particular Jesus as God incarnate, in ways that are congenial to natural and historical understandings. If our account of Jesus "reduces" to talk about natural and historical processes and their personal and social meanings, why should it not do so? If God *is* incarnate in *this* world, in this nature and this history, we must not seek supernatural and superhistorical explanations. God is now here precisely in this nature and history; therefore, it is in naturalistic and historical terms that we must now speak of God.

My intent, of course, is to reject at the outset the common conservative claim that liberalism is to be dismissed because it is reductionistic, especially when it comes to Christology. Liberalism is indeed reductionistic in a sense, of course, but it is so precisely in the sense, liberals think, that is required by the affirmation that in Christ God is at one with the world. In order to understand Christ, too—no, in order to understand Christ, especially!—we must speak in ways that are naturalistic in character, in terms that are compatible with the rest of what we say about the world because it is in the natural order that God is incarnate. Liberals may or may not speak adequately about Jesus as Christ, but the charge of inadequacy ought not to hinge simply on the fact that we use "this-worldly" categories in the effort so to speak.

This interpretation of the liberal approach to Christology is not meant to demonstrate that an alternative, conservative view is somehow self-evidently wrong. The point is not to condemn or convert, but to convey an understanding of liberalism as a *Christian* imperative. Of course there is a conservative reply to my account of the liberal's starting point. But the process of hearing that reply and the liberal's rejoinder, etc., etc., will be productive communication only if at the outset we can each see how the other's starting point might be a place of integrity.

I have said that we liberals think ourselves obligated to speak of the meaning of Jesus in terms compatible with the rest of what we say about the world. Like conservatives, liberals are compelled to state as adequately as possible how Jesus Christ makes a unique difference to us and to our history. But that statement does not seem to us to require that Jesus be interpreted in categories wholly unlike those used to analyze the font of other of the world's religions. "Aha," the conservative is likely to mutter, "you liberals think that Jesus is just another founder of a world religion." Well, yes and no. No, because no founder of a world religion is "just another founder." Each such founder or founding event, and each such religion, is unique in important ways. But, yes, Jesus is one "founder" among others and Christianity is one religion among others. This means that the ways of understanding the origins and development of religions generally are no less potentially illuminating with respect to the founder and founding events of Christianity.

Two things seem to us to follow from this point of view, one historical and the other theological. Historically, it means that we must say about Jesus what seems to be permissible according to the historical evidence. Clearly, that evidence changes. To summarize superficially, scholars in the late nineteenth century thought it would be possible to move behind the dogmatic texts of the New Testament to find the historical Jesus. They later found (though it was devastating to their theology—liberals and conservatives alike do sometimes let "the facts" challenge their theological assumptions!) the evidence intolerant of that expectation. Still later, scholars concluded that in fact we can know almost nothing about the historical Jesus, that the New Testament has little interest in Jesus so considered, and that what it does give us (and, theologically, this is absolutely all we need) is Jesus as interpreted by faith, that is, the Jesus of the New Testament witness. More recent scholarship is less skeptical regarding what can be known about Jesus apart from faith's interpretation of him.

Throughout this varying reading of the evidence, however, is the constant judgment that whether we are speaking of the Jesus who is interpreted by faith, or of faith's interpretation of Jesus, what we say can and must be developed along the same lines that would prevail if we were studying the orgins of, say, Islam or Buddhism. What the evidence suggests to be historical must be so labeled. What the evidence suggests to be the product of pious imagination must be called that. What historical investigation indicates to be the social, historical, cultural, political, and other determinants of early Christian understandings of Jesus, and the ways these came to expression in the New Testament text must in the interests of honesty be openly acknowledged. In short, the origins of Christianity must be accounted for in historical terms.

This does not mean, of course, that historical interpretations are the only accounts acceptable to the modern mind. It does not mean that we possess canons of historical knowledge that are impervious to challenge and correction. They certainly are, and they are constantly being assessed and revised. Nor does it mean that unusual things never happen. Naturalism's own self-criticism has led to the realization that natural "laws" are at most regularities, not necessities. Natural processes are now seen to exhibit far greater fluidity and "eccentricity" than the mechanistic models of the nineteenth-century scientific worldview recognized.

Perhaps, then, Jesus did walk on water or was bodily resurrected. The evidence, however, does not now support either claim in the judgment of most historians of religions and of Christianity in particular. To liberal Christians, it seems neither possible nor necessary to abandon the evidence as a convenience to traditional ways of formulating our faith. It is not possible because God's incarntion in this world compels us to take seriously the evidence of this world. But, frankly, neither is it necessary. Suppose Jesus did rise bodily leaving behind an empty tomb. How would we know that this was not simply a very unusual, perhaps to this point totally unique, natural event? Confronted by the resurrection of Jesus the Christian could say, "In spite of the crucifixion, we now know that God *is* with us," but another observer could respond by saying, "The world isn't as we had thought; we now know that at least one corpse came back to life." Each statement would be an interpretation uncompelled by the event itself. The bodily resurrection of Jesus would prove nothing theologically, and the fact that resurrection accounts in the later New Testament traditions affirm Jesus' continuing reality by speaking of a resuscitated corpse is no more normative or necessary for us today than are any of the other characteristically first-century modes of biblical understanding. Those ways of speaking were appropriate "this-worldly" or naturalistic descriptions in their day (if, indeed, they were intended to be descriptions at all). They are inappropriate descriptions today.

I have been discussing what follows historically from a naturalistic or historical understanding of Jesus and the significance of Jesus. But this approach, as I indicated above, also has theological ramifications. It means that what we say about Jesus theologically, that is, as the Christ, is tied to how we understand God and human sin. Our Christologies relate to our views of God and sin; they are not somehow read off from what are or even could be empirical descriptions of Jesus.

This characteristic of Christian theology is not peculiar; it reflects the nature of theologies in general as human ways of living in the world. Religious peoples, Christians and others, inhabit what we might call worlds of felt meaning. That is, our traditions create, sustain, and transform us primarily in the felt dimensions of our personal and corporate lives together—in our worship, in our relationship to our canons, in shared patterns of action, and in our common sensibilities. Theological systems attempt to portray the meaning of these felt worlds in reflective, coherent conceptualities. And in part because each religious world does cohere at a felt level, our theological portrayals of them also hang together internally (just as they in turn—on a liberal view—must connect up consistently with what we say about the world scientifically, historically, aesthetically, etc.).

This brief comment on the nature of theology is meant to reinforce the point that as Christians we speak of Jesus as the Christ primarily in relation to our understandings of God and sin. *What* we mean when we say that Jesus is the Christ coheres with our understanding of human brokenness, on the one hand, and, on the other, our understanding of the God who overcomes that brokenness. Particularly in the modern Western setting, Christians speak of

161

sin in a variety of related ways, reflecting the various but related ways that we experience our brokenness. Guilt for our failings, separation from God and others, bondage to oppressive structures of racism, sexism, and class, and a willful blindness to these distortions and our role in their perpetuation—these are some of the ways we attempt to fathom how it is that our lives are broken. In our relationship to Christians past, and to the canon we share together throughout the ages, we find these perceptions criticized or confirmed and deepened.

But also in this same communal relationship we find ourselves able, indeed compelled to confess that our distortions are not only judged for what they are, but also that we are accepted as we are. More than that, we are the grateful if somewhat astonished recipients of healing by a power not our own. That is, we find ourselves recipients of God's grace as it is communicated in and through Jesus, whom we therefore call the Christ. This we share as Christians. We describe this grace differently, perhaps, though our differences on this probably do not fall into "liberal" and "conservative" patterns. But as participants in the tradition of worship, reflection, and action, with its underlying wellsprings of intuition and sensibility, we experience ourselves judged, accepted, and transformed. Both historically and experientially, this tradition centers in Jesus as witnessed to in the New Testament. Thus, liberal and conservative, we acknowledge Jesus as the Christ, the Mediator of God's redemption.

How was and is Jesus the Mediator? It is difficult to see how we can deny, or would even want to, that God is redemptively present always and everywhere. At least the liberal Christian, ever in search of continuities, is likely to hold that Jesus is the re-presentation of a divine grace that is mediated in varying ways in all times and places. Like Christians through the ages, however, the liberal today wishes to confess, to report, that the power of redemptive grace is mediated to *us* in and through Jesus and the tradition that embodies and celebrates his life, death, and continued presence.

Jesus, then, is more than a "model" of what we should be. That understanding of Jesus has frequently played an important role in Christian piety. Sometimes it has been the central liberal understanding of Jesus—the human Jesus as a model for human life. Taken alone, however, it is inadequate. First, there is the difficult question of how a life lived in first-century Palestine could in fact be a very significant model for the many different kinds of lives lived in each of the subsequent centuries, including our own. Easy claims that it can be seem to me to flirt with obfuscation. The more important problem with a model Christology, however, is the fact that we do not simply need instructions on how we ought to live and be. We need empowerment. If Jesus is the Christ, then Jesus is more a model of God than he is of true humanity. God is incarnate in Jesus. Jesus is a sacrament making present the power of God to transform life in ways that we do not manage on our own.

How does Jesus do this? How is it that in and through Jesus this power is made present? In one sense there is no answer. Every theory of atonement (i.e., every effort to answer this question) is best understood, perhaps, as an effort to identify another facet of a mystery. But the liberal will want to point out that this mystery has important analogues in ordinary human relationships. Here, too, we experience the unpredictable communication of transforming power in the presence of another's love. This transforming power is a mystery in part, it seems to me, because it is efficacious at a level of precognitive feeling only marginally amenable to rational elucidation. If we are able to make sense of precognitive modes of efficacy (as I think we are, for example, in process philosophy), then the power of Jesus as Christ to transform lives is a mystery, but not a mystification. That power is mediated in multitudes of unintellec-tualized actions—in rituals, stories, proclamations, symbols, deeds of care, etc.—before we can even speak of them, much less begin to understand cognitively what they mean. That mystery is as natural as the power of love always is.

The key elements of most Christian accounts of the power of redemption through Jesus are the Cross and the Resurrection. The ways these categories are made key vary, not only in the New Testament but also in the subsequent Christian history. It would be a pity to try to reduce that variation to one supposedly correct point of view—a temptation of conservatism. It would be no less a pity to refrain from trying to say something, partial though it may be—a temptation of liberalism.

One way of understanding the meaning of Cross and Resur-rection is to note that without the latter the former may represent the defeat of all that Jesus is said to embody. For example, if in our theologies the meaning of Jesus is liberation, then the death of Jesus, taken alone, can be taken to reveal God's rejection of our yearning to be free. If the meaning of Jesus is God's presence with us, then Jesus' death may disclose God's absence. If theologically the meaning of Jesus is God's love for us, then Jesus' death, without the resurrection, may represent God's indifference.

To Christian faith, however, the death of Jesus does not stand alone. Jesus became, and remains, a power alive to the believer. Paul attempted to account for that presence by portraying it as a veridical vision. Later traditions spoke of it in the imagery of an empty tomb. Still later, as we have already noted, Christians spoke of a resuscitated corpse in order to explicate their claim that Jesus is alive. What I said above about precognitive modes of efficacy is also a speculative effort to say "how" Jesus is present. Many liberals will offer other, perhaps more elaborate, theories.

The "weight" of all such explications, however, is less to say "how" than to say "that" Jesus is a living reality. Once that presence is manifest the Cross changes radically in meaning. Now it is transmuted! From the standpoint of the Resurrection, the Cross becomes God's unlimited oneness with us. In the Crucifixion, God takes oneness with our humanity to the final act, oneness in suffering and defeat. God accepts our reality as the divine way of working in the world. More than that, God accepts our reality, with its joy and pain, as a reality in the divine life. The Cross, viewed from the vantage point of the Resurrection, is the ultimate sacrament; it is the ultimate manifestation of God's solidarity with us.

In speaking of all these things, it is perhaps inevitable that we should ask, what must have been true of Jesus of Nazareth and the events of which he is the center, in order for this power to be present to us today? What "facts" must have been true? The New Testament began to develop speculative answers to that kind of question using categories natural to the first century. The Christo-logical councils and almost every significant theology since have to some extent indulged the same question. Whatever we think of these efforts, their primary intent has obviously been less to say how Jesus enables salvation than it is to say that Jesus does enable salvation. The proclamation has always been far more important than the explanation. If we wish to address the secondary question of "how," if we must propose an explanation, we will no doubt listen as carefully as we can to the accounts of first-century and subsequent writers and, learning from them, use the categories of explanation most appropriate for today to communicate that same witness: in Jesus, God's transforming power is made present. To the liberal these seem rather obviously to be the categories of historical understanding, the "natural" language of our day.

The question that seems especially to divide liberals and conservatives today has to do with the superiority of Christianity. In terms of Christology, the question can be stated: Is Jesus the only mediator of God's finally efficacious grace? It is common for conservatives, no less than liberals, to acknowledge what I said earlier, that God may indeed be "savingly" present in other and perhaps in every religion. But typically conservatives want to hold that salvation through Jesus Christ is best and most complete, the only wholly efficacious grace.

I have no doubt that Christianity is by and large more redemptive in some respects than are some other religions in those same respects. For example, it seems to me (and, incidentally, to some Buddhists), that Christianity is more effectively transformative in areas of social justice than Buddhism is. I also think, however, that Christianity is notably less adequate in its attitude toward the created world than are most Native American religions. There are traditional Christian resources for saving us from our sinful abuse of the environment, in my view, and I would guess that Buddhism can find distinctively Buddhist resources for a more efficacious social vision. But my basic point is that the redemptive grace, as we Christians might call it, that flows through each religious tradition seems to some degree inadequate. Empirically considered, it is hard to argue that the grace of Christ is absolutely the best.

But the question—Is Jesus the only or best mediator?—is perhaps misplaced. Let me explain. A few decades ago, when space travel was initiated, the question was asked more or less seriously, can Jesus Christ be relevant to life in outer space if it, though intelligent, is radically unlike our own? Self-assured Christians easily said "of course" until their imaginative interlocutors began to propose forms of intelligent life that lack, for example, our distinction between self and other. Without that distinction, how could the motif of reconciliation even be understood, to say nothing of being relevant? (The imaginative reader can manufacture other such "puzzles"!) "Well," the answer became, "God could become present in that form of life, but in a manner quite different from God's incarnation in Jesus." However, if that were the case, and given such radical differences as we might imagine, what sense would it make to ask which "incarnation," the one on earth or the one on that other planet, is better? How is comparison even possible?

I am less interested in a "christology" for outer space as such than in what it suggests about the relationship of Jesus as the Christ, and thus Christianity, to other religions. It is quite possible that, for example, the Buddhist, Confucian, and traditional Native American ways of understanding the world are so radically different from each other and from our own that comparing the adequacy of Christ and Christianity with the adequacy of other ways for other peoples may not make much sense. Radically different worldviews have radically different understandings of the human problem and thus require radically different answers. In the face of such apparent diversity, I do not know how comprehensive judgments of "more adequate" and "less adequate" salvation are even possible. We can make tentative judgments on limited issues (racism and sexism, the environment, spiritual development, etc.), but that is all we can do if we are faithful to the evidence at hand.

Of course, Christians can simply assert the superiority of their way. Anyone can do that. I see no reason to do so. If there are other paths of healing, we should be grateful and see what we can learn from them. The way of Christ has usually dwelt in a pluralistic world, and it has been most vital when it has encountered alternatives most openly. It has survived and it will continue to do so, I trust, as long as its power of healing bears fruit. The power of Christian faith does not depend on our assertions of its superiority.

> *Pinnock: Although you have a right to do so, are you not using the term "incarnation" in a much reduced sense when compared with the meaning of the traditional category? Is Jesus in your thinking not more of an inspired prophetic figure than a metaphysical singularity?*

Brown: I do not think that I am using the term "incarnation" in a reduced sense when compared to what is central to the New Testament witness. Moreover, I think what "incarnation" came to mean in traditional theological categories is itself a significant reduction of the broader and richer New Testament witness.

Crucial to my position, of course, is a distinction between the New Testament witness and the theological categories that were crystallized in the later tradition. The former I understand to be pluriform and dynamic, speaking forcefully in first-century motifs about the meaning of God's presence in and through Jesus. The latter I view as circumscriptions of the earlier witnesses to the Incarnation. The development of the later theological categories was essential to the definitional project of the earliest Christian centuries. More than that, the doctrines that were formalized in the later centuries are instructive for the Christian today, both as witnesses to possible meanings of the New Testament witnesses that we might otherwise overlook, and as models of the kind of inquiry that we must undertake as Christians for our own time. But at the same time these later theological categories, as one kind of formalization rather than another, are also (and necessarily) reductions of the broader, and frankly more imaginative, witnesses to the meaning of God's presence in Jesus that we find in the New Testament.

The later theological categories pertaining to incarnation, however, are also reductions of the New Testament witness in another sense, a sense that is substantive rather than merely formal. Employing as they do ancient understandings that are most fully developed in Greek metaphysics, they suppose, for example, that the only way to attribute genuine uniqueness to Jesus is to attribute to him some kind of absolute metaphysical uniqueness. Those ancient understandings reflect the judgment, or at least the intuition, that the world is composed of different kinds of sub-stances or things, and that the relationships between them can be distinguished from the things themselves. Within this framework, the way to attribute uniqueness to Jesus is to claim for him a distinctive kind of substance.

Few today will want to hold that substance metaphysics is part and parcel of Christian faith. And if for good reasons a Christian judges it preferable to think about the world metaphysically in, for example, processive and relational terms, then the ways of thinking about the uniqueness of Jesus are going to be quite different. More than that, adherence to the options available within a substance framework will seem to be unfortunately restrictive.

From a processive/relational standpoint, which I think to be preferable, Jesus can be said to be unique in any number of ways.

167

One can hold that God was present to Jesus to an utterly distinct degree (though not in a manner entirely different in kind from God's presence to us). One can hold that what God intended in and through Jesus is unparalleled elsewhere in the creation. There are liberal process theologians as well as evangelical ones who make these kinds of claims. While I do not deny such claims, I think the more meaningful, and in fact more biblical, way of thinking about the distinctiveness of God's presence in Jesus is in historical and relational terms. I hold that God is everywhere incarnate, but that God is nowhere incarnate in precisely the same manner. I assume that God's general purposes are everywhere the same speaking at the most general level, but that these purposes are expressed in radically different ways appropriate to differing conditions. I hold, too, that the quality of God's presence and the efficacy of God's purposes in each instance depend partly on the special circumstances present there (including, for example, the volition of the person or persons who might be involved) and partly on the circumstances of events to follow.

I take it that these assumptions allow me to affirm with respect to Jesus a radically unique salvific role in our lives. I do not attribute to Jesus some sort of metaphysical singularity. Nothing in history, so far as I can tell, is metaphysically singular if that means either being unique in every respect or having a uniqueness that is logically necessary. I don't think either of these characteristics ought to be attributed to Jesus or were attributed to him in the biblical tradition. But neither will it do, in my view, to speak of Jesus for us simply as an inspired prophetic figure, as if Jesus is one of a class of such persons or even the highest member of such a class. Jesus does have, in my view, a distinctive and irreversible significance. It is through Jesus and Jesus alone that salvation in the Christian sense of that term is possible for us.

Having said all this, however, I confess to considerable doubt that I have really answered your question, for you or for me. The problem, as I see it, is that we approach the topic of the significance of Jesus with very different analytical categories, different metaphysical perspectives. This difference makes comparative judgments difficult. I suspect this is the place where our similarities and differences are as yet the most obscure.

> *Pinnock: Is it not a severe reduction of the biblical proclamation and faith of the church when you deny Jesus the position of being the one and only Mediator between God and humanity and ascribe to him a much more modest role?*

Brown: The difference between us here is clear! You hold that Jesus is the only Mediator, by which I assume you mean that it is only through Jesus that we or anyone can be saved. I hold that *we* are saved only through Jesus. I do not categorically deny that Jesus could be the only means of salvation for all people, but I do say that we can in the nature of the case not know whether this is true and, personally, I doubt that Jesus does serve this exclusive role for all human beings everywhere. I assume that God is able to and does effect the salvation of people in other traditions through other mediations of divine grace.

We are back to the concern about "reduction"—Is my view a severe reduction of the biblical proclamation?

My view affirms the New Testament claim that God is uniquely present in Jesus, in principle making available there to all a salvation that is full and complete. My view affirms the judgments of the successive Christological councils to the effect that the divinity incarnate in Jesus' humanity is full divinity, that the humanity of Jesus in which divinity was incarnate is real humanity, and that this incarnation in Jesus pertained to the whole of Jesus' person and vocation. My view entails that Christian faith is a missionary faith in two senses. First, it is a faith that is compelled by joy as well as injunction to share with all others the reality of God as made available to us in and through Jesus. Second, assuming as I do that all religious traditions are not equal, it is also compelled to share its witness because of a conviction that Christianity may have something to offer to others that is in fact superior to what is already available to them.

It is true, nevertheless, that the view to which I subscribe does "reduce" the traditional expression of Christian faith in certain ways. It does not insist that the way of salvation open to us in Jesus is the only way available to anyone anywhere. It does not claim that, if there are other ways of salvation, we can be certain that Christianity's path is superior to them in every respect. It does not suppose

169

that we Christians can have nothing to learn from other religious traditions of substantive importance about God's intentions for our lives. It provides no advance guarantees of the superiority of Christianity.

In my view, questions about alternative paths of salvation and their relative merits are genuinely open questions. They may be decided now in tentative and fallible ways on the basis of the best evidence open to us; but in the nature of the case, as I see it, these are not judgments about which we do or even can have evidence sufficient to base absolutistic claims. Only God can have the comparative perspective sufficient to make such judgments with finality. The human task of making tentative judgments can be accomplished only in the context of genuine encounters among the religions within the exigencies of life where the fruits of each tradition can be manifest over time.

If this constitutes a reduction of Christian faith, it seems to me to be a reduction worth having. It is the loss of claims to a kind of knowledge about empirical states of affairs that in the nature of the case we cannot possess. More importantly, it is the elimination of any theological basis for the triumphalistic and imperialistic tendencies to which Christianity has not infrequently given expression.

> *Pinnock: The Cross is surely a manifestation of God's transforming love. But evangelicals with the historic church also see the dimension of sacrifice and substitution in it. Are you able to affirm this dimension, too, or is it out of the question?*

Brown: Because it can be said of the Incarnation in Christ as such, it can also be said that the death of Christ represents literally, and not only symbolically, the substitutionary and sacrificial action of God.

That God acted to become manifest to us in Jesus means that it is God's initiative rather than our own that makes divine grace available to us. In our salvation, God's action takes the place of our action. Whatever can be said about this initiative in Jesus' life as a whole, as that is witnessed to in the New Testament, can be said preeminently about Jesus' faithfulness in suffering and death. We cannot take seriously the Christian doctrine of creation without also holding that God's grace is everywhere present, but Christians report that we recognize divine grace everywhere because we witness it in the act of God in Christ. God's initiative in Christ, then, substitutes for our own in making possible our knowledge of divine grace and its potential to transform human life.

That God suffered death in the death of Jesus means that Jesus' sacrifice is also God's. What did God sacrifice? The answer will vary from theological system to theological system. For me, the answer is that God relinquished the option of indifference to the human plight, affirming instead full openness to our suffering. It is true, of course, that God's oneness with Jesus in death represents God's intended oneness with us at all times and places; this is necessarily so if God is, as Christians say, always loving. But it nevertheless follows that God's action in Jesus' death is literally, and for us uniquely, a substitutionary and sacrificial action even if, from God's standpoint so to speak, the divine grace that we see specially in Jesus is a grace that is potentially present everywhere.

This interpretation of Jesus' death differs from the traditional versions of the so-called substitutionary and sacrificial theories of God's atoning action in Jesus. In particular, it does not attempt to limit what may be said about the agency of the Incarnation as a whole to the act of Jesus' death alone. Nor does it not try to spell out mechanistically the transformation accomplished by God in Christ. To demur from these traditional elements of atonement theory, however, is not particularly unorthodox. No one of the traditional theories of atonement has ever had the command of orthodoxy that, say, Christological theories have enjoyed. Moreover, the atonement theories have each sometimes been expounded in such ludicrous forms as, almost intentionally it seems, to repel assent in any precise way. I think, therefore, that the various atonement theories are best viewed as complementary attempts to convey intuitively what one of them cannot convey fully, and all of them together cannot convey with precision. Among other things, they witness to the Christian's conviction that we do not and cannot accomplish our own salvation. They convey, too, the conviction that the God who enables our salvation is present with us in our sin, bearing with us the burden that sin brings, even unto death. They witness, in short, to the presence and the power of God's grace extended without reserve to us in Jesus Christ.

171

My own view, incidently, is that the atonement theories, never fixed in formulation or status, have functioned more fruitfully in Christian tradition than have other doctrinal affirmations when the latter have been pressed into rigid dogmas. The tentative character of the atonement theories has allowed for openness, and their frankly speculative form has invited the imagination of Christians as they attempt to speak of the meaning of Jesus, including the death of Jesus, for our lives.

● Pinnock's Rejoinder to Brown

I appreciate the way you speak so warmly and movingly of the saving power of God in Jesus Christ. I can identify with such language from my own experience of God's grace. One might say that I in my chapter am focusing more on how Jesus can be the efficient cause of salvation by virtue of his person and work, while you in your essay are wanting to focus on the actual transforming impact on people today of the Christ event. Perhaps I am speaking more of the cause and you more of the effects of salvation through Christ, but both of us in our own ways are addressing both sides of the issue.

Going deeper in, I have great difficulty with your notion that the logical implications of the Incarnation are that Christ's life would be natural, in the sense of being continuous with the Western paradigm of reality, which is lacking noticeably in the supernatural. Surely, all the Gospels report the mighty deeds that Jesus did in the power of the Spirit and his glorious triumph over death in the bodily resurrection of the third day. But you would put them all aside. How can we permit a modern presupposition like Western secular naturalism to function as a critical principle for reducing the New Testament picture of Christ. Now I would agree to use the term "normal" of Jesus' life, too, so long as you would agree to redefine what "normal" means after the manner of biblical thought. In that sense, I would speak of Jesus' ministry as normal and call on Christians today to move in the direction of this kingdom normalcy and engage in signs and wonders through the Spirit. Somehow I don't think that is quite what you had in mind.

As to the deity of Christ, I cannot accept for a moment that the problem between us can be solved by referring to substance vs. relational categories. My problem is that you drop out Jesus' own claims to singularity and the claims made about him by the apostles in the New Testament epistles. But I think you are right to say that issues of philosophy do enter into it. For example, I would not be impressed if a Hindu were to tell me that he thinks Jesus is God incarnate if I know that he thinks we are all God incarnate. After all, everybody is God incarnate according to monistic philosophy. Now I have something of the same problem with your being a process theist. You can utter the words "Jesus is God incarnate" because in your philosophy God is incarnate everywhere anyhow. Whereas when I say those words, being a theist not a pantheist, they really mean something special. Although I am sure that the biblical witnesses are theists, too, and that you are misreading what they are intending, I have no space to try to prove that now.

But there is a real difference between us in Christology. As a process theist, you see redemptive grace everywhere in the world in principle quite independent of Jesus, though evoked for us by him. God's grace is independent of Jesus in principle. He does not in any way cause that grace to exist. Rather, he is the symbol of it and the sacrament of it. But the real Savior of humankind is the God who suffers with us all the time and not Jesus, though he points to him. Yours is really a pattern Christology, not a decisive event. Were the Incarnation not to have happened, things would not be different from what they are, except for the community of Jesus and its access to knowing about that pattern.

On the question of the uniqueness of Christ's salvation, we are a little closer than I might have suspected. Often liberals are parallel pluralists and seem to hold that any religion is more or less salvific and one should not grade them. (To say otherwise does not sound polite.) But you still think that Christianity is possibly superior. So you are not so far from orthodoxy as you might be.

PART FIVE
THE DOCTRINE OF SALVATION

SECTION 9

Delwin Brown's presentation on the doctrine of salvation, Brown's answers to three questions put by Pinnock, and a rejoinder by Pinnock to Brown's answers.

It is difficult for me to believe that there are radical differences between reflective conservatives and reflective liberals on the topic of salvation. There are differences, of course, but they are largely matters of emphasis. And such differences as we do have are another example of where we each need to profit from the point the other is emphasizing.

In denying that reflective Christians have radical differences, however, I must underscore the word "reflective." There are, unfortunately, representatives of each perspective, liberal and conservative, so wholly intent on preserving the past that what they say is more mechanical than thoughtful.

Some conservatives, for example, still reduce the concept of salvation to "heaven" and "hell" and then advocate an utterly literalistic view of each. That is not even good fundamentalism. Classic fundamentalism always insisted that Scripture is to be taken in its plain sense—literally when it was intended literally, metaphorically when that was its clear intention, etc. I do not see how any thoughtful reader can pretend that New Testament talk about the future life is literalistic. That the New Testament reflects a belief in a

177

literal future beyond the historical present and beyond personal death goes without saying. Moreover, New Testament writers and editors believed that what happens now, individually and corporately, literally makes a difference to that future, for better and worse. But the imagery employed to say what that future will be like is, it seems to many liberals and conservatives, as clearly "picture language" as one could imagine. We see most of the past and the present through a dark glass; we certainly do not see the future clearly. Thus guesses and expectations, cast in imaginative language, are "natural" with reference to the future, for us and for the New Testament.

Some liberals are also thoughtless. We have rightly been offended by the terribly individualistic orientation of conservative doctrines of salvation, and repulsed by conservative addiction to the rhetoric of guilt and eternal punishment. This binge within conservatism has been even more destructive, if that is imaginable, because it has weakened a redemptive concern for this life and this world by fastening human attention onto a life to come.

The liberal reaction has been to concentrate on salvation here and now. That, I think, is a fundamentally valid witness if it is not divorced from hope for the future, historical and personal. But in a good deal of liberalism, it has been. That "divorce" is thoughtless, I think, because it is so parochial. It is relatively easy to dismiss the hope for historical change and personal salvation if one is a fortunate, white, male, middle-class person of real or imagined power. But if one belongs to the other ninety-nine percent of the human race constantly exposed to justice denied, joy overwhelmed by pain, hope for this life disappointed, then a broader perspective is in order. What could make a life that is largely suffering and struggle ultimately worth the living? That, I believe, is a reasonable question, and within the experienced framework of most human beings, the notions of "historical hope" and "personal reward" are ingredients of a reasonable answer.

In sum, our discussion of salvation should prescind from our liberal/conservative disputes of the recent past and, as it were, go back to the basics. What legitimates Christian talk about salvation is not what the immediately preceding generation said and not even what the Bible said; it is the experienced reality of our broken and distorted lives. The Bible and the subsequent history of Christian witness and experience are essential to how we talk about salvation, since that is just what forms us as Christians. But salvation talk is justified by the experienced fact that we need it—salvation—and we know it.

In that sense we must say frankly that Christology is not enough. The Christian doctrine of sin is about the strangely distorted condition of our lives—a kind of willing enslavement that seems to immobilize us in our exploitive and unjust social and political systems, in destructive personal relationships, in self-understandings that distort and destroy, and in an uncanny sense of alienation from that which, however we describe it, we take to be basic to reality, that is, from God. Christology is the contention that, in fact, God is with us. Whatever else they do, the "cross" manifests the radicality of God's entry into our humanity, God's solidarity with our suffering and brokenness; and the "resurrection" manifests the permanence, indefeasible even by death, of that radical presence in our lives. But talk of Cross and Resurrection does not quiet our questions, and it should not. It is not irreverent to ask what difference is made by the Cross and the Resurrection, by God-with-us. The doctrine of salvation is the answer.

GRACE, FORGIVENESS, AND POWER

Christian history is in part the story of a struggle between two differing understandings of the power of God's saving presence in our lives, and, somewhat (though not precisely) related, between two metaphors having to do with the locus of this salvation. The first struggle is between understandings of grace.

On one view, grace is experienced as forgiveness. The presence of God in us is evident as God's acceptance of our brokenness, distortion, self-deception, etc. The miracle is the inexplicable fact that God should enter into relationship with us as if we are whole, faithful, and pure, when obviously we are not. In spite of the fact that we are not what we ought to be, God is with us.

The realization of God's grace as forgiveness is alone sufficient to produce a whole new perspective on life for the believer. But it is the perspective that is new, not the reality. While we should not underestimate the importance of this change of vision, life itself otherwise remains pretty much the same. The experience of God's acceptance is *not* accompanied by any change of basic character, in our character or the world's. We and the world stay the same.

179

Transformation of self and world—that is to be an eschatological reality; it is not realized in this life. Grace is present here and now as forgiveness, as God's acceptance of us. But salvation in the sense of a transformation of the substance of the world and the character of ourselves must await the life to come. The sixteenth-century Protestant Reformation, especially in Luther's formulation, is the classic representation of this viewpoint.

The second view affirms not only grace as forgiveness; it also asserts some measure of grace as power, some degree of the substantive transformation of individuals and the world in this life. God is present to us as forgiveness *and* as power.

The variations on this doctrine are many, reflecting differences on what is changed, how much it is changed, and how the change is effected. Historically, Roman Catholicism has held that God's transformative power is mediated through the sacraments of the church, and is efficacious for individuals and to some extent the church and world as well. John Wesley's doctrine of sanctification, too, is a version of this general affirmation. For Wesley, the transformative agent is not the sacramental life of the church, however, but the infilling of the Spirit. Some sectarian groups, Wesleyan and others, share this general orientation. Typically, they hold that personal disciplines, such as prayer and Bible study, in combination with the activity of the Holy Spirit, empowers one to reach perfection or near-perfection here in this life.

Generally, Protestant liberalism has also affirmed grace as power. In the liberalism of the late nineteenth century, transforming grace was viewed more as a natural power than as a special divine gift, a kind of spiritual evolution comparable to the biological evolution posited by Darwin. Much popular liberalism today probably still rests on that sensibility, more or less unconsciously, even though it is clearly inadequate. Whatever transformative power is at work in us, its efficacy is hardly inevitable!

Today, the most interesting and influential version of the understanding of grace as transforming power is liberation theology. Liberation theology is partly a critique of liberalism, to which, I think, liberals must listen if our hopefulness is to become comprehensive and realistic. But the importance of liberation theology transcends its role as a critic at one stage in Christian intellectual history. It proposes a construal of Christian faith that cuts across the line dividing liberal and conservative theology by

180

obliterating sharp historic distinctions between spiritual and material, and between creation and consummation. In this way it enables
us to take with full seriousness the vision of salvation made explicit,
for example, in Matthew 25, Luke 4, and Romans 8. "Salvation is
one" is the key; it includes what *we* call the material (physical,
social, psychological, economic, political, etc.) no less than what we
refer to as the spiritual, and it begins to break in now at every level
(in personal forgiveness and reconciliation; the overcoming of
racism, sexism, and classism; the restoration of the environment,
etc.) even if its consummation must be beyond history.

However much we may wish to affirm this liberation vision,
there is something to be said for the realism and the insight of a
Luther or (more recently) a Niebuhr, or, for that matter, a Paul and
Augustine in their more sober moments. Their analyses of human
nature and motivation are, I think, the most perspicacious in all of
Christian anthropology. Their viewpoint ought always to be preserved among us. But, finally, I think that they are wrong if, as
liberalism today holds, we live in an open, contingent universe.
Their kind of realism makes sense in a closed universe with fixed
structures, prescribed interactions, and predetermined limits. If,
however, the world at every level is open and contingent, then we
cannot rule out the possibility of a God who by a power within us is
able to do far more than we can ask or even think. In an open
universe, the surprise of radical transformation can never be ruled
out.

I have been discussing differences between Christians concerning the extent or nature of the salvation that we might expect in
this life. Reference to "this life," however, reminds us of the second
issue noted earlier, that having to do with the struggle between two
biblical metaphors dealing with the locus of salvation. These are the
metaphor of the "kingdom of God" or, better, the "reign of God"
and the metaphor of "eternal life."

THE REIGN OF GOD

Throughout Christian history there has been the assertion that
God's reign, God's kingdom, would come on earth as it already
exists in heaven. The metaphor of the reign of God implies that this
history, which God created along with everything else, is destined to

move toward some kind of fulfillment. What is the reign of God? It is the fulfillment of God's aims for history in history.

How is the reign of God to be achieved? In the messianic model of the Hebrew Bible this fulfillment would take place as a normal maturation brought about by a leader who would "rise up" when the time is ripe and make it happen. Messianic fulfillment is developmental, even evolutionary. But in the apocalyptic model, in the New Testament and subsequent Christian history, the fulfillment of history is said to be a cataclysmic, revolutionary change. It will be instigated by the "son of Man" who will "come from above." Fulfillment will come by virtue of some active intervention in history from the outside. There are differences in the Bible, then, about the means that will accomplish the fulfillment of history.

When will it come? Here the discussion, especially in the New Testament, is wisely paradoxical. The reign or kingdom of God is neither simply present nor simply future. It is neither purely actual nor purely potential. It is a future that is already breaking into the present. The kingdom of God is the future in active relationship with the present.

The biblical image of the reign of God would be a far more insightful model for the liberal's formulation of Christian hope than is the concept of natural evolution carried over from the nineteenth century. This particular biblical image is not entirely adequate, however, because if there is a dynamic God and a dynamic, everlasting world, then there will never be a time entirely beyond history when the reign of God will be a fully realized reality. There will always be the paradoxical relationship between the future and the present. A better future will always be trying to break into the present age—usually slowly, messianically, but occasionally cataclysmically, apocalyptically.

Liberalism would do well to understand the reign of God in a thoroughly historical way. As such, God's reign refers to the reality of every possible advance of good in history. When each is achieved, however, new goals will become apparent because new forms of destruction will then raise their heads. To the extent that we eliminated racial segregation, for example, we discovered other forms of racism of which we previously had been only dimly aware. That is the way it will always be in history. No achievement in history will ever be without sin; every good will be partial and provisional.

Thus, there will always be some new achievement whose coming we are called to serve.

But God's reign really does break into history, albeit in bits and pieces. There is real redemption in real history. It is every cup of cold water: the achievement of women's rights and the rights of homosexuals, the end of political discrimination in the United States and to apartheid in South Africa, success against disease, an individual's triumph over addictive or abusive behaviors, the conquest of famine, the experience of forgiveness, the acceptance of God's presence here and now. These are what God is seeking, if we understand the reign of God in real historical terms.

The idea of the kingdom or the reign of God is a theological metaphor to which liberation theologians appeal, with good reason. It is an insightful way to speak of grace as power in nature, in persons, in society, in economy, in history. The God who created the world at all of these levels seeks its fulfillment at all of these levels, and calls each of us to serve that divine aim. That is the fundamental witness of liberation theology, a witness all Christian theology, liberal and conservative, ought to affirm.

But questions remain, questions that lead us to try to talk about things "beyond history." Is there any ultimate meaningfulness *of* history? Is there any ultimate permanence of what is lost and what is gained in history? Is there a judgment of history beyond it?

These questions lead us inexorably to the rest of the doctrine of salvation which, more often than not, has been developed in terms of a second biblical metaphor, the metaphor of "eternal life." Salvation has to do with what happens *in* our history. But it also has to do with what happens *to* our history and all that is a part of it. We will consider these "extrahistorical" issues in the next chapter.

As long as we are speaking of salvation within the historical process, there is one other topic to which we must give attention—the church.

THE CHURCH

In attempting to understand the relationship of the church to God's saving activity in history, two extremes must be avoided. One is the supposition, common to classical Christianity, that the church is the privileged location of salvation. Expressed in its baldest form, this is the claim that there is no salvation outside the church. The

183

other extreme is perhaps a reaction to the first, but it is no less unsatisfactory. It is the supposition, to which Protestant liberalism has sometimes tended, that the church is incidental to the salvific process.

Actually, liberal and conservative Protestantism in our time both represent dubious understandings of the church. Conservatism's theology, where it has one, is too often an emendation of the classical doctrine in all of its self-righteousness—the claim that this particular conservative sect or that (and not "the Catholics" and certainly not "the liberals"!) is the citadel of the saved in a wicked, wayward world. More sensitive evangelicals have abandoned such arrogance. What they have put in its place, however, is less a better theology than a variety of mechanisms for success—strategies for church growth, social mobility, good feeling, economic accomplishment, etc.

In other writings Clark Pinnock has characterized liberalism as the substance of modern culture wrapped in a thin Christian veneer. I do not accept that as a description of what I mean by liberal Christianity, but I do think it aptly characterizes much of today's evangelical movement. Far too much of modern evangelicalism is almost the purest form of "liberalism," in Pinnock's sense, that one could imagine. It is a modern ideology of class, race, or nation, or all three, sprinkled with splashes of a woefully diluted biblical witness. It does work, however. While much of modern evangelicalism is an abomination from the standpoint of almost any biblical or historic understanding of Christian faith, it does do one important thing right: it recognizes that people are more than minds.

Liberal Christianity today has a theology of the church, when it has one, that is no more adequate than that of much conservatism. In fact, recent liberal theologies have been remarkable for their silence about the church. Some of that silence is understandable and even, in a certain sense, admirable. It reflects a desire to join the world, as God has done, to affirm the world and to live responsibly within it. If the world is indeed to be taken seriously as the scene of divine action, what reason is there for the church?

But there is a reason why the church is essential to Christianity and, indeed, to God's saving activity within our history. It is a "liberal" reason, that is, one consistent with liberal Christian sensibilities. Liberalism has missed that reason, however, because liberal Christianity has continued to be so much a captive of the Enlightenment.

In the first chapter I referred briefly to the Enlightenment's emphasis on reason. The Enlightenment's affirmation of critical human inquiry was an important gift to Western history. Protestantism assimilated this emphasis by making doctrine central to its focus. This focus appeared among conservative Christians in the guise of late nineteenth-century fundamentalism, but its most effective expression was liberal theology, which sought in each generation to demonstrate the compatibility of Christian belief and the best of modern knowledge. With the qualifications that I have already indicated, I affirm this liberal vocation.

In liberalism, however, what gradually occurred was the narrowing of Christian existence to the element of belief. When this was followed through consistently it meant that the church attended to the intellectual reality of the Christian, who was now viewed primarily as a "believer," to the neglect of the noncognitive dimensions of Christian personhood. Especially neglected was the ritual life of the community wherein Christians-in-relationship affirm through bodily enactment the realities, achieved and hoped for, of Christian existence. In liberalism, liturgy was "progressively" stripped of independent importance. Affective expression was "progressively" repressed, "emotionalism" abhorred. Christian worship in liberal denominations came closer and closer to the model of a New England town meeting or, better, the lecture hall. The sermon was the center, sacrament the periphery.

The intellect is crucial to an adequate human existence, and thus the sermon, or some means of feeding the mind, is crucial to the life of the Christian community. But we do not live by thought alone, or even by thought primarily. More than that, even belief is most effectively sustained and transformed at the affective level. The power and the point, even the cognitive point, of the Christian mode of existence is transmitted in eucharist, in hymn, in story, in liturgical reading, in symbol—in short, at a level where bodily feeling is primary—far more vividly than in the most reliable disquisition.

Conservative Christianity, perhaps because it has always been dubious about the Enlightenment anyway, was largely spared this whittling of Christian existence to a frail reed of truth analyzed and rationally defended. Thus conservative churches, however dubious their theologies, have had a power that liberal lecturing could not defeat. Conversely, liberal theologies, however insightful and perhaps even preferable for their times and places, have remained at the margins of popular Christianity—a blessed critique, certainly, but little more—because they have not been integrated into a ministry that addresses the fullness of human personhood.

The church does not own or isolate God's saving activity in human history. God's healing of human brokenness may best be made present—we simply do not know—in art, music, family, legislation, or the kind of caring that sometimes transpires at the corner bar. And the church certainly is not the repository of what has been saved in history, the collection of those who have been made whole. The church does not control the inbreaking of God's reign or embody in any noticeable way the consequences of that always-coming presence.

The church is that community whose simple reason for being is to remember, to explore, and to struggle with the saving power of God as it is variously witnessed to by the voices of the Bible so that, if possible, it may now serve this power as it works within our hearts and our history. But the church is people, and people are bodies as well as minds who live by symbols as well as thoughts and rituals as well as analyses. Thus the church's remembrance, exploration, and struggle are in celebration as well as assessment, sacrament as well as sermon.

More orthodox and evangelical forms of Christianity have seldom forgotten the importance of the noncognitive. Thus whether through the stately formalism of the high church liturgy, the grand cadence of Black preaching, or the ritualized spontaneity of a sectarian prayer meeting, they have communicated their version of Christianity to the whole person, mind and body. From them liberal Christianity has much to learn.

> *Pinnock: I agree with your point that salvation is power (Rom. 1:16). Evangelicals love to testify to a born-again experience and to the presence of the Spirit of God in their lives. Are liberal Christians able to speak in this way?*

Brown: Liberal Christians are certainly able to speak about the power of God in their lives as well as the experience of transformation through the Spirit of God. The term *born again* was popularized by, and is closely associated with, a certain strand of evangelicalism so that it is not commonly used by liberals or other types of conservative Christians to describe their experience. Even so, the emphasis upon a distinctive form of experience for the Christian was a hallmark of liberal Christianity, especially in its classic period. So, too, has been the affirmation of the presence of the Spirit of God in human life, individually and communally. In the contemporary period, however, talk about experience and the presence of the Spirit in liberal Christianity is muted, for some good and bad reasons.

One unfortunate feature of liberal Christianity has been its tendency toward a narrow intellectualism. It has sometimes been a shallow intellectualism really, but even as the mere shadow of responsible intellectuality it has worked against any significant appreciation of the noncognitive elements of Christian faith. Thus, for example, the person who for theological reasons is led away from conservative Christianity may find in liberal and mainline Christianity something that mends the head but little that tends the heart. The result is that people often remain in the fellowship of conservative Christianity long after they have left its theological perspective simply because it meets their emotional needs better than liberalism does. As I have explained, I think the neglect of the emotional life in liberal Christianity may be understandable historically, but it is hardly defensible on theological or anthropological grounds. My own view, also stated earlier, is that the renewal of a vital liturgical life must take place in liberalism today if it is to meet the full range of human need. But whatever the prospect for that, right now I must say only that liberals, theologically speaking, can speak of transformative experiences. But in fact we do not often do so because, in part, such talk has for so long been unfortunately and needlessly devalued in liberal Christian communities.

Some of the liberal reluctance to speak in this way, however, is well grounded, in my judgment. The witness to salvation as power has frequently been associated with an individualistic emotionalism. Much that is covered by the phrase "born again" bears little or no resemblance to what that phrase signified in the New Testament. More importantly, in my view, what the term does refer to is a relatively minor theme in the New Testament compared to the far more pervasive call for justice that we find there. Hence, as legitimate as the witness to being born anew can be, in fact it often seems to be little more than a code word for a form of self-righteousness that remains astonishingly oblivious to its own eccentricity when judged in terms of the full range of the New Testament witness that it so professes to love. The power of God is usually said in the New Testament to have results that are observable and interpersonal as well as individual and interior. Its aim is the kingdom of God within the entire concrete, created order. Liberalism has affirmed this understanding of the locus of God's power and what it seeks to accomplish. Hence, liberals have been right, I think, to suspicion whatever works to reduce God's transformative power to a purely interior and individual experience.

Still, there can be little doubt that recent liberalism has been as one-sided as the "born again" narrowness against which it has been reacting. Yes, we liberal Christians can speak of the power of God in our personal lives as well as the experience of transformation through the Spirit of God. But right now we are not often doing so.

> *Pinnock: Evangelicals think of salvation as the breaking into history of the new age of the Messiah. We wonder whether liberals do not overreact to this emphasis by practically equating salvation with raising the minimum wage or cutting off funds to the Contras. Is there not an undue horizontalizing of the concept going on in liberation theology?*

Brown: The question equates liberal theology and liberation theology. I think that is a mistake. Liberation theology, at least in Latin America, is largely a Roman Catholic movement that emphasizes the Bible as the privileged norm of theological reflection. In this respect it is more like evangelical than liberal Christianity in North America. It is unlike both, however, in one major respect. It holds that the authentic place for, or locus of, Christian theological reflection is in committed solidarity with the poor and oppressed. This view was approached by some evangelical theology in the United States before the Civil War and some liberal theology around the beginning of this century. But even then

188

it was in both cases more of a moral sensibility than a methodological premise. Today liberal and conservative theologies in North America more or less assume that Christian theological reflection can be conducted equally well any place—the suburb and barrio, the university and the hospice. Liberation theologians find that assumption to be profoundly unbiblical. The Bible discloses that God, while loving all of us equally, has chosen to side with the poor and oppressed. Theology that seeks to be faithful to this biblical view of God, say liberation theologians, must also stand in solidarity with the "least ones."

Speaking, then, simply of liberation theology, the question is, does it not reduce salvation to social and political progress? The question is shocking to anyone familiar with the literature of Latin American liberation theologians. It is not shocking to anyone familiar with North American literature about liberation theology. In a prominent segment of this literature, which has extended onto the newspaper editorial pages, there frequently appears what seems to be an almost intentional distortion of liberation theology. The distortion may relate to the fact that liberation theologians in Latin America are sympathetic to communitarian, nonbureaucratic forms of socialism, and highly critical of the impact of American economic interests in their own countries. Much of the distortion of liberation theology comes from those determined to defend the American economic experiment, or "democratic capitalism" as they sometimes call it, against all alternatives actual or possible. There are fairer ways to defend economic theories. There are certainly better ways to understand, and to criticize, liberation theology.

Liberation theology has significant weaknesses, in my judgment, but I do not think it horizontalizes the concept of salvation. It resolutely affirms both political action and spirituality, both the salvation of history in and through it and salvation beyond the historical process, both human action and divine initiative. I should think this inclusive, full-bodied concept of salvation would be more widely appreciated than it seems to be in evangelical Christianity.

My answer with respect to liberal Christianity is a little different. In the United States after the Civil War evangelical Protestantism became terribly privatistic in its concept of the Christian life and other-worldly in its view of salvation. Partly in reaction to this, liberal Christianity took on a "social gospel" orientation that increasingly associated salvation with the amelioration of social ills. The two were seldom if ever equated, but there emerged such a neglect of the broader dimensions of salvation that the casual observer is probably justified in supposing that salvation in liberal theology had become fully horizontal.

As you note, recent evangelicalism has begun to abandon excessive other-worldliness, its undue verticalism, now more and more affirming a view of "salvation as the breaking into history of the new age of the Messiah." However problematic that view might be in some of its forms, it is at least a move toward the more biblical concepts of salvation that are so important to evangelicalism. I think liberal theology, too, is now becoming more balanced, acknowledging the need for personal as well as social transformation, and addressing issues beyond as well as within our human history. I believe we, liberals and evangelicals, are both becoming more inclusive in our views of salvation precisely in response to the prophetic voice of liberation theology. It would certainly be beneficial to both of us if we could cease to overreact to each other's excesses and discuss together the elements of a doctrine of salvation that answers to the full range of willfulness, brokenness, and loss in our common human existence.

> *Pinnock: Taking the gospel of salvation through Jesus Christ to the ends of the earth and discipling all nations is central for the New Testament. Missionary work is also something for which evangelicals are well known. But liberals seem to have given up on world mission and are into a theology of religious pluralism instead. How do you justify this major shift?*

Brown: Liberal Christianity has not given up on taking the good news of Jesus Christ to all nations. It has, however, become reflective about those forms of missionizing that confuse sharing the gospel with imposing Western culture.

Liberal Christians began the twentieth century with the expectation that this would be the "Christian century." Their efforts to take the Christian gospel to the corners of the earth are well known. What is only lately becoming equally adknowledged among Euro-American Christians is the extent to which this program was conducted in a paternalistic manner, insensitive to indigenous cultures and the enduring values they represented. What is true of liberal and mainline missions is scarcely less true of evangelical missionizing. Virtually all Western missions have a record that is highly ambiguous at best, even in the eyes of those whom they have converted. It is not uncommon to hear indigenous Christian leaders, including evangelical ones, insisting that Western missionizing should be suspended for a period of time! Even when it may have been well intended, a great deal of what we Western Christians might call "discipling" is not welcomed in other lands and rightly so. It is not worthy of the name "Christian."

Liberal Christians are in the process of asking what has gone wrong during the past seventy-five or one hundred years. This process has included the effort to understand more adequately the various cultures upon which Christians have previously sought to impose themselves. A corollary of this inquiry has been an increasing effort to understand other religions as they are, to the extent that is possible for outsiders, and not simply as we imagine them to be for our own illusory edification. And both of these kinds of questions, about other cultures and other religions, have properly provoked theological reflection. How, within the resources of Christian theology, are we to understand these "other" people and their religions? Are there Christian resources for meeting them in a manner that is not paternalistic and imperialistic? How can we think, on the one hand, that we have "good news" to share with others, and, on the other, that we might learn something of importance from them? Theologically, can we approach them with as much openness as we hope they will have toward us? Can we meet them with an expectation of mutual challenge and mutual change?

These, it seems to me, are urgent questions, and they are vexing. In our own "hermeneutical" age we know the exceeding importance of communication. We know something about the way power relationships insinuate themselves into communicative situations, corrupting what on the surface seems merely to be the giving of a message. We therefore see how those who went to proclaim the gospel became, willy nilly, the none-too-humble purveyors of the values of their own class, race, and nation. In short, we begin to see why "missionary go home" can be such a widespread sentiment even when it is not publicly proclaimed. But, alas, it is not easy to see what the alternative form of communicating the gospel in an alien land ought to be. An African student recently complained to me, "Western missionaries today love to think that they are different from their predecessors, but they are not, except that they are now more subtle and effective in their forms of domination." He happened to be saying this about evangelical missions in his country, but he could as easily have been speaking of mainline and liberal missionizing. Apparently, we still are not doing much better than our predecessors.

Sharing what we have found to be the Good News with all people everywhere, and seeking to understand these people and their cultures fairly and fully, are not antithetical aims. Indeed, they require one another. Trying to understand others without being forthright about our own convictions can be deceptive, and stating our views without trying to understand the persons to whom we are speaking can be destructive. Western missions have too often been sharing without hearing. There are signs now that liberal and mainline Christians are beginning to move beyond soul-searching to experiment with new forms of communicating their Christian views of reality. Service-oriented missions (reasonably common among evangelicals, too) is one example. Interreligious dialogue is another, as is the development of theologies of world religions and pluralism. I will be frank to say that to date I am not enthralled with the results of the latter undertaking. They seem to me too anxious to assimilate religions, at their "deepest" levels, to one another. But in principle I do view these theologies of pluralism and theologies of world religions as appropriate efforts. They are attempts to make Christian theological sense of the religious diversity in which we dwell. The earliest Christians, many of whom lived in very pluralistic settings, sought to understand their reality ·theologically. We are obligated to do the same.

• Pinnock's Rejoinder to Brown

I appreciate both the wisdom and conciliatory tone of what you had to say on the doctrine of salvation, both in the essay and in your answers to questions. I suspect that we have discovered some common ground at this point because this is an area of truth that transforms rather than truth in the more cognitive mode. It seems that we fall to quarreling most when the doctrinal content of faith comes up. But I could easily and enthusiastically identify with the way you spoke of salvation as God's free forgiveness and transforming power, etc. It was good to step onto ground where being liberal or evangelical did not make so much difference. I hope we can find more of it.

I want to pause and remark also on your great patience and sensitivity. You prove conciliatory even when I ask impertinent questions. For example, you did not take offense (at least in writing) when I asked why liberals don't profess they are born again or why they are so incurably trendy or why they leave missions to the evangelicals. You take such questions seriously, you reply to them, and then rather gently and briefly expose the hidden assumptions. I frankly find it moving to see you respond like this. Your example of Christian gentleness makes me a better person and it helps me trust you even more.

You were candid when you spoke about liberals and personal testimony. I was aware of the value liberals ideally place on personal experience. Schleiermacher, father of liberal theology, was a Moravian and Pietist who sought to move theology away from purely rational considerations onto more experiential ground. He certainly valued religious feelings and practiced the presence of God. But then you admitted what I had suspected, namely a certain aridness in liberal Christianity at the present time and traced this to a degree of overintellectualism. I would add that orthodoxy too can be as dry as dust, and evangelicals need God's breath to come sweeping over us as well. May God indeed touch the entire church with new life. It would do more to center and unite us than any book like this.

My question about the dangers of a too horizontal salvation in liberalism was a fair one. The news out of the churchly conventions in early summer each year is fairly predictable. The old agendas of the bureaucrats housed at 475 Riverside Drive, New York, get a little stale. But part of this, I grant, was in reaction to privatistic evangelical salvation. And, besides, aren't we seeing more and more political theology from evangelicals that equates salvation with right wing politics? So, like you say, what we need is better balance and more common sense.

About foreign missions, you gave a reassuring answer I wish were true. You say liberals are in a time of reexamining missions as they should be and not in a time of withdrawing from the field altogether. You say they are searching for ways to do mission that are not paternalistic or insensitive to what's out there culturally. Liberals wanting to understand other religions, for example, is part of wanting to communicate Christ to people and does not spell any abandonment of evangelization. Well, I'll take your word for it, and I hope you're right about it. But I worry about your possible rationalizing the severe drop in the numbers of missionaries sent from liberal denominations nowadays. I worry that the real reason is relativism infecting liberal ranks and snuffing out all zeal for spreading the Good News throughout the world.

SECTION 10

Clark Pinnock's presentation on the doctrine of salvation, Pinnock's answers to three questions put by Brown, and a rejoinder by Brown to Pinnock's answers.

We can speak of human salvation because sin, which creates the need for it, is not intrinsic to the human condition but has intruded in upon it through the misuse of freedom. We live in a creation that is essentially good but that has fallen into disorder and estrangement. Its fallen condition is a contingent, not a necessary, expression of human nature. Alienation in all its forms— alienation from ourselves, from nature, from other people, and especially from God occurs in our existential condition and does not belong to the essential being of our humanness. Thus salvation is possible and entails fulfillment of those potentialities that were inherent in God's creation of us, rather than a liberation or an escape from the world as such. The whole person, indeed the whole world, is destined to be restored and redeemed by God. The physical creation along with the human race now engulfed in conflict, disorder, suffering, and confusion has fallen away from its essential goodness, which now has to be and can be recovered and brought to the glorious fulfillment God has promised and has always intended.

Evangelicals have always placed a strong emphasis on

salvation. It is a hallmark of ours to highlight the experience of personal salvation through commitment to Jesus Christ as Savior and Lord. It means a great deal to us to be able to announce that we have been saved and born again. Maintaining the theme of salvation through Christ is always our major emphasis in any ecumenical dialogue where we may be present. But there are problems, most seriously in the narrowness of definition often given to the category, in particular the focus on the salvation of individuals understood vertically in relation to God.

More and more this is unacceptable even to evangelicals as well as to others. Though it includes the justification of individual sinners, salvation must be understood as a broad, encompassing category. It is wrong to place salvation in opposition to the corporate, physical, and this-worldly realms. Salvation according to the Bible encompasses the individual and the corporate, the spiritual and the material, the temporal and the eternal. Salvation is bound up with other categories like the kingdom of God, so central to the preaching of Jesus, and is inclusive of physical healing, conversion, social concerns, deliverance, and cosmic regeneration. Salvation is all that is involved in the blessings of the rule of God. God's kingdom is breaking into history confronting, combating, and overcoming evil in every one of its forms and spreading the peace of both personal and communal well-being, in anticipation of the consummation of all things made new. Salvation is a broad and not a narrow topic.

Jesus came to save us from our sins and from all the consequences of our sins. The Bible does not restrict God's concern to save the fallen creation to any one aspect. Salvation will not be complete until the whole creation is liberated, involving persons together with the environment. For God to do otherwise would be to save half a human being. For the body is not the prison of the soul. Body and soul dwell together in the unity of our humanity. Our link to society is not an inconsequential but a fundamental feature of our lives. And nature is not incidental but basic to who we are as persons. Salvation addresses humanity in its wholeness.

I appreciate these words of John Stott: "There is a constant tendency in the church to trivialise the nature of salvation, as if it meant no more than a self-reformation, or the forgiveness of our sins, or a personal passport to paradise, or a private mystical experience without social or moral consequences. It is urgent salvation from these caricatures recover the doctrine in its biblical fulness" (*Involvement* I, p. 46).

Evangelicals can increasingly agree with the Chicago Call.

> We urge evangelicals to recover a holistic view of salvation. The witness of Scripture is that because of sin our relationships with God, ourselves, others, and creation are broken. Through the atoning work of Christ on the cross, healing is possible for these broken relationships. Whenever the church has been faithful to its calling, it has proclaimed personal salvation; it has been a channel of God's healing to those in physical and emotional need; it has sought justice for the oppressed and disinherited; and it has been a good steward of the natural world. As evangelicals we acknowledge our frequent failure to reflect this holistic view of salvation. We therefore call the church to participate fully in God's saving activity through work and prayer, and to strive for justice and liberation for the oppressed, looking forward to the culmination of salvation in the new heaven and new earth to come. (*The Orthodox Evangelicals*, p. 94)

This is not in any way to negate the importance of individual salvation but simply to place it in the larger context of God's renewing of all things. Biblical salvation is a broad category that includes the vertical and the horizontal, the spiritual and the bodily, individual and social, present and future, justification and sanctification. This salvation is the renewal of human beings in the totality of their lives and relationships. As such it means that the concerns that salvation deals with are found across the spectrum of ordinary human experience. There are points of contact for the gospel without number.

To avoid minunderstanding in emphasizing this point, let me add that I oppose with equal vigor an opposite tendency more typical of liberal theology to reduce salvation altogether to the temporal, as if it were only the offer of material and political benefits. Such a version would have abandoned the truly spiritual and transcendent dimensions of salvation in Christ and be little better than human ideology. We would not want to reduce salvation to the dimensions of the Old Testament, which stress salvation as social and historical and ignore the way the New Testament speaks so eloquently of a salvation that is spiritual and internal as well. We are

197

saved from guilt, from the fear of death, from Satan, from sin's dominion, etc. Israel's exodus was from political bondage in Egypt, but our exodus is from the bondage of sin through the death of Christ. One would not want in the course of correcting a view of salvation that is too spiritual to replace it with a less than Christian substitute.

AN EVANGELICAL DOCTRINE OF SALVATION

Let me present an evangelical doctrine of salvation in three dimensions: salvation as communal, personal, and societal. I begin with salvation as communal. It is perhaps uncommon for an evangelical to discuss "church" before "individual," but there are reasons for doing so. For one thing we need to counter up front the bias toward individualism. In many ways it makes sense to place the community before the individual. It is not because the individual is unimportant but rather because a person becomes a self only in context of community. John Donne rightly said, "No man is an island." The human self in fact is a delicate flower that depends for its flourishing on social and historical contexts. There are no truly self-made men or women. Not one of us could long survive on his own without the help of others. In the same way we Christians exist also as members (membranes really) of Christ's body. It is by being baptized into the community that we are joined as individuals to Christ and then to other people. Our humanity, both as creatures and believers, is really fellow humanity. Human existence is profoundly communal in nature despite Western individualism.

Evangelicals by and large neglect the ecclesial nature of Christianity. Salvation has been historically mediated. Christ established a community as an important means of grace. He is present in this body; as Spirit he dwells in this temple. Thus salvation comes in the form of new community. We comprise a fellowship of those whose lives have been transformed by the act of God in Christ through the outpoured Spirit. God's act in Christ takes actual effect in history within this community, and history itself, feeling the impact, is beginning to be changed as well. In the church God provides a new family for the nurturing of renewed human lives. The flow of fallen history begins to be turned around, and the powers that enslave and threaten to destroy humankind are checked.

The relevance of this is substantial. People today are hungry for meaningful relationships and regard them as supremely important. This is no doubt partly due to the depersonalization of the modern age. It feels important to belong to a group, whether to family, church, or nation. People need to belong, they need to be loved. They crave the intimacy and caring of community. In the face of these needs, Christianity is well equipped to respond, owing to its ecclesial nature. Salvation has a social dimension. People gather to sing and share their faith. In the fellowship of the church they experience mutuality, communication, and interdependence. They experience the warmth of one another's faith, the compassion of one another's tears, and the vibrancy of one another's joy.

One can view the church from several angles. On the one hand it is an institution. The church is an organization. It has an address, it is a place where people can be welcomed and introduced to Christ through many activities. The church as institution involves buildings, ceremonies, officers, and rituals. It is set up to facilitate interpersonal relationships in the context of the praise of God. What makes it special is its goal to be a structure that mediates the grace of God to people. It does so in all sorts of ways, through sermons, by baptisms, in the Eucharist, in fellowship, singing, Christian education, and through group prayer. All of these activities are means of grace that can transmit life-giving reality to those who come into contact with it. The church as an institution is likely the chief way in which people are confronted with Christ and come to participate in the renewing work of the Spirit.

But the church is a community as well as an institution. It would be in trouble if it were not. It is also an organism in which people are built up and gifted by the Spirit. This is in fact the goal of the church as an institution, to bring people into a saving relationship with Christ and involve them in the renewing work of the Spirit. The institution is a means of creating a community, which is the body of Christ, that can grow and develop.

Finally, the church is also a bridge that stretches out its arms to the world, which God wants to reconcile as well. It is not meant to be the circle of the saved but rather the firstfruits of the new creation, which portends the harvest of all nations. It is the light meant to lighten the world. This ought to be a major orientation, to reach the nations with the gospel and to disciple the peoples of the world. The church exercises a priestly mediation between Christ and a lost world. If the goal of the church as an institution is to create community, then the goal of the church as a community is to gather in the nations. As God's servant people, the church exists for the sake of the world. It is a function of God's mission in the world. By being new community in the midst of the world, the church impacts the old order as salt and light and by reaching out in word and deed, through prophecy and prayer fulfills its own calling to be apostolic.

The church is not always what it ought to be. It often exists as mere institution with very little life or mission. It is frequently not all God means for it to be. Therefore, it needs to be revitalized, to become alive and vital as in the beginning. It needs to receive afresh the gift of Pentecost in order to become experientially vital again; to be filled with praise and joy, mediating the kingdom of God in the power of the Spirit; for the grace of God again to become a personal possession; not for its own sake but for the sake of the world. As the Psalmist prayed, "May God be gracious to us and bless us and make his face to shine upon us, that thy way may be known upon earth, thy saving power upon all nations" (67: 1–2 RSV).

SALVATION AS THE RENEWAL OF PERSONS

God's purpose in salvation is to adopt people as his children and make us his covenant partners. God loves us and wants to renew and remake us. Jesus Christ was the true covenant partner, and God wants to bring us into conformity with Christ. Jesus displayed in his life the way to conformity with God's plan, and God wants us to walk down Jesus' path. He wants a new people who will live to his glory. Salvation means that through Christ we are being changed into his likeness.

Jesus Christ is the original image of God according to which human beings were made. He is also the goal, the image into which we are being remade. The origin and the destiny of humans are in Christ. Conformity to the image of God is the goal, growing into the full measure of his stature is what God intends (Eph. 4:13). The true likeness to God is to be found not so much at the beginning but at the end of history. This goal was present from the beginning but remains an unfinished project until now. Our destiny is to be like Christ, and we are being changed day by day through the Spirit.

The best way to understand topics such as justification, sanctification, and the new birth is to see them as overlapping metaphors of salvation in the rich tapestry of scriptural soteriology. They are not precise categories meant to be arranged in an exact order or discrete pieces of a puzzle wanting to be fitted together. They are more like complementary models. Justification points to God's acceptance of us; sanctification points to the process of salvation in us; and regeneration points to our new being.

In Christ persons are justified, accepted by God, and acquitted. God's judgment is annulled and we are given a new beginning. We receive grace, which is the exact opposite of what we deserve, and this engenders in us a sense of liberation and relief. Through faith we look to the promises of God and accept his gift of pardon. We surrender to him in trust. We appropriate for ourselves God's gracious turning to us. We are secure in our adoption as God's children and covenant partners.

Freed from egocentrism and reoriented to God and our neighbors, we are now enabled by grace to move in the direction of holiness. Free of anxiety because of what God has done for us, free of preoccupation with ourselves, we can yield up our members to God as instruments of righteousness. There is freedom and love, dying and rising. Never ending struggle but also steady progress toward conformity with Christ as salvation becomes effective in this life and moves in the direction of complete renewal.

Evangelicals have a dispute with each other in the area of personal salvation. From the Reformation comes the doctrine of predestination to salvation, as if salvation were meant only for some and not for all. Many evangelicals hold that God chooses the elect to be saved and leaves the rest to perish. By leaving no hint of conditionality in salvation, they hope to magnify the sovereignty of God in salvation and grace alone. But they succeed in casting a dark shadow over the gospel. It is a theory that must be resisted. Surely salvation is offered sincerely by the New Testament to all people. God was in Christ reconciling the world to himself (2 Cor. 5:18). God desires all to be saved and come to a knowledge of the truth (1 Tim. 2:4). Christ is the propitiation for the sins of the whole world (1 John 2:2). It would help if we thought of divine election in corporate terms as in the Old Testament, the election and calling of a servant people to serve God's purposes in the world and be a light

201

to lighten the nations. Individual persons are then invited to become part of that corporate entity by faith.

Obviously, this would introduce a human response into the application of salvation. There would be a two-sidedness. Salvation by grace through faith. By grace salvation is offered and through the response of faith it is received and accepted, as Mary responded to the Annunciation, "Be it unto me according to thy word." "Without faith it is impossible to please him; for he that comes to God must believe that he is and that he is the rewarder of them that seek him" (cf. Heb. 11:6 RSV).

But how are sinners able to respond to the message? By the power of God accompanying the preaching of the Good News and by the exercise of that feedom that rises from the image of God in us. If God calls sinners to receive salvation, one can only assume that it is possible to do so unless God is mocking them. Jesus being lifted up now draws everybody to himself (John 12:32). God calls sinners to respond because they can respond and God holds them responsible for responding.

THE SANCTIFICATION OF SOCIETY

According a third dimension of salvation, God is not only putting his stamp on individuals, bringing them into conformity with Christ, he is also working on the context of their lives in the world. God is renewing persons in the totality of their relationships. God is not interested in saving only half a person, but also cares about the totality in which we all live. Since it is God's desire to save and renew humankind, it is his desire also to save and renew the world as well. This idea of the renewal of the world itself was a major theme of the Old Testament Scriptures. It underlies the hope for history, which shines there. The leaven is going to leaven the whole lump before it's done.

God does this primarily through Christians in their communities, living out the gospel in society and salting it as they live out of their hope and act out of their love. In favorable circumstances one might even speak about the sanctification of the world. Although the structures of society cannot literally be sanctified and the powers of this age cannot be completely overcome, those structures can be shaped in ways that channel positive human values and activities. They can assist sanctifying forces rather than impeding them. Though structures cannot make people good, they can make it harder for them to be bad, harder for them to beat their children or cheat other people. The Bible suggests that God desires social forms and institutions that provide the best possible channels for the forces of his love to flow down, and that counteract as much as possible the forces of sin and egotism and death.

I can see this happening in our North American society, where the gospel has entered and impacted it. Christianity has made a clear empirical difference to this culture, though the difference is fading due to secularism. Our culture has deviated from the normal (fallen) human pattern in various ways: in the care of the sick, in concern for the poor, in the rejection of the divine powers of the state, in freedom and basic human rights. We see it in the notions of love, matter-of-factness, and history as goal-oriented, which have made this culture dynamic, emancipative, and expansive relative to others.

Recently the news reported that some students at Stanford University were demanding that Western culture not be taught in freshman courses but that in the name of fairness equal time be given to other world cultures. They seem to be unaware that the very things they hold dear: abolition of slavery, the emancipation of women, freedom of speech, political liberties, even the study of other cultures themselves are part and parcel of the Western legacy and Christian culture. It is extraordinary that, when the rest of the world seems to be desiring to adopt the very differences that are enshrined in Western civilization shaped in part by Christianity, many of our own citizens seem to be tiring of these same blessings and benefits. The remedy for such sickness would likely be to take a long hard look at alternatives.

Though it is not fashionable to admit it, I think that there is a degree of progress in history. I detect such progress wherever I notice a decisive move away from sinful social patterns and toward a better possibility for human development. But there are intrinsic limits, too. There is the struggle. The kingdom is present but not yet in power. There is still the opposition. And the irony by which the very same process creates secular people, people who busy themselves picking the fruits while cutting the roots. But there is also intensification as certain developments become ingrained in the infrastructure of the world. I retain the hope that the nations will wake up to the fact that their liberation lies in the gospel of Christ. Apart from that, the future looks grim.

Liberation theology deserves credit for recovering a sense of social sanctification. Although it often fails to uphold the dimension of the Spirit and its wedding liberation to the ideology of the failed left, which can hardly inspire optimism as to a liberating praxis. Nevertheless, we may be getting beyond that now. There is a witness in the public square that can be borne. Jesus Christ is Lord of the whole creation. What Christ did as the Redeemer is grounded in the purposes of God the Creator. Our vision of the coming kingdom should lead us to align ourselves with the features of that kingdom in advance of its coming. We are on the side of the future and should promote policies that seek prudently to establish justice and peace.

At the same time we know that we cannot bring in the kingdom by our efforts; it is God's gift and not a human achievement. Our finest attempts to establish peace and justice will never be wholly successful. What we can achieve in history will be relative and not absolute, proximate and penultimate and never final. The now of the kingdom gives us vitality; the not yet places a reserve on our best efforts.

The work of salvation is not yet complete. Although God has formed up a new community and is putting his stamp upon countless individuals to make them like Christ, and although God is changing society to make it more humane, obviously everything falls far short of completion. Even now it is only a small beginning. We have to look to God to overcome the final barriers. The completion of the renewal lies ahead of us. For it to be realized there will have to be a leap forward made possible from God's side in order to free the forces his Spirit is activating in the world. Paul images it in terms of pregnancy, labor, and then birth (Rom. 8:19ff).

One might distinguish between constrained and unconstrained visions as they relate to possibilities for social change. These visions differ as to how they view human beings and how much can be changed in the world now. Because of the doctrine of man as creature and as sinner, there are definite limits to what can be done and a prejudice in favor of programs of incentive rather than idealism to achieve results. The constrained vision has a certain realism when it comes to social policy; skepticism toward the moral perfectibility of the human, toward utopian visions; skeptical of the wisdom and good intentions of state powers; little faith in the ability of the planners to design a blueprint that can solve all the problems that we have; skeptical of an egalitarianism of results; anxious about the ongoing willingness of people to hurt one another in the name of their dreams for the world; the necessity to restrain evildoers and maintain the peace. We believe that the constrained vision has the data of reality as well as biblical eschatology on its side. Nevertheless, our efforts can always be more effective than they are, when the church walks in the power of the Spirit and when the church experiences revitalization and impacts upon society more forcefully.

Does salvation still make sense to modern people? I think that it does, whether under this term or some other. The fear of death, moral guilt, dark depression, moral inability are all still with us. The human condition has not basically changed over the centuries. In some respects things have become worse: the fear of self-destruction, aimlessness, meaninglessness. Salvation in the large biblical sense still speaks to all these problems. There is a hunger for salvation in the world today. For the sake of the next generation let us proclaim salvation in Christ, explain it in modern idioms, and gather in the nations.

> *Brown: Is it not the case that you and I share a holistic view of salvation because of a kind of cultural accommodation? While we now see this emphasis as a central element of the biblical witness, did we not come to see it largely because of developments in modern political theory, psychology, etc.? In this sense, have we not learned much about a more adequate Christian view of salvation from secular culture?*

Pinnock: I agree with you up to a point and want to affirm the positive role of culture in Christian theology. God is at work in the world as well as in the sphere of the church. The church is a witness to the kingdom of God, which is a much larger reality than the church is. In referring to this fact, evangelicals have always spoken about what we call general revelation and common grace. So I am not embarrassed to admit the definite possibility that modern developments in culture have made us sensitive to certain aspects of the biblical witness that have been neglected until now. I think it was in part because of the circumstances in which he lived that Calvin was able to come up with the idea we refer to as "Christ the transformer of cultures." In particular, he was able to entertain the idea of history as more dynamic than earlier theologians had and he capitalized on that. What I am saying is that theology is done against a background of two horizons: the perspective of Holy Scripture in dialogue with the contemporary world.

This observation would be a problem for me as an evangelical only if it could be shown that Scripture denies and rules out the construction of the nature of salvation we are agreeing about. I would have a problem if something from the modern horizon were brought in to alter significantly the biblical guidelines. I take your question to be somewhat autobiographical. Apparently, you accept the idea of holistic salvation because modernity insists on it, whereas I would not admit to that. I would credit culture with tipping me off to a possibility perhaps, but still maintain that salvation understood in this way is profoundly biblical.

And it is not difficult to prove that. Salvation and the kingdom of God according to the Scriptures are plainly holistic categories. Thus, my problem is a different one from the one you raise. My problem is to wonder how it is that the church has accepted reduced versions for so long without being corrected. Let me try to answer my own question. I think it was partly due to the personal orientation of New Testament faith in the face of a hostile world order. With the persecution of the church, there wasn't much time in the first century to think about the sanctification of society. But the foundations were there for thinking about it when the occasion rose. I refer to the social teachings of Torah and the oracles of the great prophets. I also have in mind the ministry of Jesus among the poor and the theology of Paul concerning human interrelationships. All in all, I see in the Bible a far-reaching global salvation just like the two of us have set forth.

If I were to mention just one factor that bears on this issue, I would point to the theme of the kingdom of God, so grievously neglected in the tradition and so highly relevant to this question. It simply astonishes me that Christian theology has for so long ignored what for Jesus was the central category of the Good News. Once it is recovered, the neo-Platonic version of the message as a mainly other-worldly salvation is blown away.

In this way I think it is understandable why such a view as ours was not immediately exploited as it is today. In reply to your query, I think it is clear that a holistic-model salvation is not a novel idea that you or I just picked up from secular culture.

> *Brown: The evangelical insistence on "personal deci-sion" as a central element of salvation is legitimate. But, given your own emphasis on the breadth of salvation, should personal decision not be understood as a choice to commit oneself to serve the cause of God's holistic salvation, rather than as a choice which therein results in salvation? Isn't the latter view—common, I think, in conservatism—insufficient?*

Pinnock: I am pleased that you acknowledge something that evangelicals consider to be very important, namely, that a decision in relation to Christ has to be made. Like the prodigal son in Jesus' story, we need to be challenged to recognize our alienation and distress, to come to ourselves, and to rise and go home to our loving and waiting Father (Luke 15:17ff.). The proclamation of the Good News demands a response from hearers. Therefore, we call upon persons to be reconciled to God, to turn to him and be converted. On the basis of the work of Christ, God declares to be in a right relationship with himself those who turn away from sin and believe in Jesus Christ.

But you are right to issue a challenge at that point. Cheap grace and easy believism are not good enough. We are called to holiness and obedience, to do works worthy of repentance. In reference to a current dispute among evangelicals, salvation is "lordship salvation." Accepting Jesus and not following him is comparable to asking a woman to be a lover and not necessarily one's wife. Good works, while not the basis of our justification, are certainly meant to be the consequences of it. Paul exhorts us to yield our members unto God as instruments of righteousness (Rom. 6:13) and calls us to make holiness perfect in the fear of God (2 Cor. 7:1). You and I both appreciate John Wesley's emphasis on what we can become as new creatures through faith in the power of God.

I see this process of sanctification as a complementary model alongside justification in the scheme of salvation. The two metaphors when they stand together present a rounded, balanced picture of the Christian life. God has both justified sinners and set us apart for himself, Christ himself being both our righteousness and the power of our holiness. The Spirit of Jesus working in our lives can bring us to the goal, which is conformity to the image of God. For this we were created and then converted. Like Paul, we are predestined to be conformed to the image of God's Son (Rom. 8:29). He wants us to become his covenant partners in fellowship with Jesus.

I take the relationship between justification and sanctification, not as a strict order in which one follows after the other, but as two complementary truths. Justification speaks of our relationship with God while sanctification speaks of our being set apart for his service. God acquits us and also calls us to right relationships in the world. Though not based upon ethical attainment, justification must lead to sanctification.

For myself, I would want to add a third point, a word about empowerment alongside justification and sanctification. Traditional theology has not paid much attention to the filling of the Spirit, although it is prominent in the New Testament. But how can we become faithful disciples unless we are baptized with the Spirit of God? Christians need to be empowered to testify to the mighty acts of God and to follow Christ radically. We need the Spirit to equip us to be instrumental in the coming of the kingdom.

In short, I am very much in agreement with the tenor of your question and want myself to avoid cheap grace at all costs.

Brown: I agree that liberal theology sometimes tends to reduce salvation to its political benefits. Is there not an even more dangerous reductionism at work in conservative theology? Is it not the case that much of "evangelicalism" today is popular because of its promise of material success or, more subtly, its suggestion that material success is a sign of spiritual superiority?

Pinnock: Everybody has some dirty laundry. Let me respond to these two unsavory facets of our religious spheres. To get my licks in first, dwelling on your admission about liberal theology and politics, when do you think liberals will stop identifying left-wing

THE DOCTRINE OF SALVATION: SECTION 10

politics with the kingdom of God? I understand how in the late sixties people bought into Marxist analysis and praxis to try to explain and respond to Third World poverty. I myself loved to blame capitalism and found considerable hope and inspiration in some undefined form of socialism. We used to call the churches to come down on the side of the poor in a class struggle with the rich. But that was in the sixties, and in the past two decades the reputation of socialism as a solution has been destroyed along with the validity of Marxist analysis. Now that the peoples of the socialist sphere in Eastern Europe and Russia know that, when can we expect Protestant liberals to come right out and say that they too reject Marx?

Why, just this past summer (1989), it was reported that Paul Cardinal Arns of Brazil was praising the Cuban regime on its thirtieth anniversary. When will this sort of folly cease? When will liberals begin to say more sensible things in the sensitive area of political theology: does this liberation theology proclaim Jesus Christ as Lord and Savior or does it make human beings the center of history and the source of their own salvation? Does this theology really want to turn the church into a partisan political organization or is it willing to let Christians come to differing economic and political decisions? Does it promote class hatred and violence as a solution to social conflict or seek social reconciliation? Does it really want socialism, which has oppressed the poor and failed to overcome their collective poverty, or does it want democracy, human rights, and free economic initiatives, which have historically brought freedom and prosperity to millions of the formerly poor? Gustavo Gutierrez seems to have begun to ask these questions. Will mainline Protestant liberals soon begin to ask them, too?

Having got that off my chest, I will comment on your idea that evangelicals might be enjoying some of our current popularity because we promote material prosperity as proof of spiritual well being. First, I would say that I find the proposition slightly bizarre. I know there are some who teach in this way, but my impression is that these people are very untypical of evangelicals, even of Pentecostals. The recent histories of evangelicalism by Marsden, Bebbington, and Ellingsen, for example, do not feature any such trait in the definition because it is not an important feature of evangelicalism and not the source of their appeal. I consider the health and wealth gospelers to be a lunatic fringe and an unhappy impediment who make us look stupid and avaricious. Obviously, the gospel calls us to follow Christ and to suffer with him. If following Christ has in fact led to long-term prosperity in Christian countries (as it surely has), it is not because we aimed at or were promised it going in. Conversion certainly does not offer the individual prosperity; indeed, it constitutes a serious danger when it comes (Deut. 8:11–20).

Having said that, it is still true that there is a health and wealth gospel (though there is little gospel in it) making its rounds in North American religion. "Serve God and get rich" say people like Brother Al and Rev. Ike. Name it and claim it, says Kenneth Hagin. God promises it, so claim it and it's yours. There are other people saying that sort of thing, if in subtler forms, as if God promises the financial prosperity of each of his children. I would say the same thing about this cult of prosperity as you would. It is a most unscriptural message. The kingdom values that Jesus preached are very different from that.

Perhaps we do need a proper theology of prosperity to counter this falsehood. God does bless people, some even with great possessions. The Bible does not view wealth as intrinsically evil. Possessions of every kind can be dedicated to God and can be used for good. Even a rich person can live in a servantlike way. The key may be detachment—having our priorities straight so that our love of God determines how we use material things rather than our appetites. I suppose that the health and wealth gospel is a good example of how conservative religion accommodates to culture, much as religious liberalism does in its own way.

● Brown's Rejoinder to Pinnock

In this discussion we agree that modern culture can make a positive contribution to theology, and that salvation has a social as well as a personal dimension. I have not always found us so close on these issues. We continue to disagree on what it is that warrants our accepting a belief (such as the claim that salvation is holistic), that is, we disagree on methodology.

In response to your suggestion, I doubt very much that I accepted a holistic conception of salvation because modernity "insisted" on it, unless by that term you mean that the cumulative and critically assessed evidence in a number of modern fields of study provided overwhelming and complementary support for the judgment that humans (and thus their undoing as well as their healing) are holistic and interrelated. In fact, as you say, this modern view of personhood is consistent with the anthropology of the biblical (and other ancient) traditions. Still, my reasons for affirming a holistic view—in distinction from the factors that cause me to be attracted to it—are, finally, what I take to be the cumulative and complementary experiential and (broadly speaking) scientific evidences for it.

What if biblical exegetes were to conclude that they had been mistaken, and that, in fact, the Bible rejects a holistic view of the person and salvation? (Dominant exegetical conclusions, after all, have been rapidly overturned.) In that event, I would certainly be open to considerations, ancient and modern, that counted against holism. But if these considerations seemed to be without compelling merit I would continue to subscribe to a holistic anthropology, and I would think myself as a Christian to be entitled to do so.

One way of clarifying our actual differences, methodologically, would be to determine whether and how your answer to this hypothetical situation would differ from mine. I have said that our beliefs, insofar as we are Christian, are formed in our continual struggle with the biblical text. You have said that our beliefs, as Christians, are normed by Scripture. Does that mean that you would be bound to renounce a holistic view of human nature, in spite of the massive evidence in its favor?

Sometimes, of course, Christians disagree about non-theological issues. Your response to my last question in this section occasions an illustration of that. I think you are simply wrong to claim that liberal theology identifies "left-wing politics with the kingdom of God," and that liberals are reluctant to reject Marx. I think it is grossly unwarranted to suggest that liberation theology makes "human beings the center of history and the source of their own salvation," that this theology is unwilling to "let Christians come to differing economic and political decisions," and that it promotes "class hatred and violence as a solution to social conflict" I believe it is terribly simplistic to lump together, as you do, all forms of socialism, to ignore the fact that for well over half a century some of the most penetrating critics of bureaucratic socialism have been other kinds of socialists or to speak as if Marx said nothing at all from which we might learn. I believe it would be equally simplistic to

211

lump together all forms of capitalism, to ignore the fact that some of the most penetrating critics of bureaucratic capitalism have been those who espouse other versions of capitalism or to suppose that capitalist theorists have nothing to teach us.

Christians ought to encourage responsible analyses of the strengths and failings, in theory and in practice, of the various socialisms and capitalisms. Blanket approval and blanket condemnation strike me as theologically unjustified and as less than penetrating. We have seen that to be the case in analyzing liberal and conservative theologies. Political theories ought to be assessed with the same care.

Your discriminating assessment of the relationship of prosperity to Christian life is an example of the kind of care needed as well in our political analyses. It is certainly true, as you note, that the promise of material success has not been a prominent feature of evangelicalism historically, and therefore that the appearance of a health and wealth "gospel" today is a sad betrayal of the evangelical promise. It is insightful to add, as you do, that prosperity as such is not a vice, just as poverty as such is not a virtue. It is less persuasive to contend that "following Christ has . . . led to long-term prosperity in Christian countries." (I would like to see the empirical data for that claim!) You might better have said that the reduction of Christian faith to a gospel of worldly success, measured in terms of money and power, has frequently been a sin of the liberal and mainline churches, too. There is, sadly, plenty of evidence for that.

PART SIX

THE DOCTRINE OF CHRISTIAN HOPE

SECTION 11

Clark Pinnock's presentation on the doctrine of Christian hope, Pinnock's answers to three questions put by Brown, and a rejoinder by Brown to Pinnock's questions.

Hope is a central category in evangelical theology because we begin with the givenness of the faith attested in Holy Scripture. The gospel of Jesus Christ is filled with hope. According to the biblical witness, God, having posited created reality alongside himself, is working in history in order to realize his purposes. Christians understand the world to be an expression of God's purposeful activity, and look forward to the fulfillment of his purposes and the renewal of all things.

As we saw earlier, God by his very nature is an agent who acts with purpose, who projects and realizes goals. The whole world is an expression of his purposes: in creation he called the world into existence, in providence he orders the historical process in meaningful ways, and in eschatology he promises the goal of salvation toward which he is moving the whole of history. Thus, all reality is expressive of God's purposive activity, as created, as providentially ordered, and as moving toward a goal beyond its present condition.

Christians are able to view everything that happens in this basic framework. We seek to apprehend every object in the world, every experience, every event in relation to God's purposes as realities that are somehow grounded in God's purposes. We see history full of meaning, a linear forward-moving process composed of unique events, impregnated with meaning, and undergirded by purpose. It is a pattern of events created by God's interaction with humanity as finitely free and purposing agents. We enjoy the confidence that, although human beings individually may accept or reject God's purposes for them, God's rule will be established finally. We believe that history is directional, morally grounded, and goal-oriented.

This worldview has been influential in Western culture and underlies it, contributing to much of its success. The confidence in the worthwhileness of life is what has helped to make it so expansive and dynamic. Meaning and fulfillment tend to follow when people attune their lives to God and his plan for them, while confusion and misery fall upon them when God's divine purposes are ignored or rejected.

This does not mean, however, that the divine purpose is everywhere visible to the finite observer existing anywhere in history. To use an analogy, as in ordinary human projects there is an inner dimension to purposive activity that does not reveal itself completely until the project is finished, so it can be difficult to discern God's purposes until the objective is reached and the purpose becomes visible. As in the human analogy, often it is impossible to discern just from external observation exactly what a person is intending by a certain action. This is something known fully only to the purposer as the subjective principle according to which he or she is working. For example, were we to observe a person chopping down trees in the woods, we would not necessarily know what the purpose of his activity was: is he gathering firewood for warmth? is he obtaining wood to make a table? does he want to improve the view from his window by removing the trees? Just seeing him chopping down trees does not tell us exactly what he is up to. External observation cannot answer all of our questions. Only the woodsman himself knows for sure what he is doing, and we will not know until he is finished unless he reveals his purpose to us before that.

It is much like this in our Christian faith and hope. We claim to know what God is doing in the whole of history, but not from observing it closely and figuring it all out. No one has ever done that. It would be impossible for a mortal to achieve that knowledge.

No, our claim to know what God is doing comes through revelation on the basis of God's disclosure of his purpose to us through Jesus Christ. As Paul puts it, "God has made known his hidden purpose to us" (cf. Eph. 1:9–10 RSV). So this is an insight not gained scientifically but theologically. It is faith knowledge, and the basis on which we are able to confess that history is full of redemptive purpose. Jesus Christ is the one who makes it possible for us to see history as a theater of God's action and hope for the realization of his intentions.

This is why faith is so important. Just as in the middle stages of a purposive human activity the inner principle cannot be seen by the external observer, faith is called for. We are always having to trust that agents know what they are doing. In much the same way, we find ourselves having to believe that God really is working out his purposes in history and in our lives, even when it does not appear on the surface that he is. Isn't it the case in ordinary life that in any long-term activity, such as preparing for a career, there are numerous bypasses and delays in the overall plan and that it is not clear to the external observer exactly what it all means? In a similar way, God's providential activity will not always be comprehensible to us. We may not know what God's purpose is in some particular event until much later, if we ever do in this present life. We are compelled to trust God and believe that he knows what he is doing. There are dark and mysterious moments to go through in life and at such times we have to confess the goodness of God's purpose by faith. We have to believe by an act of the will that things have meaning even when for the moment they do not seem to.

In this present chapter we are looking at the consummation of the purposes of God, as the goal of all his work. Creation affirms that the world's source and ground are in God. Providence says that every phase of history is under God's direction. But both creation and providence are steps toward the realization of God's ultimate purposes. So let us look at the goal, which imparts order and significance to everything else. Of course this does not mean having recourse to prophetic charts or the setting of dates, follies that have seriously marred the evangelical reputation in the minds of many. It will mean looking at the image of the future given in the gospel, which inspires our journey through history. Eschatology is about the image shaped by the revelation of God in Christ, which tells us what God's purposes are and projects their ultimate realization. It chiefly concerns the hope that, despite all that opposes the kingdom of God, the Lord will come in glory and his purposes will prevail. The day will come when the kingdoms of this world will become the kingdom of our God and of his Christ and he will reign for ever and ever (Rev. 11:15). History is the story of how the creation is going to become the kingdom of God and embody the reality that was revealed in and inaugurated by the coming of Jesus.

Eschatology should not be thought of as an obscure area of doctrine, although some have tried to make it obscure. It is in fact very meaningful and links up effectively with ordinary human experience. The call to hope for salvation correlates with a deep human instinct in everyone. Human beings have a strong propensity to hope. Never being altogether satisfied with the present, we dream of future possibilities. The questions spring up: has life meaning? has man a destiny? where is history going? is hope justified? We are creatures of hope. It is something hard to live without but at the same time something not always easy to find and therefore a precious commodity.

Christians do not believe that hope can ultimately be justified without God. Merely earthly resources cannot satisfy the dimensions of the hope we feel the need for. But the Christian message makes it possible for us to account for the hope that dwells in human beings and to satisfy those longings. Just as Kant postulated God on the basis of the moral impulse within us, in a similar way we can postulate final salvation on the basis of the hope we feel. The gospel makes such good sense at this point in the way it meets our inner aspirations and speaks to our anxieties and concerns so directly and profoundly. Hope can be justified if this message is true. Then one can account for its presence and satisfy its longings.

Hope is basic, history has meaning. We do not need to fear the future. We are not locked into a cyclical view in which everything repeats itself or into a meaningless sequence of events. History is the realm of the working out of the purposes of God. Therefore, we can live in hope.

THE FLOW OF BIBLICAL ESCHATOLOGY

Hope is fundamental to the message of the Bible. Believers in both Old and New Testaments lived in anticipation of the future salvation of God. Their faith is based on and structured around the promises of God. They are essentially a forward-looking people. Hope is not simply some small part of their outlook but central to their entire self-understanding. They anticipate God's intervention in history both in the near term and in the long term. This is what gives them energy to run the race set before them.

The Old Testament displays this hope primarily in this-worldly terms. It gives us a vision of well-being in the world of space and time. Hope was born in God's promise to Abraham and his descendants: "I will be their God and they will be my people" (cf. Jer. 24:7 RSV). This is what people were meant to be, God's covenant partners, and this is what God is determined they will become. The prophets of Israel, certain about God's faithfulness to his promises, articulated the same hope. Though they often had to expose false hopes, they projected a glorious future, a time of peace and prosperity. They spoke about a new covenant and a messianic deliverer. The prophets foresaw the future rule of God, which would be righteous, peaceful, universal, permanent, and the cause of great rejoicing. They insisted that God's purposes were going to be worked out on the earth. Salvation would not mean escaping from the world; the world itself is going to share in the transformation that is coming. They did not know exactly how or when these things would happen. The future and the present stood in tension in their minds. The prophets viewed the present against the backdrop of the ultimate goal. But they knew that God was going to act even though they did not know whether the thing that was about to happen was the final set of actions.

For Jesus, too, this earthly dimension holds true. He taught us to pray, "Thy kingdom come, thy will be done on earth as it is in heaven" (Matt. 6:10 RSV). But he introduced a degree of discontinuity and an apocalyptic dimension as well. The powers of evil are such that they are not going to be defeated by human effort alone. A supernatural act of God, a world-transforming intervention of his is going to be necessary. This point had already been made. Biblical writers like Daniel also directed attention to the world beyond and to resurrection. There will have to be a transformation by the power of God. In the New Testament, then, God is still trusted to change the world, but the hope about that has become larger and grander in scope. A break is posited between this world and the one to come.

The essential nature of New Testament eschatology points to fulfillment in two stages: the drawing near of the kingdom and later its consummation in a new age. On the one hand, the time is fulfilled, the kingdom of God has drawn near, a new era has begun—evidenced in miracles, the casting out of demons, the preaching of forgiveness. But then there is something more. The new age has dawned, but it has not come in fullness and finality. The blessings of the present age are only a pledge and guarantee of greater blessings to come. There is to be a future consummation of God's purposes based upon the victory Christ has already won, the D-day and V-day pattern. Thus, we proclaim both the presence of the kingdom now and the coming of Christ at the end of history. The kingdom has been inaugurated, but God will have to come and break the deadlock. God will have to complete what he has begun in history.

This spells tension for believers between the already and the not yet. The kingdom is both present and future. The power of God has broken through to change the world, but there still remains a future crisis. The new age coexists with the old age. So we have to live in the tension between who we are in Christ now and what we shall become in the future.

Just as in the Old Testament, the prophets were not exactly clear when the future events they spoke about would transpire, so the New Testament writers experienced a similar running together of present and future. The foreshortened perspective that belongs to prophecy crops up in the New Testament as well. This created a hurdle for the early church to get over because of the expected soon return of Christ, which is implied in many texts. Believers found themselves having to cope with an apparent postponement of the Second Coming, which has now stretched into two thousand years. It meant they had to settle down to the process of institutionalization, which in turn lead them to place their emphasis in eschatology on what happens to individuals at death. The last things that were expected in the near future in the New Testament, such as the Second Coming, the Resurrection, and the judgment were removed in their thinking to the more distant future.

Nevertheless, the future was still important to the New Testament writers. They still expected that God would make all things new, if only eventually and in his own time. They still expected God to raise up the whole person in body and soul. They surrendered entirely to Hellenism. One should not exaggerate how completely New Testament eschatology was changed by subsequent generations. The key factor for them, too, was that Messiah has come and the Spirit has been poured out. So however long it might take, the Spirit of Jesus can bridge the gap for Christians experientially. He can bring us the life of Christ and share with us the blessings of the age to come since he himself is the subjective guarantee of its coming. Through the Spirit those in Christ receive a foretaste of the blessings of the age to come. Therefore, we do not lose hope as we await the consummation of the kingdom of God when we will enjoy God's blessings to the full.

Eschatology, then, was a central concern of the biblical writers and must be a basic doctrine for Christian theology. It just cannot be the tail end of a doctrinal system. Christian truth as a whole is permeated and penetrated by the subject. Jesus' proclamation of the kingdom of God was eschatological in its very essence and core.

CHALLENGES OF MODERN THOUGHT

The tendency of the modern era is toward human-centeredness and this has meant that man himself has become the maker of history. Humanity and not God is thought to be the primary agent in history. We can change the world without God's help, to bring it into line with our own ideals and purposes. This amounts to a secularizing of the biblical hope of the kingdom of God. Any future salvation must refer to a this-worldly, harmonious social order to be brought about by human efforts. The kingdom is reduced to a symbol for the best we can do with history and society. It expresses our own aims and ideals. It is eschatology without God. It is a kingdom of this world, dependent not upon the will of God but upon unaided human achievement. Enlightenment liberalism tied the kingdom of God to the idea of human progress toward a new social order that will come about as a result of human activity. This is a belief in a teleological process in which the kingdom is gradually realized in the present ethical achievements of humanity.

This development of ideas in Enlightenment culture was sharply challenged early in the twentieth century by the rediscovery of New Testament eschatology and by dramatic changes in Western culture. On the one hand, the biblical hope cannot be reduced to a humanist agenda in this manner, at least on scholarly grounds. On the other hand, the optimistic liberal culture as a whole entered into a state of disintegration due to the horrors of war. Suddenly, the older biblical eschatology seemed relevant once again. Initially, Karl Barth took eschatology not to require real events in the future, but in his mature period he acknowledged actual future fulfillment in history. The coming of Jesus would be an event that would be the decisive proof of what had been already revealed in Jesus Christ. There would be a final unveiling of God's revelation of his grace and salvation.

Although theologians like Bultmann still reduced eschatology to the element of bare futurity in the temporal structure of human existence, seeing it chiefly as a factor of meaning in each existential moment, others took up the future orientation of the New Testament. In the work of Moltmann and Pannenberg, the future horizon is solidly present and stressed. They refuse to dispense with hope for the future of all things, for all nations, and even for cosmos. For them the kingdom of God refers to an actual circumstance that God will bring about, an event that gives us an incentive to bear witness against injustices and proclaim the Good News.

Thus there is occurring a renewal of biblical eschatology in theology at the present time. Its comprehensive hope is being recovered, with many good effects upon our thinking. The recovery is helping us overcome the false dichotomy between this-worldly and other-worldly eschatology, enabling us to hold out hope for human history and for eternity as well. The gospel speaks to both the personal and the social. Kingdom reality can be embodied in actual social structures as well as in the lives of individuals. There is hope for both individual and social fulfillment in the Good News of the kingdom.

Evangelical eschatology was postmillennial before 1850. It expected to see society substantially Christianized before the coming of Christ. Such hope seems incredible to many of us today. Under the influence of premillennialism and cultural pessimism, any this-worldly aspect of eschatology was pushed off into the distant future in our thinking. That was what encouraged many evangelicals to leave the transformation of society and culture to the liberals. This was surely wrong and is beginning to change.

Owing to our biblical orientation, evangelicals have helped to keep future hope alive in modern Christianity. But one of our weaknesses has been in the area of the hermeneutics of eschatology. We tend to see statements of biblical prophecy as bits of information or as pieces of a puzzle to be fitted together. From these statements we also try to draw information about specific dates and to interpret prophecy literally. This practice has led to many embarrassing failures. We are now learning that it would be better to view eschatological texts like creation texts, as images of the future but not as precise pointers. In this way the prophetic Scriptures can serve every generation and not lead to great disappointments.

IMPORTANT ISSUES IN ESCHATOLOGY

I now take up some specific matters of importance.

(1) It is important not to forget that world mission is itself an eschatological sign. As Jesus himself said, "This gospel of the kingdom will be preached throughout the whole world, as a testimony to all nations; and then the end will come" (Matt. 24:14 RSV). Christ cannot return according to this saying until the task of world mission has been accomplished. The task unfinished actually delays the Parousia, while pursuing it hastens the day according to Peter (2 Peter 3:9, 12). Thus world mission is a primary sign of the end. This is why Paul insists that the gospel must be preached to the Gentiles (Rom. 1:14; 1 Cor. 9:16). Jesus promised the Gentiles a share in salvation; between the Resurrection and the Parousia is the time of the ingathering of the Gentiles. The distinction between Jew and Gentile will disappear. As the Old Testament promises, the nations will put their trust in the Lord, come to his sanctuary, and participate in the messianic banquet. The missionary task is grounded in the promise of Jesus. It means cooperating with the divine purpose to gather the Gentiles. It is part of the final fulfillment, a vindication of the exaltation of the Son of Man, eschatology in the process of realization. In mission we cooperate with God in the power of the Spirit in preparing for the time the table will be spread for all peoples (Isa. 25:6–8).

All history is moving toward the goal of a restored and glorified universe. This does not mean, as I said earlier, that we understand the meaning of every twist and turn in history. Far from it. Nevertheless, it enables us to be deep optimists, based on our faith. The chief characteristic activity of this age between Christ's first and second comings, as we said, is missions. But this is not simply a question of saving individual souls. Missions is also a history-making activity, for it brings into the world a new understanding of man and his nature and a new basis for the unity of humankind. The power of the Resurrection even makes itself felt in the transformation of people and their cultures. It means deliverance of captives, healing of the sick, the settlement of differences, the elevation of the poor. The preaching of the kingdom throughout the world is a major contributor to the struggle for genuine human existence. Christ is the hope of the world.

In the area of world mission, evangelicals are making a decisive contribution today. Not so much in articulating in theology the full scope of what God is doing, but in actually getting the job done. The world mission of the church is actually getting done, thanks largely to the forces of evangelical missionaries. Liberals and even Roman Catholics seem to have left the job to them.

(2) Is there life after death? Evangelicals treasure sentiments like Paul's: "This slight momentary affliction is preparing for us an eternal weight of glory beyond all comparison" (2 Cor. 4:17 RSV). The Christian hope indeed calls for the resurrection of the whole human being. As Jesus said, God *is* (not *was*) the God of Abraham. He is not a God to let his people perish. There will be an eschatological verification of our belief in God. Even now we are moving toward transcendence when we will see him as he is, when there will be an integration of body and soul in resurrection rather than natural immortality. Belief in life after death is fully intelligible if one believes in the God who is love. This is the basis of our hope rather than any philosophical arguments for immortality.

How tragically unfair it will be for all but the fortunate few if we do not live again after death. It might not be quite so bad for materially comfortable humanists to forego the privilege of eternal life but what about the vast majority whose lives are unsatisfactory? Multitudes lack not only salvation but a decent life as well. And how will evil be overcome if history is the limit of possibility? Only a final deliverance can morally justify a world so full of wickedness and suffering as this one is. How can human existence as most people have experienced it be considered a good thing unless it leads to fulfillment in life after death?

(3) What is life like beyond the barrier? Christians often say that we go to heaven when we die, but this is not really an accurate way of speaking biblically. Scripture speaks of a new heaven and a

new earth, of a universe transformed and perfected, fit for God who is present with his people. The world beyond is something as real and solid as the present order. Of course, it is hard to imagine or describe exactly what it will be like. There is a reason why the Bible itself employs the evocative language of poetry and imagery to describe it. But from its language there are some things we can say with assurance. We can say with confidence that God will be there, that his presence will permeate the place. We would expect glorious worship such as we have never known. We can be sure that evil, death, sorrow, and Satan will not be there. We know that sin will be removed and love will govern existence in all its aspects. There will be true community, perfect oneness with others. And we expect it to be a place of activity, not boring inactivity. There will still be dynamism, change, and progress. From one point of view we can speak of eternal rest, but I think we can speak also of eternal activity. And there will be continuity with this world's cultures. The creative achievements of human beings will be carried over into the new order (Rev. 21:24, 26). We will experience the fulfillment of God's purpose for us. Life may be said truly to begin when God lifts us up out of the penultimate, provisional and alienated forms of life and takes us home into his gracious presence.

Life everlasting, though exalted above what we now know, will not be altogether foreign to present experience, since we have already been participating in some of its reality through the Spirit who is the down payment and foretaste. Thus, to an extent we can extrapolate from our experience now of new community and new life to what it must be like across the Jordan. And we know enough about the destructive effects of sin to be keenly anticipating its exclusion from any future world.

(4) Will all be saved in the end? Evangelicals have always believed that they will not. This opinion does not rest on evangelicals' own wishes (universalism is an agreeable thought) but because of what Scripture indicates. At the same time we can speak of a universalism that is biblical. The scope of salvation in the New Testament is large and generous and not at all niggardly. God loves the world and desires to save everyone (1 Tim. 2:4). Scripture is full of the most wonderful predictions about the throng without number around the throne of God. It says that God was in Christ reconciling the world to himself and that God is the Savior of all, especially of those who believe (2 Cor. 5:19; 1 Tim. 2:4). It says that the grace of

God has appeared for the salvation of all (Titus 2:11). Jesus himself said, "I did not come into the world to judge the world but to save the world" (cf. John 12:47 RSV). And later he said, "I, when I am lifted up from the earth, will draw all men to myself" (John 12:32 RSV). In many ways the New Testament is hopeful about the salvation of the world, and it is time for evangelicals to sound just as hopeful.

At the same time, we have to say that God respects human freedom. He allows us to rebel against him and will accept "no" for an answer in the area of salvation. The absolute universalist must ask himself, "If God is going to save all people, will it be with or without asking them about it?" It seems to me that a real choice needs to be made; therefore, the matter is open as to the outcome. "Whatsoever a man sows that will he also reap" (cf. Gal. 6:7 RSV). It is not God's desire to condemn anyone that leads to condemnation. It is people's preference for darkness. It is their own decision that brings judgment. The universal-sounding texts of the New Testament are serious, but they all contain a conditionalist implication. God will save everyone, "provided" (Col. 1:23).

(5) So what about the dark side, if it is possible not to be saved in the end? What is the destiny of those who finally reject God's love? What is the hellfire about which Jesus often spoke? On this subject evangelicals have often said some terrible things. They have taught that there will be a literal fire in which people will be tortured forever and ever. But surely this is both morally intolerable and fortunately biblically unnecessary. The case can be made from the biblical texts about judgment that hell points to destruction, not everlasting conscious torment. The belief in hell as everlasting torture is probably based upon the Greek view of the immortality of the soul, which crept into Christian theology and extended the experience of judgment into endless ages. But eternal life is a gift and not a natural possession according to the Bible.

Here we have a clear example of how moral sense causes us to reopen an exegetical question. I was led to question the traditional belief in everlasting conscious torment because of moral revulsion and broader theological considerations, not first of all on scriptural grounds. It just does not make any sense to say that a God of love will torture people forever for sins done in the context of a finite life. It implies a vindictiveness in God that I cannot imagine in the Father of our Lord Jesus Christ. It makes no sense to suppose that, alongside the new creation, tucked away in some corner of it, there exists a lake of fire with souls burning ceaselessly in it. It's time for evangelicals to come out and say that the biblical and morally appropriate doctrine of hell is annihilation, not everlasting torment.

(6) Finally, what about the billions who have never been able to decide for or against God's grace in Christ because they have never heard the Good News but lived their lives outside the New Covenant? This group might well be the majority of human beings who have ever lived. On this facet of eschatology, too, I think we have to make some bold changes in traditional thinking. Evangelicals may hold out real hope for the unevangelized and be consistent. First, because the redemption of innumerable people, which the Bible forecasts, requires it. Second, how can God allow those who have been downtrodden and the victims of oppression to perish? Having received no mercy in this life, will they receive no mercy even then? Third, God will reject his enemies but only his enemies. He knows who they are, though we do not. They are such as have trampled down his people, who have blocked the way to life for others, who have decided against God knowingly and willingly. For them certainly the judgment will spell condemnation and shame. But surely only for them. Surely the judgment of persons who have never heard the gospel will be according to the light they have received and they, too, will receive mercy.

The gospel gives us great hope as we move toward the goal of Christoformity and divine glory. And what a difference such a hope can make! Compare the child with eyes bright with hope and the sullen teenager bent on self-destruction. How we need the hope the Bible sets before us. "We have this hope as the anchor of our lives" (cf. Heb. 6:19 RSV).

> *Brown: What do you mean when you refer to God's intervention in history in the near term and in the long term? God's activity may at some times be more efficacious than at others, but is God not always equally active? Must evangelicals assert that God occasionally interrupts the pervasive patterns of causal relatedness in order to accomplish the divine purpose? Do you hold that such an act of God will occur at the end of history?*

Pinnock: In raising the issue of God's mighty acts or miracles you have touched upon something very important to evangelicals. The question reflects (I think) the belief of most religious liberals that nature operates uniformly according to scientific laws and that God does not intervene, displace, or set aside normal causal relationships in order to bring about effects that cannot be accounted for in terms of the factors ordinarily at work in nature. However God is thought to act, it is not (according to liberal theology) by intervening in history, even though denying such divine interventions overthrows an important presupposition of classical Christian doctrine, based as it is on that very assumption. At this point evangelicals charge liberals with rejecting an important dimension of the Christian faith.

But you want to know how I see this. First, I agree that God is always at work everywhere in the world to sustain and uphold the creation. One might use the analogy of force field theory. God is definitely not to be thought of as existing only outside history, waiting for an opening to jump in and do something. This would give the impression that the works of God are odd and extraordinary. I want to say that God is the creator of the whole universe and sustains all things every moment by his power. On account of this, reality as a whole reflects his purposes and is being directed toward good ends. We could say that the whole creation is a master act of God and expressive of his purposes. So far I think we would agree.

Second, I believe in other modes of divine activity than ordinary ones. God is free to interact with the world in a variety of ways. Special occasions rise in history that call for distinctive divine actions. So I would prefer not to speak of "equality" in this case. God is free to act or not to act by way of ordinary or extraordinary providence. God is a free agent and retains his options in this regard. I do not think of God as limited to working only in ordinary ways. There are times when God chooses to act in ways that surprise us.

Thus, I find miracles an intelligible concept. They are novel and extraordinary ways of God's providential rule over all things. They cause surprise because we have become used to the abnormality of sin and need to be jolted by them. The most noteable case recorded in the Bible is the resurrection of Jesus, a miracle that vindicated his claims and inaugurated the new age of the kingdom's nearness. It was and is a signal and singular revelation of

228

the grace of God and the powers of the age to come and a foundational event of our faith. Evangelicals find any theology bankrupt that casts doubt upon the bodily resurrection of Jesus. To us it seems both biblical and intelligible to celebrate God's demonstration of his own existence and purposes by extraordinary signs and wonders.

Our problem in consenting to this is, I think, the Western worldview, which blocks so much reality out. This materialistic orientation prevents us from seeing the supernatural and spiritual realm. We are culturally conditioned to be naturalists in our thinking and perceiving. We are imbued with the prejudice that the way to know anything lies along the path of reason and science. Need we wonder why even our religion is lacking in power? What do we expect if we are little more than practicing deists, totally lacking in expectant faith? We need to change our habits of thinking and acting.

You asked what I think about God's actions in the last days. I don't know much about them but I feel comfortable with Paul's hope: "The creation itself will be set free from its bondage to decay and obtain the glorious liberty of the children of God" (Rom. 8:21 RSV). I presume this means that there will be a break with everything we have known and the advent of a new heaven and a new earth. This leap-event, which will carry us over the gap that separates this age from the age to come, so far transcends anything we can achieve that it obviously must come from God's side. This glorious prospect is referred to in terms of the Parousia of Jesus, the regeneration of all things, the consummation of the kingdom, the resurrection of the dead, and will spell the destruction of all that is evil. I take great comfort in the promise: "Behold, I make all things new" (Rev. 21:5 RSV). I would not claim to grasp the nature of what is prophesied but can only glimpse it by faith through revealed symbols and picture language. On this subject I would not wish to assert either too much or too little.

> *Brown: Why, in terms of your methodology, are you free to dismiss "the hell of fire" about which you say Jesus often spoke. Why is belief in hell as eternal punishment not mandatory for evangelicals? Aren't you playing the game you attribute to liberals—"picking and choosing" what you want to believe?*

Pinnock: Your question betrays a misunderstanding, since I do not in fact deny hellfire. Rather, I am simply raising the question whether it is correct to interpret hell (like Augustine did) as everlasting conscious punishment or to understand it instead as the annihilation of the finally impenitent. My own view is that the traditional idea of hell as everlasting conscious torment is a mistaken interpretation of the Bible (as well as a morally outrageous idea) and that the destruction of the wicked is what the Bible and Jesus actually teach. Nor am I the only evangelical to think this way in that John Stott, P. E. Hughes, and others have espoused it, too. I am happy not to stand alone.

But you are right to inquire after my method. How exactly did I arrive at this nontraditional conclusion? Let me be candid and admit that I was led to doubt the traditional doctrine initially because I found the notion of endless torture even for the most wicked morally intolerable and not because first of all I doubted its biblical status. But because of my theological method (as you say), which takes the Bible to be primary and normative, I was compelled to consider what the Bible teaches about hell. Even though I value moral intuition, I believe that doctrine must rest on something more substantial than that. So what I did was to sift through the biblical data and found more substantive ground in the biblical language and imagery about the judgment of the wicked, which predominately conveys the idea of destruction. Jesus warns that God can destroy body and soul in hell and this language is typical of the whole Bible (Matt. 10:28). Having reviewed the biblical material, I felt justified in concluding with some confidence that hell is indeed a place of destruction rather than torture.

Other factors than exegesis entered into the decision of course. I have already mentioned the role played by simple moral revulsion. Then I had to consider the biblical understanding of resurrection and immortality, where it became obvious that the traditional view of hell rested on the Hellenistic and unscriptural belief in the immortality of the soul. I also had to look at the issue of justice as it bore upon the concept of hell and consider the metaphysical implications in terms of an everlasting dualism implicit in the traditional doctrine. Finally, I was forced to look at the few difficult passages that seem to teach everlasting conscious punishment but which, I found, do not necessarily do so.

You are right to wonder how this decision worked from or

affected my theological method. I was confronted with the powerful role of tradition in evangelical theology, despite its pretensions. Why can a traditional belief like hell not be questioned in the name of the Bible? It forced me to ponder why biblical readers do not agree on issues like this. What issues in their thinking and experience are influencing what they are seeing in the text? What is the precise authority of moral intuition in theology? Obviously, it drove me to reconsider an established exegetical opinion. Reason and philosophy also played a role in thinking about the metaphysical and justice issues. So all in all, it forced me to think more about the fact that multiple factors affect evangelical theology, even when Scripture is given pride of place as the norm.

> *Brown: You speak of missions as a history-making activity, not simply the saving of souls. But you also think that missions is necessary because the gospel must be preached to the Gentiles before the Parousia. Why is that the case if, as you believe, people who have never heard the gospel can nevertheless be recipients of God's saving grace? Would you say more about the nature and motivations of missions?*

Pinnock: I am glad you asked this question. First, I welcome the question because you put your finger on a severe inadequacy in evangelical thinking about missions and evangelism. So many seem to think of it individualistically in terms of rescuing lost souls from hell and as bare verbal proclamation. Our thinking about salvation and missions has been much too narrow. This gives me a chance to help reform evangelical thinking. Second, I welcome the chance to speak about the urgency of missions and evangelism.

Thinking too narrowly about the motives for missions is closely related to the problem of thinking too narrowly about the gospel and salvation. Evangelicals are much too influenced by neo-Platonic thinking where salvation is viewed as fire insurance, deliverance from eschatological wrath. In contrast, the New Testament tells us that God is moving in on the world to bring his rule to bear. There is Good News for the whole of creation not just for souls. God's kingdom has drawn near so that people can enter and participate in it, even while it remains to be consummated in power and great glory. Therefore, the Christian mission is to initiate people into the kingdom of God in its present aspects and in its future hope. It is not a bare announcement or primarily the rescue of souls from hell, but it encompasses all the ways in which people are initiated into the coming of the reign of God. Missions is an instrument in God's plan to transform and redeem history as well as to reconcile humanity.

Missions challenges people by word and deed to respond to God's offer of the kingdom through Jesus. It gathers believers to celebrate the God who is near and who is coming to reign over us. It proclaims the Good News to the world in the broadest sense. Our motive in missions is a concern for the glory of God our king and a desire to see the nations find fulfillment and salvation in his praise and service. We want everyone to know and enter into the fullness of who God is and what God has done for the race in Jesus.

You asked about the point I made about God's grace being active even beyond the reach of the gospel and the possible impact of that belief on missions motivation. Why would it be necessary, you wondered, to preach the Good News if this is true? What would the motive be?

Let me say why I believe it necessary to preach the gospel to the world and deal with your question in the course of it. There are three major motives for evangelizing the world. First, because Christ commands it explicitly and unequivocally. Second, because all peoples need and have a right to know who God is and what God has done for them in Jesus. Third, because any who have already responded to God will want to know about Christ. This last motive is the one you are inquiring about. Why would any who have responded to God in their own religion and culture need to have the gospel preached to them?

The answer is simple: all people have a right to know the true source of the light they have responded to and who the God is whom they have sought after. It is important that they should enjoy full access to God's grace and power in Jesus, that they be fully initiated into the kingdom of God. The motive then for taking the gospel to such people as have already responded to God is to bring the faith already present in them to fulfillment. Cornelius was a God-fearer according to Luke (Acts 10). Although he enjoyed a relationship with God, he had not been saved by Jesus or filled with the Holy Spirit. Being a God-fearer isn't the same as being saved by

Jesus and the gospel. It is ignorance of the coming of the kingdom into history. Why would we want to deny anyone a knowledge of this Good News?

● Brown's Rejoinder to Pinnock

Your contribution to the reform of evangelical thinking about salvation and missions is salutary, and I know that your effort is joined by that of other conservative theologians. Traditional Christian thinking on this issue seems to us today so obviously narrow that one must wonder how individualistic missionizing ever got to be widely accepted among Christians. If the area of missions is a place where we are learning and being corrected through dialogue with alternative positions, then we should be encouraged to redouble our efforts to seek genuine dialogue in other areas— theological, political, economic, social, etc. In any case, your contribution to the dialogue on missions is one I greatly appreciate.

Your "reform" of the traditional view of hell is a considerable improvement, in my judgment, but I have some trouble with your account of the process whereby you reached your conclusions. Notice that I do not fault your method either, only your account of it! You want in the end to say that what the Bible "really" teaches is the destruction of the wicked, not their everlasting torment. Is it not more nearly accurate to say: (a) the Bible contains differing views about what happens to the wicked, (b) there are several more or less plausible ways to construe the biblical message as a whole, and (c) the broad interpretation of the biblical witness that you can defend (but not prove) leads you on this particular point to deny conscious everlasting torment and affirm a doctrine of hell as annihilation?

If this were the proper account of your method, it certainly would not follow that you are simply picking and choosing. I want to make the same point about liberal theologies: they are not fairly characterized as the arbitrary selection of that within the Bible which liberals happen to want to believe (in blind conformity to the dictates of modernity). We are not picking and choosing anymore than you are. Like you, we find ourselves drawn to the biblical witness and compelled to listen to its manifold voices. Like you, we struggle, amidst the wealth and diversity of these voices, to come to some interpretation of that witness as a whole. Like you, we then

233

assess that witness in relation to all the rest that we think to be true, and we try to do so openly, analytically, and self-critically.

At this last step we apparently differ. Generally, you seem committed to affirming what you understand to be the biblical witness on a particular point even if it runs counter to everything else that you would otherwise think to be reliable evidence. Liberals, generally, are not bound in that way to the text—not, however, because we do not take the text as seriously as you do, but because we have a different understanding of what it means to live as Christians in relation to the biblical text. In short, we—liberals and conservatives—construe the meaning and the role of the biblical text differently.

SECTION 12

Delwin Brown's presentation on the doctrine of Christian hope, Brown's answers to three questions put by Pinnock, and a rejoinder by Pinnock to Brown's answers.

    Christian hope is hope for the world, hope for history, hope for human beings individually and in relationship. It is spiritual hope, political hope, economic hope, environmental hope. It is all of these hopes tied together because all of the dimensions to which they refer are connected in life.

    This "holistic" conception of hope is something supposedly modern, and indeed it is warranted by our contemporary studies of human reality. But, in fact, the ancient Hebraic conception of who humans are and thus of what humans may hope for was also emphatically holistic. That "historical holism" also permeates the New Testament, especially in the reign or kingdom of God motif, as we have seen. Although the challenge of Marxism may have provoked our modern Christian recovery of this perspective, we Christians do not take our hope for history from Marxism, as some allege. A holistic hope is present in the Hebraic foundation of our Christian historical experience (and it is probably from that source, too, that Marxism derives its own hopeful view of history). Christian hope is one because salvation is one, and salvation is one in

Christianity because the God who authors the "entire creation" seeks its freedom from bondage to decay and death.

HOPE IN HISTORY

But what precisely can we hope for in the historical process? Christian answers to this question have ranged from the most despairing to the most utopian. As we have seen there are Christians, on the one hand, who reduce God's grace in this life to the experience of forgiveness, and, on the other, there are those who affirm the possibility of personal and social transformation within history. Liberalism generally has been on the latter side, as I am, but for it and for any other hopeful Christian viewpoint sobriety still is in order.

Having hope in history is dangerous business. There is danger, for example, in the effort to determine whether progress has in fact been made, and there is even danger in hoping at all. What hopeful expectation can lead to is the facile assumption that "we"—our own time (that's the liberal form of the assumption), or our own particular group (that's the conservative version)—just might be instances of the transformation we work for and anticipate. The result is that we become blind to our own potential barbarity and therefore uncritical about what we do. The bent toward self-righteousness is enormous. The belief that divine grace can transform us seems to activate that inclination. It is plagued by the persistent temptation to think that we already have been transformed, that we already are what we hope for, that (though we say it in quiet humility) we are at least a bit better than that obvious sinner (no doubt a conservative if we are liberal, a gay person if we are straight, etc., etc.) who is praying on the other side of the courtyard.

Whatever the risks of hoping, however, our confidence in an open history and an active God forces us, I think, to accept those risks. If we are to be faithful to our confidence in a God who through us is able to do more than we ask, more even than we can imagine, then we must emphatically reject any effort to put a limit on the kind of personal and social transformation that might be accomplished in history, even in our own time.

The testimony of Christian realists, however, can help us be self-conscious about the risks of hoping. Their testimony exposes the frequency with which Christian hope has given way to social and personal delusion, and the frequency with which goods gained at one point have been lost shortly thereafter. If we listen to the realists, as I believe we should, we may come to doubt that there are nearly as many advances as are alleged, or that they come as easily as is sometimes supposed, or that they are as gigantic as some people claim, or that they are as stable as we all might wish, or that they are ever inevitable. Especially at the personal level, skepticism about progress seems to be in order. If there really is personal growth in grace (and I think there is), it is doubtful that we would ever know it about ourselves. Those who are called "saints" by others never find saintliness in themselves, and those who fail to find it in themselves are probably always right.

Nevertheless, to repeat, whatever the risks of hoping, those who believe in an open history and an active God must run those risks. We cannot ever accept the supposed wisdom that this or that is the point beyond which progress is impossible. The claim that the structures of our personhood, psychological and spiritual, are incapable of change must be denied. The claim that there can be no historical progress beyond current political and economic structures must be rejected. The claim that efforts to eliminate poverty, disease, and war are futile must be viewed as faithless. If history is open and a good God is active within it, then transformation for the good is possible in history at any and every level, however cautious we must be to claim it for ourselves and our time. Maybe we should never be so presumptuous as to announce progress, but we must be bold enough to believe it possible and work for it.

At this point, I think, conservatism is too frequently guilty of a failing. Perhaps motivated by its respect for the past, it hesitates to expect much of the future. As simple realism, that hesitation can be respected. But conservative Christianity sometimes translates this wise dubiety into a perverse alliance with the political and social status quo. How many times, for example, does one hear evangelical Christians say, "Well, certainly capitalism has its faults, but we should be content with it because it is obviously better than the socialist alternatives." For the sake of argument let us suppose that on balance capitalism is better. But how can one who believes that history is open, and God is at work in it, conclude that capitalism and socialism are the only alternatives? The same point can be made about every one of the other obstacles that now inhibit the search for greater peace and justice in the world community. Conservative Christians are too frequently co-opted by those who benefit from the status quo. If evangelicals truly believe in a God who is able to do far more than we can ask or think, they are not entitled to that kind of "conservatism." Christian conservatism should hope in history.

HOPE FOR HISTORY

Progress in history, however, is not everything. We liberals, especially, need to be reminded that even a continuously transformed world—a world always in the process of improvement—would not necessarily be a world of abiding significance. Even a "perfect" society could be meaningless, ultimately speaking. Our achievements could come, flourish for awhile, and then perish into a whiff of cosmic nothingness—their positive and their negative outcomes alike being ultimately pointless. What about ultimate meaning?

In "A Free Man's Worship," the philosopher Bertrand Russell wrote,

> Brief and powerless is Man's life; on him and all his race the slow, sure doom falls pitiless and dark. Blind to good and evil, reckless of destruction, omnipotent matter rolls on its relentless way. . . .

Is Russell right? Is there no significance or "point" to our lives apart from the differences they make to the future within history? The meanings our lives have in history are real and they are important. But even our finest contributions to the historical future are imperfectly preserved, and at best they fade into comparative irrelevance eventually. Do our lives have a significance beyond their fallible historical destiny?

As we saw in the last section, one metaphor of the redeemed future in the tradition of Christian reflection is that of the "reign of God" or the "kingdom of God." It portrays salvation in terms of the ideal historical future, a future that is already breaking into the present and yet is always still coming. As central as this portrayal is to the historic Christian witness, it alone does not address the question of ultimate meaning.

Another and quite different metaphor of the redeemed future, also rooted in the New Testament, is "eternal life." The fourth gospel speaks of eternal life as a special quality of life in the present, the quality of eternality in time. It is something the believer already possesses.

> In truth I tell you, the one who believes already possesses eternal life.

> Anyone who gives heed to what I say and trusts the one who sent me, has hold of eternal life, and does not come up for judgment, but has already passed from death to life (cf. 5:24 RSV).

In my view, there is real sense to this kind of talk, even if it is not precisely the sense given to it by traditional theology. If God genuinely knows and loves us, then our lives and their historical consequences make a difference to God. And if God knows perfectly and everlastingly, then our lives in their fullness make an everlasting difference to God. Whatever the meaning or significance of our lives within this history, our meaning beyond it in God is firm and complete.

In God our lives have an eternal reality. In that sense, our lives have an everlasting, abiding meaning or worth in God. And the Gospel of John is right: that eternality has already begun. Each moment of our lives, good and evil, as it happens, is taken into God's reality so that already our lives have what the fourth gospel calls "eternality,"

More than that, if our lives embody both good and evil, as they do, then these, too, have eternality. Therefore, in a nonliteral but nonetheless absolutely real sense, there is heaven and hell. Heaven is the permanence of every fulfillment, however relative, and the permanence of our actions as they contribute to that fulfillment. Our positive achievements in history are tenuous at best—weak in their emergence, frail in their endurance, soon forgotten. In God they are treasured fully and everlastingly. Every good achieved in history, whether personal or social, abides permanently in the life of God.

But hell is real, too. It is the permanence of every destruction, of every lostness. These, too, make an everlasting difference to and in God's life. God cannot rewrite history, including our own. It will always be the case that we have destroyed each other and ourselves in the ways that we have. That, too, is an indelible fact in the reality of God. God's forgiveness is not forgetfulness. Forgiveness is grace, that is, God's acceptance of our lives "in spite of" the destructive side. Divine grace makes sense only if there is some real meaning to "hell," and if grace is everlasting then so is the permanence of lostness.

There is meaning to "heaven" and "hell" if in history there is both transformation and destruction, both liberation and oppression, both healing and disease, both communion and alienation— and if each becomes something permanent in the life of God.

How do we become permanently a part of the life of God? Do we contribute to God as we contribute to each other now, as dynamic and self-conscious selves? Or do our lives become a part of God's life as the lives of others in the past are now a part of ours?

Some liberal theologians contend that even in the New Testament it is God alone who enjoys immortality. These liberals insist that aspiring for personal immortality is unwarranted and immature. God is the only individual who always was, and God alone is the only individual who always will be. The human desire for immortality is like the temptation of Eden, it is hubris—the longing to be like God. We do not complain that we were not before we were born. Why should we complain that we may not be after we die? What counts is God's immortality and the knowledge that our lives are permanently meaningful in it.

Whether or not the desire for life everlasting, immortality, is suspect, it does not seem to me inappropriate that those whose lives are here unfulfilled should aspire to a more abundant continuation of life beyond this one in order that their sufferings here might be compensated there. We do not ordinarily think it a sign of hubris that a person should want to live the rest of the day, or tomorrow, or another ten years. We may have goals to reach, matters to make right, good things to enjoy. It is no more a sign of hubris to desire another life after this one, a life in which the things here denied might be realized. Much of the hope for "life beyond death," I suspect, is of this sort. Especially for those whose lives now are filled with injustice and suffering, it is a hope to be respected.

In fact, however, the imagery of "eternal life" connotes something different, something still more. Belief in eternal life is the conviction that our lives, even now, have an ultimacy, an abiding meaning in an everlasting God. "Eternal life" is not the same as "life after death." The latter, after all, can be just as meaningless, from an ultimate standpoint, as life before death can be. Another and happier life might be compensatory for the suffering of this one, but that life could still be pointless beyond itself.

Do our lives have an ultimate point, an irrevocable meaning? The question can be asked whether the lives we are asking about last for seven years or seven million years, whether they occur in one installment or many, and whether they are on balance happy or sad. The idea of eternal life has to do with the ultimate significance of life. It is not about how long we live; it is about the eternal significance of our living whatever its duration. The affirmation of "eternal life" is the claim that, now and always, all that we do and are abides fully in and for the everlasting life of God.

If the concept of the reign of God suggests that there are real potentials within history that we have not yet dreamed of, the concept of eternal life affirms the everlasting importance of that history and our lives within it, individually and corporately. The details of our lives—what we bind in history and loose in history, what we heal and what we destroy—abide forever in the God who is the heart of the universe.

The two ideas—salvation in history, and salvation beyond it—are not incompatible. The Christian today, liberal or conservative, need not choose between them. Indeed, this cannot be our choice. If we believe that a faithful God brought all things into being, then we will believe that this love still seeks in history the good of every thing at every level—what *we* call spiritual, psychological, sociological, economic, political, ecological, etc. But if we believe in a God whose love is everlasting, then we will also believe that in ways our pitiful images cannot possibly fathom, the future, our own and that of the entire creation, is somehow safe in that love.

IMAGES AND EXPECTATIONS

Without diminishing the importance of "eternal life," however, I want especially to affirm the significance of an active Christian hope in God's historical reign. This metaphor is so important because it runs so counter to one of the predispositions that infects us all, liberal and conservative.

What this metaphor says, curiously, is almost precisely identical to the dominant metaphor of Christmas except that the liberals' and conservatives' point is made in opposite ways. The Christmas claim is that the supreme power of the universe is a child in a manger, that is, the strong is weak. The "reign of God" reverses the imagery. The power of this already-present, ever-coming "kingdom" is not impressive. It is hardly even noticeable. Yet, according to the metaphor, the One whose aims are manifest in the slow, patient, working of love—a "reign" so weak as to be embarrassing, according to the standards of this world—is finally the supreme power of the universe. The weak is strong.

The image of the reign of God comes as quite a surprise. We think the world belongs to the governments, to the wealthy, to the managers, and—sometimes when we feel very confident—even to ourselves. Listen to our talk, pay attention to our newspapers, look closely at our actions. We think the future belongs to the mighty.

The image of God's reign says that is wrong.

If true, that would be a happy surprise. If the dominant powers of the world are really the governments, the titans of industry, the managerial elite, or, heaven forbid, ourselves, then there is little reason to suppose that the future will be much better than the past. But if, in addition to the observable powers of this world, there is another power, and if this is a power for good, and if this power for good is capable of surprises small and large, usually when we least expect them, then surely the future of this world is worth our commitment. After all, if God does reign—however quietly, however strangely disguised—the world could turn out to produce some pretty interesting surprises.

Yet we must keep in mind that "eternal life," "reign of God," "heaven and hell," and all of the other terms Christians have employed in thinking about the future are not literal descriptions. In this cluster of linguistic symbols we find intuitions that we mine like the rich ore deep within the earth. But what we mine is ore, not precise, finished products. We are never sure what the metals we mine can or will become. We take them out of the earth, look at them, imagine their possibilities, and work with them. We shape them into beautiful and valued things. We know, however, that these precious metals preexisted our discovery of them by millions of years. They will live beyond the forms we give them, someday to become other, better, even more valued things.

Pinnock: You emphasize objective immortality. Do you share the vivid hope, which evangelicals treasure, that we will consciously experience personal fulfillment in the new community in the presence of God and in the new creation?

Brown: I treasure the hope that we, personally and socially, as well as all of the creation will be fulfilled in whatever way is possible (see my response to your third question, below) and appropriate, both in the temporal process and beyond it in the everlasting economy of God.

I sometimes think the language of conscious personal fulfillment is an appropriate way of expressing that hope. As my initial statement indicates, theologies written by privileged people have sometimes minimized this way of speaking quite inexcusably, in my judgment, ignoring the aspirations of the great majority of human beings in whose lives pain and loss have predominated. Until recently, evangelical Christianity has been most in touch with the North American underclasses. It has also been the form of North American Christianity, in intention at least, most attentive to the Bible, which is by and large the literature of an underclass tradition. It is understandable, then, that evangelicalism even today should be so insistent on the legitimacy of a language that vividly encapsulates the aspirations of many of these people.

When pressed toward clarity, however, "conscious personal fulfillment" language expresses the hope for fulfillment quite inadequately, it seems to me. What can unqualified fulfillment mean for us? For us, the values with which we are familiar can be achieved only at the expense of other values. For us, the experience of joy depends in part on the context of contingency and uncertainty in which it occurs. For us, fulfillment has meaning only in relation to a struggle fraught with obstacles. In short, what can value and joy and fulfillment be for us apart from the "contraries" in relation to which their meaning for us depends. But if we could think of a fulfilled existence in which these contraries were absent, in what sense would this kind of existence be *our* existence? In what sense would the value, joy, and fulfillment bear any resemblance to what we mean by these terms?

These are only examples, quickly stated, of antinomies that seem to me to be inherent in talk about conscious personal fulfillment in any unqualified sense. (If fulfillment in the life to come is not unqualified, then it would merely be more of the same, better than this life, if at all, only to a degree.) For me, these antinomies do not indicate that hope expressed in the language of conscious personal fulfillment is inappropriate, but rather that the language of Christian hope, whether expressed in personalistic imagery or any other, is to be viewed as metaphorical.

This returns me to what I said in my initial statement—what we affirm about the future of this life beyond this life is necessarily metaphorical. The task is not to exclude this imagery or that, but to remain open to the multiplicity of metaphors that might express the Christian's aspiration for fulfillment. We long, as Saint Paul said, not only for the salvation of "we ourselves," but for the fulfillment as well of the whole creation groaning in travail until now. I do not think any one metaphor can be considered the normative statement of such a great hope.

Your question is about my personal view, not about the view of liberal Christians more generally, and thus to this point my answer has been personal. In fact, affirmations of continued conscious, personal existence in fellowship with God have been about as common in liberal piety as in the piety of evangelicals. Nor have they been exceptional in liberal theology. The fairly consistent differences between liberal and conservative theologies on this matter have been twofold.

First, liberals have been more tolerant than conservatives of a variety of views about the ultimate fulfillment of this life, even to the point of doubt about fulfillment in a life to come. This openness to doubt is not entirely a matter of smug class interests. The contention that immortality belongs to God alone, and that the human desire for life after death is really a form of the sin of pride, is not without theological insight. It cannot be blithely dismissed even if it also cannot be canonized.

Second, liberals have probably been more self-conscious than conservatives that such talk—indeed, any talk about postmortem existence—is the imagery of hope, not literal language. I will defend this second point with particular fervor. The term "vivid" in your question can only refer to the intensity of Christian hope, in my opinion, not to the clarity of its object. We anticipate the future wisely only keeping in mind that, in this matter especially, we see through a darkened glass.

Pinnock: You find meaning in the biblical images of hell and judgment. But that does not seem to include the notion of individuals having to face the living God in a final judgment at the close of history. How then do you handle Jesus' stern warnings about just such an eventuality?

Brown: This is a good point at which to state again what I understand to be the Christian's definitive relationship to the biblical text as it is variously mediated to us in history. That relationship is not one of being normed by the text, whether in its precise letter or its general spirit, but of being formed by the Bible as we wrestle with its witness. Hence, however the present question is intended, from my standpoint it cannot properly mean, why does your view not conform to the view implicit in Jesus' stern warnings? but instead it means, how do you wrestle with this text and what is the consequence of that struggle in terms of your own self-understanding? In other words, the implication of the question is precisely that the Christian should seriously "handle" the text, not that she or he should mimic it.

It is obvious, I should think, that the point of the stern warnings you refer to has little to do with the precise timetable for the deliverance of judgment. That, at least, is the understanding of the writer of the fourth gospel. John exempts believers from judgment altogether (5:24), or, perhaps more likely, John holds that the believer (and thus, by logical implication, the unbeliever as well) is already judged, that judgment being contemporary with what is being judged.

My own view, in any case, is that the importance of the insistence upon judgment is that our lives, both momentarily and cumulatively, are lived in relationship to standards and that our actual achievements, whether for good or ill in relationship to these standards, make a permanent difference in all that is to follow, for ourselves, for others, and for God. As Christians we view the standards in terms of which we live our lives as the will of God, provisionally and fallibly understood. Therefore, our lives as we live them are already judged, both momentarily and cumulatively, by God in relation to God's will. It is as meaningful to say that my life is judged at its completion as it is to say that God judges my life at any

245

point along the way. However, I do not see what is gained by positing some special point, either in history or beyond it, when these judgments are simultaneously and, so to speak, officially delivered.

I am not sure why you suppose that my appropriation of the biblical ideas of hell and judgment fails to relate to individuals. I did not mean to leave such an impression. It is true, however, that my notion of what it means to be an individual or a human person differs from the idea of a person, drawn from Greek substance philosophy, that became determinative for Christian orthodoxy well after the post-biblical period. Employing the conceptuality of process philosophy, I understand persons to be essentially dynamic and relational. This means that judment, and the related imagery of heaven and hell, cannot apply to persons conceived as some one unchanging "thing" or in isolation from their concrete contexts. This, in turn, means that isolated people cannot "go" to some "place" called heaven or hell rather like distinct apples can be assigned to baskets labeled "good" and "bad." Rather, I understand ideas of the futurity of judgment to refer to things in their interrelatedness—which by no means excludes human persons— as they are everlastingly in the reality of God. That which is destructive on earth is everlastingly destructive within the reality of God, and that which is saved on earth is so treasured everlastingly. If this means that the imagery of judgment gets complicated, it by no means gets more complicated than Paul's notion that the "entire creation," and not only the whole person, will somehow gain permanent reality by virtue of the grace of God.

Pinnock: If all the good and all the evil that men and women do make an everlasting difference to God's life, is there ever going to be a resolution?

Brown: I will begin by observing that on the topic of this last question my view is arguably more orthodox than your own idea that hell is annihilation. Even if my observation is accurate, however, it tells us nothing about which view is more nearly "right," but only that the distinctions between liberals and conservatives are happily (in my opinion) less rigid and predictable than they have been in the past.

Nevertheless, although your view may be unorthodox, it does

246

indeed conform to a conviction in the New Testament best stated, as you observe, in Colossians 1. There the persistent vision is of the eventual redemptive embrace of all things in Christ by the power of God. When this universalistic vision confronts the question of what happens to that which is (including those who are) not saved, two responses are possible. One may say either everyone and everything that ever was will in fact be saved finally, or one may say that what is not saved will finally be annihilated thereby becoming no-thing at all. Rejecting the first option in deference to New Testament talk about hell, you hold, as I understand your view, that what is not saved becomes no-thing. Thus you are able to say, in the spirit of Colossians, that all "things" will be reconciled to God in the end because what is lost, on your view, is so radically lost as to be no thing at all, that is, it is annihilated. Hell is nothingness.

According to the alternative and more dominant view in the New Testament, hell represents something that has an everlasting reality. This, of course, is the view that became orthodox. You are properly harsh in your criticism of orthodox talk about hell as a literal place, to say nothing of its heinous conception of hell as a place of everlasting torment. If, in order to be Christian, we must believe that anyone, however evil, deserves such a punishment, or that God would have a hand in delivering it, then we should all renounce Christianity! But this more orthodox or customary view of hell need not be literalistic, and it certainly need not be sadistic. It can be understood to reflect the conviction that destruction gains a permanence that is never wholly eradicated, however much it might be forgiven and compensated. The Holocaust, for example, will never be wholly undone; its evil lives on in the temporal process as well as beyond it. So, too, does all of the destruction that we suffer and impose upon others by our willful disregard of the divine ideal for our lives. Loss takes on a permanence. That, it seems to me, is the underlying sense of the traditional Christian insistence on the enduring reality of hell. That is the sense in which I affirm it.

You are correct in observing that for this view loss is never fully resolved. Sin and evil unredeemed in this life may in the mystery of God somehow be placed in a larger, partially compensatory context, but it will never be made not to be. In a sense this view is more tragic than your own. The continuing reality of a hell would be a tragedy most of all for a loving God who must grieve everlastingly for all that is lost everlastingly.

247

Your view has the advantage of escaping such tragedy, if that is an advantage. The weakness of your view, it seems to me, is that it tends to minimize sin and evil. It would be too glib to say that for you "evil is nothing to worry about ultimately," but your view does trivialize evil to a degree that I find problematic.

I prefer a position that refuses in any way to minimize the ultimate evil of evil, even if it leaves us with an unresolved permanence of lostness. I think the intuition of a lostness that is never fully resolved is more adequate to the dimension of tragedy that orthodox Christianity recognizes to be a part of our life, and that I believe to be a part of God as well. What is a loss in the world is also loss for the God who loves the world. But tragedy is not despair, not for God and therefore not for us. For if evil cannot be entirely eliminated, it can be mitigated and to some extent compensated by the good that God works through us and in us and the rest of creation. Loss is a permanent part of the story, but it is not the whole story. The rest is the triumph of grace.

● Pinnock's Rejoinder to Brown

When it comes to hope *in* history, you and I share a similar outlook, which is a cautious optimism for historical progress rising from the work of God in history. The church by being the new community impacts society, and effects social change by being faithful. I see a remarkable convergence along the same lines, not only with us but across the entire church. Christians everywhere seem to be taking hold of the biblical vision that the whole creation belongs to God, and, although powers of darkness strongly resist the kingdom, Christ has won a victory over them, making beneficial social change possible. Though we cannot expect utopia to arrive from our work and cannot bring the kingdom of God to earth by our own efforts, there can still be a fair degree of transformation in history before the Lord returns. Exactly how much no one can say. Our primary obligation is to proclaim Christ and to live for him in society; in so doing the victory of Christ will impact the public realm through the church's life and witness.

When it comes to the hope of everlasting life, however, evidently we do not see eye to eye. Of course you are formally correct to say (and I agree with you in principle) that we can and must entrust our final destiny to God's loving care. We may take solace in the fact that our future is safe in God's hands. After all, Old Testament saints seem to have exercised their faith in God without knowing categorically whether they would survive death as persons or not. They trusted themselves to God without having that matter settled in their minds. They did not know whether immortality would be objective or subjective, to use our modern jargon. So you ask why couldn't it be the same for us. In reply I would say that obviously it could be the same, except for one small thing: it isn't the same! By that I mean the New Testament speaks of immortality being brought to light through the gospel (2 Tim. 1:10). The promise of God has been issued that there is hope for life beyond death in the presence of God. So we are not left without hope in this regard as you imply we are.

Here we are back to where we started in the book, back to the difference between us concerning the nature of the authority of the Bible. From my point of view you will not allow the Scriptures to give us information about such realities as these. You allow the Bible a functional but not a cognitive authority; that is, you will not bow to the content of Scripture but accept it only as a power that authors your life in some (to me) vague way. This means in the present case that you are not able to rest your hope on the revealed promises of God concerning eternal life in Christ beyond death. Usually I appreciate your modesty in the way you do theology, but when it comes down to your not affirming clear promises of God in the gospel, the modesty is being taken too far. Lacking guidance from the Scriptures and as if to underline my anxiety, you are forced to resolve the issue rationally and then cannot do so. Thus is the problem of liberal theology highlighted.

We do not agree about hell either. Although I appreciate your interaction with what I had to say about hell as annihilation, I cannot take you seriously in the remark about your view being more orthodox than mine. It is clear that what you mean by hell being everlasting is purely metaphorical. Your idea is that evil will never be forgotten by God but will continue to cause him grief because it happened. You are not saying hell is permanent in the sense of persons consciously suffering in hell forever. There are no souls in hell as you understand it. So you *do* evade Jesus' warnings to evildoers about a tribunal they will have to face personally one day in the future.

CONCLUSIONS

CONCLUSION
BY CLARK H. PINNOCK

Dialogues like this are needed in contemporary theology. Since all serious theologians are attempting to relate the Christian message meaningfully to the challenges of the present day without distorting it and since we often work alongside each other in churches and denominations, shouldn't we be trying to communicate more often and more effectively? That does not imply that conversations will prove easy. There are bad attitudes to overcome and serious differences of belief to deal with. It is patently obvious that we two are not in agreement on matters that are crucially important and by no means trivial. Nevertheless, it is also obvious that, in conversing together as we have done, there was mutual benefit both to us and one hopes to the reader. Surely it is important that theologians should be compelled to do their work in public, in the presence and under the scrutiny of kindly but serious critics. And it is also important that people who are not theologians should see how liberal and evangelical theology is actually done and how critical questions get faced.

The possibility of such a dialogue despite large differences was facilitated by a couple of factors. On the one hand, the perennial dialectic of the Christian message and human existence helped. In that back and forth correlation of the twin poles, the message can never be exhausted and human existence never ceases to raise fresh questions. The task of contextualizing is one that never ends and one that we all share wherever we are on the spectrum. It simply helps to talk about it and to find out how the other one is doing.

In some ways we were very different but in other ways we were not. Both of us took biblical and traditional ideas and tried to make them work. Both of us attempted to contextualize the Word of God in the modern situation. But the results were not totally predictable. I did not leave everything unchanged, while Brown did not feel he had to challenge every received doctrine or invent completely new categories.

Liberals have worked with the problem of contextualizing the Christian message in the modern world longer than most evangelicals have. They felt the pressure earlier and took steps to try to respond to problems. Evangelicals reacted strongly to their efforts, charging them with conceding too much and even changing essentials of the gospel. But we are working at the same task, and the time seems to have come for us to work more closely together on the challenges in order to help each other. In part the time is right because in recent years liberals have been admitting mistakes they have made, while evangelicals are behaving more responsibly in the willingness to face up to the pressing issues and not hide from them.

Another factor that facilitates dialogue is the fluid character of theological traditions. Although evangelicals usually do not like to admit that changes occur even in their beliefs, they do of course occur. The great variety of evangelical sects testifies to the fluidity of interpretation even of a Bible held to be infallible. Liberals on the other hand are well known for the nonconformist and individualist character of their convictions. This means that rich lodes of diversity are available for us both to draw upon. Since no uncontested liberal or evangelical positions exist that any of us are obliged to adhere to, we are free to work within the generous parameters of our different traditions and place fresh constructions upon what we receive from them.

The conversation proved to be mutually stimulating. Both of us were forced to face up to hard questions. We both held the other's feet to the fire. We experienced more than one awkward moment. It certainly forced me to address some of the challenges of modernity I would have preferred to bypass. And Brown found himself having to respond to the question of doctrinal continuity with historic Christianity after all the revision. It proved to be an occasion of growth for us both.

The dialogue taught us to respect and not caricature one

another's ideas. It proved that we simply must take each other's ideas seriously and respect the other's motives. Let us be done with the approach that dismisses a liberal theologian without trying to understand him, that ridicules the motives that energize the work of evangelicals, that refuses to admit the seriousness of the concerns that drive people to the positions finally adopted, and that refuses to own up to the fact that we are both struggling to do justice to the challenging subject matter that Christian theology requires.

Obviously, we did not come to a common mind here. We were unable to carve out a middle channel. Some really basic differences remain. While there was a rapprochement of understanding, there was no rapprochement of ideas. I appealed to a principle of apostolicity that Brown did not share with me. Brown measured continuity with historic theology not so much in concepts but in spirit and direction. I showed some flexibility in working with received doctrines but still held onto sacred content and guarded it. My liberty to make changes in theology was much more limited than Brown's and required more justification from me in the face of scriptural teaching. Brown on the other hand enjoyed greater freedom and was less inhibited in expressing what modern people are thinking and feeling in his theology.

Even when we agreed on things, it was not always for the same reasons. I would defend a belief like human sinfulness primarily because it is taught in the Bible and belongs to the historic grammar of the community, while Brown would hold to it because it rings true to the way he sees the world. I would rejoice if a biblically authorized truth did ring true to modern experience, but that would be a bonus rather than the basis for my believing it. Brown on the other hand would not think that the fact that something is mentioned in the Bible automatically makes it believable, if it were not credible on other grounds.

In closing I would add that Jesus told us to be anxious for nothing, and that applies even when it comes to theology and the church. God promises to care for us. He will not let us perish. Who knows exactly what God has in store for us?

CONCLUSION
BY DELWIN BROWN

When we began this project, Clark Pinnock and I naturally expected to write a joint conclusion. Just as naturally, however, we abandoned that plan, not with a sense of failure but with the comfortable recognition that we still have different languages, different concerns, and, yes, different conclusions. To me, our separate conclusions suggest something far more valuable than the common statement we certainly could have produced. They suggest that dialogue is best not only when it undertakes to clarify differences and be changed by the encounter, but when it undertakes as well to appreciate and preserve the differences that remain.

What are our remaining differences? Without attempting to rehearse them all, I will venture to suggest, and to comment on, some of the basic ones.

We remain far apart on method. Pinnock is probably more critical in his use of the Bible theologically than many evangelical theologians, and I am perhaps more insistent on the role of the Bible in theology than many liberal theologians. Even so, we differ sharply at this point. The difference, in my view, is not that liberalism takes the Bible less seriously than conservatism does, but that liberalism has a different understanding of how the Bible contributes to Christian life and Christian reflection. Liberal Protestant theology distinguishes two questions: What does it mean to say that this belief is authentically Christian? and, What does it mean to say that this belief is true? The first question is answered in relation to the Bible; a Christian belief, I have said, is one that is formed by and sustained in a continual struggle with the biblical canon. The second question is answered in relation to the fallible and revisable criteria of modern knowledge.

Pinnock is not convinced that my method gives the Bible adequate accord. For my part, I certainly am not convinced that, systematically speaking, Pinnock takes modernity as seriously as he ought, or even as seriously as he sometimes may wish to take it personally. On these issues, we do enjoy some common grounds on which to challenge each other's point of view (e.g., we both reject fideism), and we have done so. But, here as with other issues, we recognize as a primary obligation the task of trying to understand how the other's position "fits together," and how it "feels" as a place wherein intelligent and responsible Christians can dwell.

We differ in our language. This is a difficult factor for me to calculate in assessing our differences. Clark Pinnock, for example, repeatedly edges up to the blunt accusation that liberals do not "really" believe in the Incarnation. This liberal, at least, finds that to be a very peculiar charge. Still, I understand why he makes it. My language about the Incarnation employs the resources of a modern metaphysical system because those resources seem to me to fit, and facilitate, what Christians intend to say about the meaning of God in Christ. Pinnock finds process metaphysics inadequate. But I am not sure that he understands what I intend to say by employing it. However, the important question is whether we are hearing one another correctly, and whether we are translating accurately between our conceptual systems. As I say, it is hard for me to know. Thus, while I am very sure we disagree significantly on Christology, I am not sure how much of our disagreement is substantive and how much of it is merely verbal.

We certainly differ about what theologically is most adequate. That is, even when we think we agree on the meaning of terms, we still disagree on basic theological judgments. Let me illustrate with a suggestion. One can interpret much of historic liberal Christianity as the effort to understand the meaning of the biblical witness by making fundamental to it the claim that God is incarnate. Thus, liberals are perfectly comfortable with viewing God's action within the patterns of the natural order, and we think that doing so reflects a Christian and biblical perspective. After all, this is where God is incarnate. Historic conservative Christianity can be understood as

258

taking God's transcendence as the key to the biblical witness. Thus, conservatives resist the "reduction" of God's actions to natural processes. After all, conservatives say, God is not simply incarnate. Liberals might respond, "Of course not, but 'transcendence' refers to a feature of God's incarnate reality," and liberals will then try to explain what that might mean. Conservatives may well retort, "That is not enough," and try to explain why. Each side acknowledges a place for transcendence and for incarnation in its theological framework, but those places differ. My point is that, differences of method and meaning aside, we also differ because our substantive theological starting points differ significantly.

What are we to make of these many, significant, and persistent differences? Obviously, they change somewhat. Sometimes a difference here or there will actually be overcome. But for the most part our perspectives, liberal and conservative, continue to contrast markedly, even if not absolutely and even if not always predictably. How shall we view this inability to get to basic agreement?

I want to suggest that our differences, like our dialogues about them, are essential. The fact that Christians differ theologically is appropriate, for three reasons.

The first reason has to do with being human. Humans differ, Christians differ, because our views are limited and others are able to see that. This is not an expression of personal generosity; it is an epistemological judgment, a judgment about the nature of human knowledge, including Christian theological knowledge. As much as I appreciate his spirit and his perspicacity, I am sure that Clark Pinnock is missing something. He seems no less convinced that I am. It is possible that we are both right because, in another sense, we are both wrong—we are indeed each missing something. Liberals and conservatives alike can agree that the human mind is fallible, and often obstinate. We are always able to see the evidence for narrowness in every other point of view that we examine. Why should we not assume it about ourselves? If we do, must we not begin by assuming that the opposing position just might be expressing something we have missed (and are probably not going to hear easily because we are not going to like hearing it)?

There is also a historical reason for valuing Christian diversity. The biblical witness in relation to which we live and think is a rich and diverse tradition. We noted above, for example, that among its many contrasts the Bible expresses both the "transcendental" and

259

the "incarnational" mode of approaching the world. It is no wonder then that Christian people in fact exemplify these contrasting ways of seeing things. A canon with many facets will form a people of manifold views. Since ours is a plurivocal canon, we have diverse traditions and we are a diverse people. For purely historical reasons, then, we should expect to be different. The diversity of the Bible produces our diversity.

Finally, there is a hermeneutical reason for valuing our diversity, a Christian hermeneutical reason. The diversity of the Bible requires our diversity. Precisely because the Bible does speak with a richness and multiplicity of meaning, we cannot hope to approach it adequately except as we approach it together with our differing experiences, traditions, and assumptions. The fullness of a plurivocal book, a book that speaks with many voices, can be approached only if it is heard with many ears. The diversity of the Bible, then, not only produces our differences; it also requires our differences if its own richness is to become available to us.

Diversity alone, however, is not enough. The manifoldness of the biblical tradition, thus heard in our manifold ways, can become a common resource only if it is communicated and appropriated. This means that we must not only be willing to accept our differences as appropriate and necessary, we must make them productive by serving one another in the critical reflection of dialogue. Critical reflection together is essential if the biblical witness in its true wealth is to be a living resource for Christianity today.

This, in my judgment, is the most compelling reason for pursuing productive dialogue. We may desire dialogue among Christians for many other reasons, but there is one basic reason: unless we explore our present differences together we cannot adequately explore our past, for that past is too rich to be plumbed from only one point of view.

This means that dialogue among Christians is an imperative. To be sure, Christian dialogue with non-Christian traditions is also important, for we have all seen how quickly our own tradition, when viewed conjointly with the representative of another point of view, takes on new meanings, sometimes embarrassing and sometimes exhilarating ones. But the curious thing is how much harder it seems to enter genuine discussion with one of our own kind, other

Christians with whom we sharply differ. Whatever the reasons for that, I believe intra-Christian dialogue is also a Christian imperative.

Dialogue is necessary not only for all of the humane reasons that mutual understanding is always an urgent obligation—we want to be open to change, we want to understand, we want to avoid prejudice, we want to stop oppression, we want to escape our mutual destruction. Any one of these alone is a sufficient, humane (and also Christian) reason for dialogue. But I am arguing that there is another, distinctively Christian point: Christian dialogue is necessary as well simply in order to be Christian. For if being Christian requires taking the Bible seriously, given its rich reservoir of multiple meanings there is no other way to take this canon than to struggle with it, together, from our multiple points of view.

Theological Crossfire: An Evangelical-Liberal Dialogue
was typeset by the
Photocomposition Department of Zondervan
Publishing House, Grand Rapids, Michigan
on a Mergenthaler Linotron 202/N.
Compositor: Nancy J. Wilson
Editor: Robert D. Wood
Designer: Jan M. Ortiz

The text was set in 10 point Korinna, first issued by
H. Berthold's typefoundry in 1904, it was later produced
by Intertype in 1934 as a metal face. As a novelty face
it was not popular in metal but has experienced a broad
revival as a photocomp face. Basing their work on
Berthold's original drawings, Ed Benguiat and Victor Caruso
enlarged the family of Korinna faces for ITC in 1973.
The display type is also Korinna.

This book was printed by Arcata Graphics / Kingsport,
Kingsport, Tennessee.